# BRITISH GENTLEMEN
# IN THE WILD WEST

# BRITISH GENTLEMEN IN
## THE WILD WEST

—◆—

## The Era of
## the Intensely English Cowboy

LAWRENCE M. WOODS

ROBSON BOOKS

This paperback edition published in 2003 by Robson Books,
64 Brewery Road, London, N7 9NT

First published in Great Britain in 1990 by Robson Books.

A member of **Chrysalis** Books plc

Copyright © 1990, 2003 The Free Press

The author has made every reasonable effort to contact all copyright
holders. Any errors that may have occurred are inadvertent and anyone
who for any reason has not been contacted is invited to write to the
publishers so that a full acknowledgement may be made in subsequent
editions of this work.

British Library Cataloguing in Publication Data
A catalogue record for this title is available from the British Library.

ISBN 1 86105 593 5

Printed in Great Britain by Creative Print and Design (Wales), Ebbw Vale

# Contents

———◆———

# Acknowledgments

———◆———

It is always a risky undertaking to acknowledge assistance for a work such as this, as any such effort is certain to neglect a number who should be specially remembered. I have therefore elected to mention only a few.

First I must mention Joseph Tomkiewicz, whose research and assistance has been invaluable; his insight has contributed much to the finished work. At the University of Wyoming, the boundless enthusiasm, knowledge, and skill of Gene M. Gressley were of great encouragement to me; and the kind efforts of Trevor West in Dublin have added so much to my knowledge of Horace Plunkett and his relationship with the Frewens.

LAWRENCE M. WOODS

# BRITISH GENTLEMEN
# IN THE WILD WEST

# Introduction

———◆———

In the summer of 1885, a young Pennsylvanian named Owen Wister came west to Wyoming Territory with two maiden ladies (friends of his mother's, who were somehow to look after him), to live and work on the VR cattle ranch, managed by Major Frank Wolcott for the Tolland Cattle Company. Though Wister—who would celebrate his twenty-fifth birthday in the West that summer—had crossed the Atlantic a number of times, only an hour's train ride west of Philadelphia already exceeded his previous western exposure in the United States.

Nevertheless, he may have known something of what he would see out there, since the British in-laws of his grandmother (the famous actress Fanny Kemble) were already cattlemen of some substance on the Wyoming plains, and word of their adventures might have reached his ear. Wister had considerable talent as a writer, as he would later demonstrate, and he saw not merely sunsets and dead trees along the watercourses, but gold and saffron vapors from "heavenly volcanoes" and monstrous spider skeletons strewn about the landscape. The journal he kept recorded these impressions and also fresh quotations that were very different from the French and English literature he had studied at Harvard; these notes and the images impressed on his mind would enrich his literary outpourings for the rest of his life.[1]

Wister's host, Major Wolcott, would later achieve notoriety for leading the big cattlemen in their ill-fated attempt to stamp out rustling by invading Johnson County, Wyoming, with a private army,

*1*

but in 1885 that disaster was still in the future. When Wister appeared on the plains there was nothing to disturb for him the image of Wolcott as a man very much in charge of the entire area stretching for some miles around the ranch headquarters on Deer Creek (not far down the Platte River from the present city of Casper).

During the time Wister was out west, he met many of the people who were important to the cattle business, and when he later wrote his famous novel *The Virginian*, those people lived on in that work, albeit as composites. Thus, the model for the Virginian himself has been claimed to be a number of westerners whom Wister met, including Sheriff Frank M. Canton (the man who filled the dual role of sheriff of Johnson County and detective for the Wyoming Stock Growers Association).

Wister also met Moreton Frewen, only five years older than himself, the son of a Sussex squire—and a man of great energy and boundless enthusiasm—who had come to Wyoming from England in 1878 to ranch. Frewen (who would later marry Clara Jerome, sister of Jennie Jerome, who was to be Winston Churchill's mother) had brought along with him a number of his friends and acquaintances, some to hunt and disport themselves in the "Wild" West and others to invest in a venture they hoped would make them all rich.

Among the latter group was Horace Plunkett, the younger son of Lord Dunsany, an Irish peer. A year younger than Frewen and much more reserved, Plunkett too was willing to suffer the privations of life with the cowhands during roundup. (He could also play tennis at the Cheyenne Club while simultaneously shouting chess plays to an opponent sitting on the veranda.) To achieve the needed scale for the profits they sought required a spacious setting; Frewen's range was on Wyoming's Powder River, and Plunkett's EK operation was nearby. Other friends of theirs were soon scattered on ranges to the west and south in the same territory.

In Colorado a Scottish earl, too, had set up his younger son in the ranching business. The earl of Airlie—descendant of a long and noble line—was chairman of the huge Prairie Cattle Company, mother of those British enterprises on the American plains. Airlie's son Lyulph settled down north of Denver, where he ranched for a time, his work interrupted only by a higher imperative to serve his queen during the Boer War. Much to Lyulph's disgust—he was dead serious about his American undertakings—the thought of having an earl's son in their presence continued to excite the local press to sometimes ridiculous extremes, as when he was supposed to have used a rooster for an alarm clock at Denver's Brown Palace Hotel.[2]

These British gentlemen had learned of an opportunity in the American West that seemed unequaled for profitability; indeed, a governor of Wyoming Territory had called it the most profitable legitimate business in the world. At the end of their third year in ranching, Moreton Frewen and his brother Dick had nearly $80,000 to divide between them, and he expected to net $1.25 million from his first five-year stint as manager of the Powder River Cattle Company—not a bad return for a young man who had had only $39,000 to invest when he left England.

The idea was a simple one: Place a herd of beef animals on the public domain, let them eat and reproduce as nature willed, and when they were fat and full grown, ship them off to market and collect the proceeds. The cost, although not insignificant, was relatively modest. All that was needed was the work force necessary to brand in the spring and collect the animals for shipping in the fall and an adequate headquarters to house the workers and their bosses when they needed such accommodations. To make the costs tolerable, the scale had to be grand—Moreton compared his range to the size of Ireland—but the unit costs shrank accordingly. When those costs were borne, the owners could expect to receive 30 percent, 50 percent, or even more as a return on their investments. It was a prospect to fire the imagination of men who were trained to lead— and to do so as gentlemen ought.

The idea of the open range did not originate with the British gentlemen, but when they came upon it they at once set out to make it better. For example, Frewen saw the chance to take over a box canyon that could readily be fenced to form a huge corral for breeding shorthorn and Sussex cattle: The offspring of this venture would vastly improve the traditional Texas longhorn breed, which had been based on Spanish imports. Consistent with Frewen's view of a proper transaction between gentlemen, he bought his pasture (which was all public land), fully recognizing that the seller had nothing to sell and the buyer acquired nothing thereby but that it was a fair deal for both.

Frewen also expanded into other functions of the beef distribution business, using the concept of a natural refrigerator atop Sherman Hill—the highest elevation on the Union Pacific Railroad, where temperatures generally dipped below freezing even in summer. There the carcasses could hang perfectly preserved until market prices in the East were attractive. That the project failed did not argue against its ingenuity, but as with many of Frewen's ideas, the timing was flawed.

In the north of the British Isles were others whose thriftiness had already been remarked around the world. They also perceived the opportunities available in the American West, but they perceived them as alternatives to other investments they could make, mostly in sound mortgages. Scottish merchants and bankers like John Clay, Jr., came west and invested, but their style and inclination were different from those of the English gentlemen, although both could enjoy the gentility of the Cheyenne Club, where Clay nostalgically sang songs from home to a grand-piano accompaniment. A bit older than Frewen and Plunkett but still only in his late twenties when he came west, Clay managed a number of ranches for the Scots and made money for himself and his masters. But there is a dour feeling around Clay, and one is led to ask whether he had as much fun on the range as Moreton Frewen did.

A Scottish nobleman whom the Frewens also knew was the earl of Dunraven, who first came west to hunt and while in Denver learned of a spectacular "park" presided over by Long's Peak, where one might have a ranch fenced in by the loftiest peaks in the continental divide. It was then late December, but he at once set out to explore the park and came away with the determination to own it. Within a few months he had amassed about six thousand acres in Estes Park and set his manager to raising cattle in this natural enclosure, now a part of Rocky Mountain National Park.

While Scottish businessmen like Dunraven built ranches based on privately owned pasture, the other British gentlemen saw a different opportunity. Perhaps it was only a historical accident, a sort of hiatus between the period in which the fertile cropland of the United States passed into private ownership and the later time when it was realized that much that was left was so dry that it could not be the domain of the 160-acre farmer. In any event, during that time the rangeland thus in unsurveyed transition was in limbo, awaiting the rush of homesteaders who never came. While everyone waited, those who cared—and dared—to act could set up operations on this land, letting their herds feast on the grasses it sustained and harvesting the return without so much as a backward glance at the owner. Governed by men who divided up thirty-six square-mile townships among themselves as readily as they might have parceled out garden plots on their estates back home, the system functioned according to rules decided on by the tenants themselves, and for a while it functioned remarkably well.

The calf dropped by its mother on the trackless prairie got up to follow her, and for its trouble was given the same brand she carried. The marking was accomplished in late spring in the first of two annual roundups, when scores of cowboys circled the range to draw the herds together for calf branding. When it came time to collect the steers for market, a second roundup was mounted and the steers and livestock were shipped east to be slaughtered. When a big outfit found a few strays with other brands, they might be sent along with the shipment and the proceeds forwarded to the rightful owner. To be sure, there were exceptions to this convenient system and the degree of compliance with it. But the watchful eyes of the stock-growers' association agents were out in Omaha and Chicago to iden-tify the foolish man who might try to sell an animal branded with another's mark.

While their operations on the range were not spartan, the civi-lized touches the British gentlemen introduced were not so much for show as in the interest of efficiency, like the telephone Frewen installed on the Powder River ranch in 1882. Since the nearest rail-road station was still two hundred miles away to the south, opera-tions in so remote a place had to be self-sufficient, and these men were determined to make them so; nevertheless, the fact that the Cheyenne Club could serve fresh oysters and fine French wines somewhat eased the rigors.

The British cattle operations were carried on for the most part through corporations, and they needed supervision to a degree here-tofore unheard of on the range: The far-off boards of directors wanted reports (sometimes as frequently as once a month), and they insisted on approving actions taken in the United States. The high cost of cables was a recurring concern as London or Cheyenne found the need to communicate—and quickly. Nor was the written word the only means employed; Frewen crossed the ocean more than one hundred times by his own count, and although few others could match that record, travel was a constant necessity. If Moreton Frewen could congratulate himself on getting a duke to be chair-man of his company, this satisfaction did not void the frustration brought on by the nobleman's insistent questioning. And the stric-tures of the foreign-based masters naturally produced friction, and sometimes scorn, in the freewheeling American West.

The English and Scottish businessmen differed in their approach to problem solving, perhaps because what was almost a natural Scottish inclination toward thrift and financial security drove them to purchase grazing land—a choice that reduced the profit that could be made but afforded greater protection when the free range became crowded. And when that happened, some of the Scots, like John Clay and Murdo Mackenzie (both of whom managed Scottish corporations), saw the demise of the free range as merely another turn in the road that had already led them from real estate mortgages to cattle. They adapted to the new conditions by developing and selling off the vast acreage they owned, while their colleagues from the British aristocracy for the most part lost interest in a world so greatly altered and chose to leave the arena, devoting their energies and money to other pursuits.

In the last two or three decades of the nineteenth century, all of these investors from the British Isles, and a few from the Continent, were present in the North American West, in the region that had formerly been only a highway to be crossed by those seeking their living elsewhere, an unbroken band of territory stretching from Alberta to northern Mexico, and including all of the front range of the Rockies in the United States.

These men were mostly young—both Frewen and Plunkett were only twenty-five when they began their ventures—and they were vigorous and willing to run the financial and physical risks that beset them in this rude and unfamiliar environment. The place they chose had all too recently been a favorite hunting ground of the Indians, and Frewen, who arrived in the Powder River Basin only two years after Custer's debacle just to the north in Montana, could still contemplate the grazing buffalo from his own porch at the ranch headquarters. An area that had been little more than a well-traveled highway could not be expected to offer many of the conveniences of civilization.

Nor was nature itself cooperative. The dry climate produced wide swings in precipitation, and in the summer, dry or somnolent streams could turn into dangerous torrents, while winter blizzards could cover the life-giving grass too deeply for even a hungry longhorn to dig up. Lightning was a much-feared occupational hazard to the herding cowboy: and a prairie fire could outrun a fast horse, sparing neither wildlife, cattle herds, nor man himself.

In spite of these obstacles, some cattle operations turned very handsome profits. The mammoth Prairie Cattle Company paid a

20.5 percent dividend in 1883 and 10 percent in each of the two following years, and others also rewarded stockholders well in the early years. But in the end, the unformed business system was destroyed by its own built-in weakness: There was no way to keep the free grass from being overgrazed by the competing herds of other ranchers. By 1886 natural increase (and natural greed) caused the seemingly endless acres to overflow with too many creatures, and when the spring thaw came after the harsh winter of 1886–87, the mortal remains of the great herds littered the hills and ravines where they had huddled to die. Even among those that survived were many too weak to live on.

In the aftermath of the disastrous winter, men like Frewen and Plunkett could do little but recognize the end when they saw it, and leave. Background and training had prepared them for success but had also given them the strength and courage to deal with adversity. The Scottish businessmen, for their part, picked up some of the pieces and kept their wounded companies alive for several more years, in some few cases realizing truly handsome profits. But it was not the same game: The grandeur of the open-range idea had expired and could not be revived. Those who remained accommodated themselves to a more constrained life, the ambit of their operation hemmed by land that was privately owned and fenced and by leases that spelled out in varying detail how many and whose animals could graze there.

Most of the British gentlemen had left the range country after the winter of 1886–87, but the big cattlemen who remained sealed the fate of the free-range system in a disastrous invasion of Johnson County, Wyoming, with a private army whose mission was to eliminate the rustlers in the area. While the U.S. Army troops arrived in time to save their lives, the trial and its aftermath left the industry mortally wounded. What nature had begun in 1886–87 was completed in 1892.

But six years before that disastrous event, Moreton Frewen had gone home, where his questing mind turned to new ideas that eventually formed a catalog too long to detail here. Some of them were to be the source of great fortune (although he sold out before he was able to share in any of it), while others were not. His political appetite was satisfied, at least in part, in the Mother of Parliaments itself.

Horace Plunkett is remembered in a different way—not for his short interval on a horse in Wyoming but for his parliamentary ser-

vice and his years of support for the organization of Irish coopera-
tives (for which he was knighted in 1903).

John Clay, Jr., stayed around the West longer and made some of
his considerable fortune there. But he continued to duck and weave
to avoid the financial perils of the western scene. He sold his interest in cattle-country banks to avoid the risk of capital calls, and by
the time he died in Chicago his fortunes were only indirectly tied
to the cattle range that he celebrated in *My Life on the Range,* his
best-known literary work. Clay had a low opinion of the English
aristocrats and his comments flavor much that has been written
about them.

The footprints left by the departing gentlemen were few. Since
they actually owned little in the way of sod and structures, there
were few tangible reminders. Still, some cattle roamed the West that
would not have been there but for the journey from the British Isles
paid for by men who knew how to improve the breed.

These men and their friends never constituted anything like a
majority of the inhabitants in this vast area, but they left an indeli-
ble mark on it; even where their legacy goes otherwise unacknowl-
edged, the hard currency they contributed to the growth of the
American West provided an impetus that was important to what
would follow. Because their western experience was brief, and afterward they went home to take up other pursuits, they cast a larger
shadow in their homeland than on our side of the Atlantic. To be
sure, they did not always succeed, for they did not resolve the Irish
question, as they had not overcome the natural disasters they faced
in the American West.

In the pages that follow, this story is traced, beginning with the
American West in the last quarter of the nineteenth century, a land
that had for so many years been only a highway to carry travelers
bound somewhere else but now stirred the interest of the cattlemen. The Indians who lived there were not pleased to see their
hunting grounds taken over by the new industry, but their free-
ranging days were ending, anyway—the buffalo that had sustained
the old life-style were gone. Strikingly, the cattlemen who followed
would use the land in much the same way the Indian had, not owning it, but grazing the "self-made" hay without the need to pay rent;
the idea was profitable but also unstable, as the future would soon
prove.

The British gentlemen who came to join the Americans already on the range were members of an aristocratic class hitherto unrepresented in American society. Their education at Eton and Harrow had trained them to be leaders, not shopkeepers, and their numbers were widely distributed around the British colonies, where they upheld the principles of conduct of the gentleman. Earlier in the nineteenth century, gentlemen sportsmen had visited the American West and inevitably caused a stir in the media when they came, but now they came to work and to manage large enterprises, so that the contrast of their members and their business style would become very apparent to the "locals."

Beginning in 1879, a royal commission investigated the new and growing phenomenon that was the American range cattle industry, and its report served as a sort of prospectus for the investments that would follow. The British aristocrats, hurrying to organize the companies that would own huge American ranches, chose the high plains that spanned the region east of the continental divide from northern Mexico to Alberta. Among those early arrivals were Moreton Frewen and his brother, Dick, who came in the fall of 1878 and settled in the Powder River basin of northeastern Wyoming. With the money from their father's inheritance, they bought sizable herds and threw themselves wholeheartedly into the business of branding and roundups, coping with fair weather and foul in a region where there were few amenities of any kind and certainly none of the sort to be found in castles and townhouses back home.

Not long after the Frewens arrived on the northern plains, other friends took up ranges nearby, including Horace Plunkett, a baron's son. These gentlemen were soon buying up cattle on an unprecedented scale. To finance their operations, public companies were organized in England and Scotland, and their boards of directors often included the cream of the aristocracy; Frewen's Powder River Company had a duke as first chairman.

These English companies often ran cattle on the public domain and bought very little land, while those managed by the Scottish merchants and bankers were more likely to invest in the rangeland itself. While the latter system particularly applied to Texas, where much of the range was owned and leased, the Scots also employed men like John Clay, Jr., to manage their operations on the northern plains, and some of them made heavy land investments (as in the case of the Swan outfit in Wyoming). Down in Texas, huge spreads were purchased and enclosed by fences that could stretch a hundred miles in a straight line.

Managing Frewen's Powder River Company was an exercise in long-distance communication, and his experience in this regard was fairly typical; western management was often entrusted to countrymen from the British Isles, and a great deal of travel was needed to oversee, inspect, and report on operations. The system of industry organization on the range permitted these huge outfits to function without many fences, and with uncounted herds roaming freely across land nobody owned. The stockgrowers' associations employed inspectors and administered laws they themselves had drawn up, so that the branding and the roundups would be conducted only when those operations could be supervised.

The center of the cattlemen's operations on the northern plains was the Cheyenne Club, where some managers maintained headquarters, and where those like Frewen who did not live there could stay whenever they passed through Cheyenne, to enjoy the hospitality and conduct business. There a rancher could make deals, learn of range conditions throughout the region, and check on cattle prices.

Relations between the foreign aristocrats and the Americans were checkered. Some were well liked and others detested, with many variations in between. It is sometimes difficult to separate truth from the colorful story or Western "tall tale," and we will look closely at both in an attempt to form a comprehensive picture of this period.

The free-range system quickly came to an end, dying from the very advantage which gave it birth: the fact that the grass cost nothing because it was not owned. Overcrowding could not be avoided, because those with herds merely drove them to the next available grassland. Frewen and some others anticipated the problem and tried to move north into Canada, but troubles with his London management delayed the move so long that only a part of the herd could enter the British dominion before the tariff barrier came down. A hard winter in 1886–87 finished off many of the foreign-owned outfits, as well as many owned by Americans. In the aftermath of that winter, a large number of the aristocrats simply left the western plains.

The memory of the British gentlemen did not totally disappear from this western region where they had once been present in some numbers. For one thing, they had brought blooded breeding stock to America, and the descendants of those animals still roam the Western ranges. And, of course, they brought millions of pounds sterling to shore up the meager Western economy. The subtle legacy of their style and training is more difficult to trace.

While the meager physical evidence they left behind was quickly obliterated by the settlers in the new states that were soon formed where first the buffalo and then millions of cattle had roamed, much that is romantic in our perception of the old West arose in this brief era. After all, Wister's Virginian was a gentleman.

# 1

# Before the Herds Came

## Prelude to the Free-Range Era

———◆———

**R**achel Fisher buried her husband in a small grove of cotton-wood trees beside the Platte River in what is now Wyoming. It was June 1847, and Rachel was now left on the Overland Trail with her husband's wagon, livestock, and the only surviving child of the four she had borne in their six-year marriage. They had been bound for Oregon, and now she had to decide what to do. "I thought of returning," she wrote, "but had no one to take me back. . . ."[1] So she pushed on, enduring more of the privations all too common for those travelers; in August the remaining child died, and she must have wondered what terrible curse followed her.

More than thirty years later, Moreton Frewen and his brother arrived in the same country to carry on a business. But even the passage of thirty years had not brought civilization, and Moreton had not been there long when he had occasion to direct an ad hoc inquest into a murder committed on the trail, a death he remarked was "rather characteristic" of the "savage" country. This land had few marks to suggest it would tolerate, let alone welcome, those whose background had so recently been filled with creature comforts.[2]

For here there were few amenities of any kind. Certainly, no traveler would find comforts he could identify with a civilized home. In 1859, Horace Greeley made a trip west and remarked that civilized comforts disappeared by stages as the party moved westward from

13

Missouri across Kansas. He last had the use of a bed in Junction City, Kansas; and by the time he reached Colorado, rough benches to sit on were a scarce luxury.

In the heyday of the overland migration, old Fort Laramie, on the North Platte River—on the southern edge of Frewen's range—was a sort of jumping-off place where the services of a small town were available. It was an anchor on the eastern edge of the high plains, an artifact of an earlier era. Even before Lewis and Clark arrived, the French *voyageurs* had come to search for beaver, and if the peltry was to be top quality, it had to be taken in cold weather. The risk to life from savage storms was added to that from Indians such as the Blackfeet, who were not pleased by the intrusion on their hunting grounds. But the mountain men were not all steel traps and pack mules. When the trapping season was over, they gathered at a great rendezvous, where the skins were traded for food, tobacco, and other supplies and barrels of whiskey—a great portion of which was consumed at the grand party, attended by their Shoshoni, Crow, and other Indian friends and by traders from St. Louis and other parts east.[3]

The rendezvous might involve eight hundred souls or so (others would say fifteen hundred), half women and children, and there would be gambling and other games of skill as well as horse racing. There was considerable trading of horses and women, too, while scandalized missionaries watched. When it was over the men might well have consumed more than their earnings from pelts and thus created a new debt to the trading company, to be settled next year, if the beaver fell in sufficient numbers and barring the intervention of the Blackfeet or some other disaster.

The venerable old fort on the Laramie River, first named Fort William, was built by fur trappers in 1834, at a time when the rendezvous system was still in full swing. The fort was finally purchased by the army for a military post in 1849, giving the region one of its few permanent white settlements and a welcome resting place for those in transit. As early as 1843 the westward migration across this highway, or band of highways, was already heavy enough for a Sioux chief to ask in wonderment whether any whites remained in the East. And the really heavy traffic was still to come. It was estimated that five to six thousand people crossed to Oregon and California in 1847, and with the discovery of gold in 1849, the flood was on; in 1850 the number was estimated at fifty-five thousand.

There was a blacksmith at the fort, and the men could work on the wagons while the women could catch up on the washing; the discipline of the group could also be sharpened for the trials ahead. Then westward again, another five hundred miles to the next permanent settlement at Fort Hall in what is now Idaho. The days could be so hot that scarce water had to be used to wet the dusty tongues of the oxen; and then the fickle weather would send winds so strong the wagons had to be anchored to the ground, or else bring roaring torrents of rain with freshets of water two feet high, like waves off the ocean, or hailstorms more vicious than any the frightened folks had ever seen. Then again, after struggling more than twenty miles without water, the travelers could be hit by a June storm leaving enough snow for snowballs, and tea might be brewed in July from freshly gathered snow.

The buffalo roamed in great numbers. Greeley reported seeing a valley more than four miles long "fairly alive" with them—he thought there were more than ten thousand in a single herd. On the trail the great beasts were both a source of food and a menace. When the Indians were on a hunt, the wagon trains had to be alert to avoid the stampeding herds of thousands, but when food was in short supply, the kill of a buffalo would provide sustenance to large numbers for a time. It was no easy task to do so, however, for the huge animal might carry his mortal wounds more than a half mile, plunge down a bluff, and swim a river before succumbing to the loss of blood. Frewen saw a herd of buffalo in 1878 when he first came to northern Wyoming and credited the great beasts with saving his life when they plowed through a snow-choked mountain pass, leaving a trail that could be followed by the party's winded horses. (But this was almost the last time such a herd could be found on the northern plains. Within a couple of years, only scattered remnants remained.)

Although the region was nearly without permanent inhabitants, one should not assume that even its limited use for highway and hunting was viewed with satisfaction by all. The government eventually awakened to the need to head off the certain collision between the Plains Indians and the hordes of travelers crossing their hunting grounds. The solution hit upon was an extension of that delightful fiction of the Indian tribe as a sort of nation within the nation. Even before the founding of the republic, the English settlers had been accustomed to dealing with the Indian tribes as treaty-making powers, much as one would deal with a foreign nation. The fiction was continued after independence, so that these treaties became the responsibility of the State Department and were ratified by the Senate, just as treaties with Great Britain or France or Russia were.

Relationships between the white man and the Indian were complicated by differences of economic condition and language, but the two societies were very different as well. The Indian policies of the United States government never comprehended the realities of Indian life-style and culture and represented only hypocrisy to the tribesmen. While the Indian agents as a group never enjoyed a particularly high reputation with either side, their failings cannot be put down to a lack of concern for the natives or to moral insensitivity. Indeed, for a time the Indian agencies were in effect subcontracted to religious bodies, so that the Episcopalians were the guardians of the Dakota, and the gentle Quakers were given suzerainty over the most redoubtable warriors of the plains—the Comanche.

It was the Comanche tribe who kept the Texas ranchers from the Panhandle region of that state, where the JA spread (the ranch was named for the brand) of Frewen's friends, John George Adair and Charles Goodnight, was ultimately located, alongside other cattle outfits of great size. Obedient only to superior power on the rare occasions when it was encountered, the Comanche generally knew no limitations to their primitive lusts except that of their own physical stamina. Making war was a part of their culture, and they conducted it with great skill. They drew maps in the dust so that the braves could commit to memory great stretches of terrain; raids were then conducted at night in periods of the full moon. During these dreaded "Comanche moons," bands could ride confidently all the way from the Red River in northern Texas and Oklahoma to Durango, in northern Mexico, and return with horses and captives over a trail broad enough to be visible for miles, beaten to a dry dust by thousands of unshod hooves.

On the northern plains, the Indians were "pacified" sooner than in the Southwest, where the Comanche roamed. In 1851, by means of a treaty signed near Fort Laramie, the high plains were for the most part parceled out among the tribes. In exchange for fifty-year annuities, the tribes also pledged themselves to permit travel across their hunting grounds and to permit the government to build military posts on their lands. (To make even more of a mockery of the treaty system, Congress later unilaterally reduced the annuities to fifteen years, and the president was authorized to cut the period further to ten.)

In the normal course of dealing with the Indians, the 1851 treaty would have been followed quickly by others to shrink the Indian presence to someone's notion of tolerability, but this progression of affairs was interrupted by the Civil War. The high plains were important to that war, but again in an indirect sort of way. They were the inconvenient territory that connected the states in the East with the valuable new states in the West. Their vastness required more troops to control than the hard-pressed Union Army could spare, and the government's policy had to be one of containing trouble rather than subduing the native inhabitants in that hostile land.

While the government was marking time in Indian affairs, the matter of providing local government in the high plains was advancing, although in a somewhat haphazard way. Before Texas joined the Union there was not a state government in the whole area, and the territories that were established by the federal government were for the most part fashioned to solve other problems. No one cared much for the western reaches of those territories, and nearly all of the interest in them focused on the settlements in their eastern regions, along the Missouri River, until some activity that was more than transient finally arose on the high plains. At first this was mostly mining, and a series of territories were organized when it became apparent that permanent settlements would rise up in the new mining regions.

A decade after the discovery of gold in California at Sutter's Mill, the Colorado gold rush was on, and in the next decade mining operations sprang up to the north in Montana and Wyoming (as well as in Idaho). These developments made possible what had heretofore been beyond the reach of those few who lived on the high plains: territorial government that was fairly nearby. Colorado Territory was organized in 1861, after attempts failed to secure immediate statehood for a State of Jefferson. Montana Territory came along three years later, carved out of Idaho, and Wyoming was organized in 1869, after the railroad arrived. Farther south, New Mexico Territory had been created out of the Mexican cession when Texas came into the Union. Now the entire high-plains area had territorial governments that, if not all that efficient, were at least subject to some political control by those residing in the region.

The government correctly assumed that the integrity of the nation demanded that the separated settled areas in the East and the West must be connected by a transportation and communication system, and this assumption spawned the Pony Express, a short-lived experiment in fast communication that could deliver a letter from St. Joseph, Missouri, to Sacramento in eight days for one dollar. Not a commercial success, the service was doomed by completion of the telegraph line in 1861.

The most important link, of course, was the railroad. The Union Pacific Railroad, chartered by Congress in 1862, faltered for three years until after the end of the conflict in the east and then surged westward, spurred by incentives that created new possibilities of riches if the task could be finished early. At the end of 1865, the terminus was at Fremont, Nebraska, but a year later it had reached North Platte; and by the middle of 1867 the new city of Cheyenne was laid out by the railroad at the crossing of Crow Creek; there the crews wintered, enjoying the hospitality of the new and very wild city that sprang up.

The construction crews and those serving them formed a mass of more than three thousand people, all of whom had to be fed. With the success of the enterprise assured, it was clear that those who provisioned this army would be paid, and paid well. An enterprising man from Colorado named John Wesley Iliff secured the beef contract for the construction crews, and as soon as General Grenville Mellen Dodge (chief engineer for the railroad) selected the site for Cheyenne, Iliff established a cow camp five miles away on Crow Creek. Early the next year, Iliff bought forty-thousand dollars' worth of cattle for delivery at Cheyenne, and from these beginnings grew a ranching operation that made him one of the cattle kings of Colorado by the time he died in 1871.

Although there were those who knew that the grasses of the plains were good for wintering stock, that knowledge did not count for much until the advent of the railroad. Iliff's operation was a direct offshoot of the railroad's construction activity, but soon others exploited another benefit the iron band could confer: access to eastern markets.[4]

Impediments still stood in the way. Indians occupied vast stretches of rangeland, but with the end of the Civil War, it was possible to turn the attention of the military to this "problem." So back to Fort Laramie the negotiators came—to strike a new deal that would reshuffle the territory so painstakingly parceled out to the Indians in 1851 in a fashion more to the liking of the white settlers.

The 1868 treaties were intended to shrink Indian landholdings.

Rather than leaving the Indians with large swatches of contiguous land that covered much of the high plains, the 1868 maps reduced the Indian holdings to reservations: the Blackfeet, Crow, and Northern Cheyenne in Montana; the Sioux in Dakota; and the Shoshonis in Wyoming. The entire region north of the North Platte River and east of the Bighorn Mountains as far as the Black Hills of Dakota was set aside as a Sioux hunting ground, although it was not a formal reservation.

The process of herding the Indians onto reservations succeeded reasonably well in the north, but in the southwest the situation was much different. Powerful tribes still roamed large areas and raided at will, making settlement and even travel impossible. The Spanish had never been able to establish more than a temporary military presence in the regions raided by the Comanche (their capitals at San Antonio and Santa Fe were essentially isolated from each other), and although the Texas Rangers, armed with the new Colt revolvers, carried out the task of exterminating most of the Indians in the eastern part of that huge state, for extended periods there was no reliable, safe communication between eastern Texas and New Mexico.

Moreover, the Indian lands were not a well-defined region in their own minds. The Comanche claimed the right to range over so much territory as they could safely cover, and their "boundaries" were fluid, responsive to any concentrations of power brought to bear against them. They sensibly avoided walled cities and forts and other well-defended areas. Consequently, when the Texans successfully established their hegemony in the regions around San Antonio, the Comanche bands ceased raiding there.

The United States government had earlier resettled a number of eastern tribes in Indian Territory (present-day Oklahoma), and the treaty-making efforts did induce some of the hostile bands to spend varying periods (often only in winter) at the Indian agencies in the territory, where rations were distributed. But the fierce Comanche never attended a treaty conference and never agreed to any reservation assignments. Led by Kwahnah, or Quanah Parker, son of a white Texas girl stolen in a raid by the tribe, this band made its headquarters for a time in the remote or Staked Plain, Llano Estacado. Despite the terrible retribution meted out by the Texas Rangers and repeated forays by the army, they still returned to raid white settlements after the armed pursuers had gone back to their fortified camps.

The end of the Comanche life-style came not by force of arms but by the decimation of the buffalo herds. For monetary gain, and with the active support of the army, the hide hunters who sold buffalo robes destroyed the food supply of the nomadic tribes and guaranteed their submission. The military action that followed was in a sense anticlimactic, but the army sent its best to do the job, a man who was first in his class at West Point. Colonel Ranald Slidell Mackenzie, a brilliant though tormented Indian fighter, commanded the Fourth Cavalry at Fort Sill; he would be called upon again and again in answer to the pleas of the Texans who came to trust his skill.

In 1874, Mackenzie took his troops to the Staked Plain, where in the summer's heat thirst-maddened soldiers drank their own blood, and the winter brought more suffering for the troops. Mackenzie caught a Comanchero (a New Mexican trader friendly to the Indians) and stretched him on a wagon wheel to extract the location of Kwahnah's hideout. The troops then surprised the tribe encamped deep in the remote Palo Duro Canyon, and although the Comanche escaped, they had to abandon their winter foodstuffs and their remuda of fourteen hundred horses. Mackenzie burned the supplies and distributed some of the ponies among his Indian scouts and killed the rest—more than a thousand—for he had already learned the bitter lesson that the Comanche were good horse thieves and especially good at stealing back their own stock. More important, he also knew that Kwahnah's band could not survive on the Staked Plain without them, and when the great fusillade destroyed the horses, both Kwahnah and Mackenzie realized that there was now no realistic alternative for the Comanche than the inevitable exile to the reservation.[5]

The Texas Panhandle was now open to settlement, and the cattlemen were not far behind the departing Fourth Cavalry. Only four years after Mackenzie's victory, Moreton Frewen first came to the Staked Plain and saw the marvelous Palo Duro Canyon, where an Irishman, John Adair, had teamed with Goodnight to create the JA ranch; this journey persuaded him to fling himself into such an enterprise.

A few years after the Texas Panhandle was cleared, the Sioux in the north also accepted the limitations of reservation life, after the irony of a victory over brevet Brigadier General George Armstrong Custer, the flamboyant, yellow-haired soldier whose spectacular end earned him the place in history that had so painfully eluded him in life. It was one of those moments when the victors conceded effective defeat and the vanquished were left in possession of the field.

In spite of their different objectives, the Indians did have at least one similarity with the cattlemen who followed them on the plains: Both believed the range should be free and unfenced. In 1810 the Shawnee chief Tecumseh (who was later to be commissioned a brigadier general in the British Army) gave William Henry Harrison (later President, but then governor of Indiana Territory) his own philosophy of public land policy. The land belonged to all, he said, and the Indians had no right to sell it, "even to each other, much less to strangers. . . ." Thus, in a sense, the Indians invented the open-range grazing system that Frewen and his friends would later exploit. The Native Americans followed seemingly endless herds of buffalo across the grasslands of the country, killing more or less at will to feed their people; the abundance of game made life bearable, if not luxurious, and there was time left after hunting for the braves to indulge in other pastimes, which often meant warfare with other tribes. Before the arrival of the horse, the Indians stalked their prey with the help of prairie fires that they set to herd the great beasts or simply to stampede them over a nearby cliff. And they regarded the land they hunted on in a way not significantly different from that of the later cattle ranchers.[6]

This philosophy was vastly different from the traditional view of property among the first English colonists. Among them, the emphasis was very much on *owning* the land. Charters from the Crown granted the land to the colonies, specifying that it was to be held in free and common socage and not *in capite* (thus, the tenure did not require military service to the king). The colonies in turn bestowed the land, often in large blocks, on those who would settle.

The new nation took over and continued the British system. If the royal governors had been generous with land grants, some of the new states were equally so. Georgia, for example, entered on an orgy of land grants; although its own law set a generous limit of one thousand acres per person, one Richard Dawson persuaded Governor George Mathews to sign warrants to him for 1.5 million acres, and there were many grants of fifty or one hundred thousand to a single person. Connecticut's Western Reserve was a 3.3-million acre tract of land in eastern Ohio, which it granted in one action to a syndicate for $1.2 million, payable in easy installments, and included in the grant the "juridical" powers, thus causing the owners to think of establishing their own state of New Connecticut. Yet these grants paled beside Georgia's sale of 35 million acres for $500,000 in the celebrated Yazoo land scandal.

Such extravagant generosity did come to an end insofar as the central government was concerned. The new nation needed revenues (it was still some years before the idea of an income tax would be palatable, and customs duties were the major source of revenue. Accordingly, the public domain began to be seen as a painless way to raise public money—at least for so long as the land held out. But if there was any concern about the size of the land inventory, that was soon dispelled by the purchase of Louisiana in 1803, followed by other cessions from the British in Oregon and from Mexico after the war with that country. The last two were small by comparison with the huge Louisiana Purchase, but on the European scale they were nation-size.

Thus it was possible for the government to sell land to private citizens and, as a result, by 1835 the public debt was entirely paid off. Indeed, a surplus totaling $28 million was distributed to the states in the next few years, but this pattern was not to continue for long. The passage of the Homestead Act in 1862 signaled a radical change of land policy. Now, for the first time, land could be had by living on it and making improvements. The old revenue imperative, leading to the minimum two-dollar-per-acre price stipulated in the act of 1800, was no longer a factor in the disposition of the public domain.

Although the rules were never stringent, violations of the land laws were always a source of trouble. But a new reason to evade them arose when the line of settlement moved out on the high plains. Here laws designed to foster small farms in the moist areas simply did not make sense, and partly for this reason, public-land-law frauds were at a high point in the 1880s. To amass the acreage necessary to make a living in this arid region one had to get around the limits in the laws, and it was not uncommon for the cattle companies to pay their cowboys to file claims, expecting the new "owners" to assign title to the company later on. Since this "obligation" could not be legally enforced, cattlemen like Frewen fretted that the cowhands would not honor the deal. As a matter of fact, apparently none of the filings made for Frewen's Powder River Company actually resulted in the issuance of a patent. While some of the filings were made by the cattle companies to obtain grazing land and control water sources, others like those of Frewen and Plunkett were only intended to acquire parcels of land around headquarters and camp locations. After all, when a range was measured in hundreds of square miles, a desert-land entry of 320 or even 640 acres was a small factor in the total being used.

Since the land was generally unsuited to the sort of farming use the law required in order to "prove up" on it, various subterfuges were resorted to. Stories abound of "proofs" describing a cabin on the property as "12 × 14," neglecting to specify the scale of the dimensions (it might well be inches) or swearing that water had been conveyed onto the property, when in fact only a single barrel of water had been placed on each of the four corners of the parcel.

Some filings were not expected to result in a patent. Frewen considered the filing fee of twenty-five cents per acre as a relatively cheap lease payment, since it permitted the land to be held for three years, after which time another filing might be made, with no effort at all to improve on the claim.

What then does one make of this land policy? Words like *efficiency* or *equity* cannot describe a policy so riddled with conflicting rules and exceptions; moreover, the free market was functioning only imperfectly, as there were efforts to interfere with the free disposition of land, in pursuance of some perceived social purpose. Thus, the 160-acre limit for homesteads was stubbornly defended, although there are as many examples to condemn it as there are those offered in its favor.

Another limitation had to do with citizenship. It was a common provision of the federal land laws to require that the grantee either be a citizen or have signified his intention to become one. Frewen and his wife both made filings in their own names, and Moreton swore that it was his intention to be naturalized. Of course, he never formally switched national allegiance, but we do not know whether a more profitable conclusion to his ranching career would have altered the outcome in that regard.

A total of thirteen states enacted laws prohibiting the acquisition of land by aliens, and in 1886 the matter came before Congress. The House Committee on Public Lands submitted a report reviewing the ownership of real estate in the territories, in support of a bill to prohibit alien land ownership there. This report included a table purporting to show the extent of foreign holdings in the entire United States (not just the territories). The total of listings in the table was 20.7 million acres, and the text could be interpreted to say that foreign holdings amounted to either 30 or 50 million acres. To emphasize the supposed gravity of the situation, the report estimated that only 5 million acres remained in the public domain where crops could be grown without irrigation, and only another 50 million where they could be grown with irrigation. With such large moral and political issues at stake it should be no surprise that the bill passed, prohibiting alien land ownership in the territories by individuals or corporations more than 10 percent foreign controlled (the railroad companies were thoughtfully exempted from the law so as to preserve their access to foreign money).

But what exactly were these foreign holdings? The report listed twenty-nine items, the first of which was the grant made by Texas to a Chicago syndicate in return for construction of the state capitol buildings in Austin. As we will note later, the syndicate did, in fact, secure foreign financing, but none of its holding of 3 million acres had ever been in the public domain, and certainly would not be affected by the proposed bill to limit foreign holdings in the territories. Another item was 1.75 million acres identified with the marquess of Tweeddale; he was chairman of the company that owned the XIT spread, and if this is a reference to that operation, it was also in Texas, and was a partial duplication of the previous item. A smaller item was for Lord Dunraven, consisting of sixty thousand acres in Colorado. This holding existed, of course, but the decimal point was misplaced; the earl's holdings in Estes Park were more on the order of six thousand acres. In fact, all of the listings were rounded to five thousand acres or greater, and one cannot have confidence that they represented more than guesses (in addition to those entities specifically identified, there were others with even more shadowy provenance: for example, "German syndicate ... 1,000,000").[7]

But neither the state nor federal laws were more than an annoyance to those foreigners possessed of the resources to evade them. The citizenship requirement was commonly avoided by having employees who were citizens make the necessary filings and then taking the title from them when it was proved up on. The alien land-law prohibition was more difficult to circumvent, but it was normally accomplished by having title taken in the name of a domestic entity (such as a corporation or trust), with the benefits flowing to the foreign beneficiary. In the end these restrictions accomplished little except litigation.

Despite the ease of acquiring large tracts of land, by the last quarter of the nineteenth century it was clear that there was still a great deal of public land "left over." Some of the land was truly beautiful, and the rise of the conservation movement had sparked the creation of national parks (Yellowstone was the first, in 1872); national forests were also established. But even after deducting these desirable vistas, there was still a huge inventory of semiarid land, totally unsuited to intensive agriculture. It was at this point that the wisdom of the Indians in their pursuit of the buffalo dawned on the cattlemen. Why not leave the public lands as they were, owned by all and by no one? The idea had a powerful economic argument behind it, for the open-range industry could not afford to buy the land for grazing. The utter vastness of the range was so great that even a tiny cost would be large if one wanted to buy or homestead a range large enough to run a big herd. Thus, when the government floated the idea of either selling the range land at five cents per acre or leasing it at one-half cent per acre per year, the Wyoming Stock Growers Association, with only three members dissenting, concluded that the cost was too great to be acceptable, and the idea was voted down.

The cattlemen's point of view was not shared in some quarters. A fair amount of the same sort of land *was* in private ownership, specifically in the hands of the railroads, which had received alternate sections in their land grants, and they were unhappy. The railroads complained that their efforts to dispose of their land for cash were inhibited by the checkerboard arrangement with the federal government and most importantly because the government was not forcing users to lease public lands, creating an impossibly low-cost (that is, zero-cost) competitor to their own leasing efforts. Still, some leasing of grazing lands did go forward. Indian lands were leased; the Matador Land and Cattle Company later held the entire Fort Belknap Reservation in Montana and three hundred thousand acres on the Pine Ridge Reservation in South Dakota and there were other huge leases in the Indian Territory.

It has often been noted that the big cattlemen acquired control over watercourses, and thereby had de facto control over the high country between the streams. While such situations existed, in the early days of the industry they were in fact atypical of the range-cattle industry outside Texas, except for those close to the land-grant railroads.

In the early years, fencing was also avoided in the open-range area. In Texas, after a brief unsuccessful effort to have the legislature ban fencing in the region, the big outfits fenced their ranges at considerable cost. Similarly, the cattle companies near the Union

Pacific often became involved in land acquisition and bought up large blocks of the railroad land. Once the purchases were made, the land had to be fenced to keep the use of the costly investment away from those who had no such stake in the business.[8]

Some fencing of public lands did occur. In 1884 the House Committee on Public Lands noted that there had long been fencing of small areas to segregate breeding stock but that now the practice had increased. In response to the committee's request, the General Land Office reviewed the situation, beginning with the complaint of the post office department that it could not make deliveries in Nebraska without the need to stop and open gates, thus leaving their "unruly" horses unattended. The Interior Department investigated and found that there was in fact some public land included in the enclosures complained of.

Other examples in the report seem chiefly identified with the so-called checkerboard problem in Kansas, Colorado, and Nebraska. Where fencing of the checkerboard lands occurred, complaints arose at once over the fact that government lands within the checkerboard were effectively made inaccessible. The government early proceeded against the cattlemen to retain access, and the cattlemen countered with the "eight-inch gap," which kept the fences from touching at the corner where the federal land abutted. In an 1889 lawsuit against the Douglas-Willan, Sartoris Company (of the Laramie plains), the government lost its argument that public lands were being fenced; only in 1895 did the United States Supreme Court decide that the checkerboards could not be fenced in a manner that prevented access to the public sections in between. The fencing problem dragged on, and in 1902 an angry Theodore Roosevelt was moved to initiate a wave of arrests for illegal fencing that resulted in jail sentences for such prominent cattlemen as Wyoming's Bartlett Richards, brother of the governor.[9]

A group of cattlemen on the northern plains was almost entirely opportunistic for a number of years, moving ahead of the settlement frontier and grazing the public lands without any effort to fence or to acquire land, except for very limited tracts at ranch headquarters. These outfits, including Frewen's 76 ranch, Plunkett's EK, and the VVV managed by Clay for Western Ranches, operated for the most part in the regions away from the railroads, and they would only fence an exceptional pasture (such as Frewen did with the box canyon he bought), where they might keep imported breeding cows away from the ordinary range bulls. It is this group that was most vulnerable to overcrowding, since anyone could move a herd onto their range (assuming the requisite courage), whereas a fenced range was, of course, limited to the use of its owner or lessee.

Therefore, while it is true that the Swan Land and Livestock Company, which acquired perhaps five hundred thousand acres of Union Pacific lands, had its land ownership scattered along stream courses, and maps of these holdings clearly establish the control these holdings represented, many cattlemen did not own any significant amount of land and did not fence. These ranchers were often quoted as being opposed to fencing of the public domain, because fencing limited the range and because of the danger fences presented during storms. (After the Union Pacific fenced its right of way, beginning in 1884, there were complaints that cattle piled up against the railroad fences during storms.) Only an XIT or a Swan could afford the enormous outlays to acquire and fence the land. The others took the risk of overcrowding and moved whenever conditions required; only when there was nowhere else to move did the system finally collapse.

While there was thus no actual ownership of the land in the public domain, the big outfit with a small army of cowboys could command a certain respect for its claim to range rights. A British lawyer for Frewen's Powder River Company described this practical fact in a letter in 1883: "In point of fact . . . these people put out their cattle in common, and if any stranger came and built a ranche and put out his cattle, we think the place would be, to use a vulgar expression, made 'too hot to hold him.'" Nevertheless, the barrister was still of the opinion that the land "rights" were of "comparative trifling value" and certainly not something one could sell debentures on.[10]

We thus have the idea of land belonging to no one and to everyone—a most appealing economic concept if it could be made to yield a profit, since, at least, the price was right and many were now eager to try their hand at this new business. For years investors in Scotland and England had made investments in the United States, at first mainly in railroad securities, which were traded in London in the 1840s; during the panic of 1873 the Scots were able to make some bargain purchases of American securities, paying for them with gold. Later they found that the return on mortgages in the United States was better than what they could get on their money in England. The Scottish syndicates sent their agents over to write mortgages, always staying ahead of the settled portion of the frontier; we are told that by 1879 Illinois had become unsuitable for such investments, because the prosperous Illinois farmers could command interest rates as low as 6 percent, which was no better than in New York or Pennsylvania and lower than the Scots were prepared to accept.

Technological improvements were also aiding the new cattle industry. As early as 1851 railroad cars were equipped with primitive refrigeration, so that several tons of butter were successfully shipped from Ogdensburg, New York, to Boston, and then in 1880 the steamer *Strathleven* carried the first meat cargo to England, using mechanical refrigeration. This ushered in the era of fresh meat shipment to Europe, an event that eventually called the attention of British gentlemen to the concept of "self-made" hay on a free range.

# A New Class in a New Land

## Who They Were and Why They Came

---

The wind was fresh off the snows lying on the summits of Wyoming's Bighorn mountains; the river was iced by the same sources and boiling like a millrace. An English gentleman and an American cowboy contemplated the river crossing and resolved to trust to the strength and stamina of their seasoned mounts. To protect their clothing, both men stripped and stowed their garments in "waterproof" saddlebags. Then into the raging Powder River they rode, the gentleman going first on his horse Walnut. Two-thirds of the way all went well, and then, in the strongest part of the current, "the old horse goes down like a stone, and we are both lost to sight for a few seconds." That underwater interlude separated man and horse in the icy water, the horse making his way back as he had come, and the man taking the shorter route to the far shore. There Moreton Frewen, younger son of an old Sussex family, and now naked as the day he was born, waited until the cowhand could bring Walnut back across the stream, where he was once more joined to the not-so-dry riding apparel of an English gentleman.[1]

This was no foolish lark, no hunting trip or safari, but the serious business of driving some loose stock across the Powder River—in short, the sort of work cattlemen everywhere were doing in those days. But it was not the usual outing for an English aristocrat back home, nor was it that usual for Frewen anywhere (although it was not the only time Frewen was to be cold, wet, and naked in the

American West), but it was the sort of unexpected event he could approach with confidence and a bit of humor.

Moreton Frewen was a gentleman, one of an undefinable breed. King James I was once asked by his nurse to make her son a gentleman; "A gentleman I could never make him," the king replied, "though I could make him a Lord." When Frewen was born in 1853, he entered the life of a gentleman in a family of substantial landowners; the father was the patron of a dozen livings, (ecclesiastical posts to which a revenue attached), and Brickwall, their lovely half-timbered Elizabethan manor house, had been in the family for three hundred years. The drawing room was hung with master works like Van Dyck and Reynolds, although financial hard times later forced the dispersal of the collection. Among other words, it included a Holbein that Moreton later recognized when he came upon it in Williams Vanderbilt's New York house; it now hangs in the Metropolitan Museum.[2]

Moreton's father was not as easygoing man, and when the eldest son, John, married a governess much against his father's will, he was disinherited. The father also petulantly refused a peerage, saying he preferred to die as the first commoner of Sussex rather than as a minor peer.

As a younger son, Moreton might have considered the clergy, but if he ever did, the consideration was short. Indeed, the family calling was more political—both father Thomas and Uncle Charles had served in Parliament—and Moreton would one day follow in their footsteps. Moreover, the calling of the cloth might have conflicted with the other joys that uplifted his soul. Once a year the family went on a sort of royal progress, to Cold Overton, a house in the hunt country, and there Moreton developed his great love for fine horses. Moreover, the handsome young man found no difficulty making an impression on the fairer sex. His own immodest assertion was that every woman he had ever enjoyed had been "completely paralyzed by the vigour" of his performance.[3]

Moreton's education was a bit different from that of most gentlemen. Although his older brother John had gone to Eton, father Thomas so disliked the result that the younger boys were tutored at home before entering Cambridge. At the university Moreton entered Trinity College, where he did rather better at polo than at Latin syntax; but his experience there marked him for the rest of his life. Although he would never outgrow his love of horses (and beautiful women), neither did he outgrow his reverence for the Empire and a patriotic interest in its governance.

Almost wholly absent in the American colonies, the aristocracy of which Frewen was a member was a class present in all its fullness in England. At its summit was the queen, who had succeeded to the throne when the fifteen children of old George III failed to produce a legitimate heir who outranked her; in 1870 she had already reigned thirty-three years.[4]

Ranking below the queen were the royal dukes, and then the other peers: dukes, marquesses, earls, viscounts, and barons. Since only the holder of a title was noble, their numbers were not large, even at the height of Victoria's reign. Indeed, the peerage had not grown at a steady rate from earliest days; instead there had been long periods when the number of peers actually declined. There are today only twenty-six dukes, and Moreton Frewen was able to get one of that select group, the duke of Manchester, to chair his cattle company.[5]

Honors were available for those who were not noble. Just below the peers were the baronets, who were entitled to be styled "Sir"; also entitled to be called "Sir" were knights, but they could not pass that honor to their heirs.

If there was no way to generalize the qualities that set gentlemen apart, there was at least a prescribed formula for the education of the sons of gentlemen. Wellington is supposed to have said that the Battle of Waterloo was won on the playing fields of Eton, and if the statement was apocryphal, at least the idea was on target. The education of upper-class boys in England was carried on at the old public boarding schools—Eton, Winchester, Westminster, Rugby, and Harrow were the "inner five"—which were not really public at all, of course, but private schools, where the parents paid for the cost of education.

These schools dominated the education of the peerage and, according to one study, accounted for 72 percent of a group of 216 peers in the eighteenth century; Eton alone was the choice of 92 in this group. As a sort of democratic touch, the public schools also received those children who could not claim their father's name, as when the marquess of Wellesley sent two of his bastard sons to Eton (where they edited the *Eton Bureau*). It was a unique system; even in Scotland the education of upper-class children was still entrusted to private tutors.[6]

Admission to the oldest public schools was almost exclusively from the upper classes, and some argued that those from the lower middle classes were unfit to attend because the improvements wrought by the school would be "contaminated" by holidays at home; yet if a manufacturer or a wealthy banker was willing to for-swear commerce for his son, the boy could take his place in the public school. For the public school boys were not being educated for science or commerce. They concentrated on Latin and Greek, and a "useful" course like mathematics was taught only as an extra subject; and it was argued with some justification that the education thus provided was not utilitarian, since most discoveries in science and technology were made by comparatively self-taught men, not public-school graduates. Rather, the boys at Eton and Harrow were being prepared for public leadership; the classics they read spoke of the duties of service and the fitness of patrician rule. Their readings from Horace inculcated the feelings of detachment and love of the countryside; and the virtues they learned to admire were order,.sym-metry, balance, and restraint. The Latin and Greek studies called for a powerful memory and, more important, formed a common bond with other gentlemen that could not easily be acquired by outsiders. These young men learned to read Greek for pleasure and could converse confortably in Latin; Robert Walpole is said to have used the language to "govern" a king (George I) who could speak no English.[7]

These early years of education were admittedly harsh, and many accounts speak of the dread and hatred children felt toward their schools, where floggings might be administered for such infractions as having a bootlace undone or not eating a piece of dry bread pro-vided before an early class. At Eton, Dr. John Keate, the headmas-ter, flogged an average of ten boys per day, Sundays excepted, and on some days the total was far more than that. On one occasion the boys determined to resist in a body, perhaps in the hope that their numbers would deter the punishment. To their dismay, Keate com-menced executing the penalty and continued until a shower of eggs caused him to suspend the proceedings to change clothes; then he resumed until all had been flogged, a total of about eighty, accord-ing to one commentary.[8]

Inside the public-school system, a strange equality prevailed. There were few servants, and discipline was chiefly placed in the hands of the senior boys; the son of even the noblest family began as a "fag" to the older boys, waxing their shoes, boiling water for their tea, and carrying their cricket balls and bats.

Such stringencies were supposed to build character, and possibly they did, although we cannot know at what cost. Indeed, the case of the marquess of Londonderry is cited as an example of the good that could be accomplished. The lad came to Eton filled with the pride and dignity that had been instilled in him by his mother and obsequious servants; the Reverend William Rogers, also a student at the school, later recalled that he asked the boy his name. "I am Charles Stuart Vane, Viscount Seaham, and my father is the Marquis of Londonderry," was the reply. Thereupon Rogers kicked the young viscount three times, "once for Vane, once for Seaham, and once for Londonderry." It has been suggested that the reason Prime Minister William Edart Gladstone disliked Dr. John Keate was because the headmaster was not sufficiently impressed with Gladstone's own evaluation of his dignity.[9]

Nevertheless, some aristocrats so hated the brutality at the public schools that they had their sons tutored at home; the duke of Devonshire chose this alternative (although we are told Lord Hartington was "unsophisticated" as a result), and Lord Chatham thought all Eton boys were "cowed for life." As has already been noted, Thomas Frewen only permitted his eldest to be educated at Eton, preferring to tutor the younger boys at home; it was for this reason that Moreton Frewen lacked one of the marks of most gentlemen— a public school education.

Still, most aristocrats sent their sons to the public schools, as did Lord Dunsany, who sent his son Horace Plunkett to Eton in 1868. Plunkett later ascribed the want of such an education as the cause for the troubles his partner Alexis Roche (he did not go to public school) suffered in later life; said Plunkett, "[Roche] lorded it over the stable boys, when he ought to have been fagged & kicked. . . ." And after a boy had come through the public school experience, his father would no longer kiss him on the cheek as he would a child; later the lad would be treated as a gentleman in his own right.[10]

Beyond public school was the university, and here Oxford and Cambridge dominated the field, accounting for half of the college education of peers during much of the eighteenth century. By far the most popular college for these gentlemen was Christ Church at Oxford. The Frewens had attended Oxford in the old days, and a portrait of their ancestor who was an archbishop of York still hangs there. But Moreton's generation went to Cambridge. Moreton found college life not too demanding, and noblemen could earn a degree without even the pretext of an examination, sometimes in spite of behavior that was less than exemplary.[11]

After formal education was complete, military service was in prospect for the gentleman, especially for younger sons, and the family

honor turned on getting posted to the best regiments or seconded
to the personal staff of a commander. Nor was the thirst for the
military solely a matter of snobbery. Some families, such as the
Ogilvys (the earls of Airlie), had long traditions of military service.
In that tradition Lyulph Ogilvy, ranching friend of Frewen's, enlisted
in Torrey's Rough Riders during the Spanish American War (although he did not see action); and when the Boer War broke out,
he embarked for the scene of battle with a shipload of horses and
mules and served the British Army as a captain.

Getting the right military appointment called for pulling strings.
(Moreton Frewen wrote to ask his wife to put in a word with the
Prince of Wales to advance the cause of his younger brother
Stephen. The effort failed, although the prince professed to be cooperative.) If the right appointment could not be secured, there
were other ways to get to the scene of action. Windham Thomas
Wyndham-Quin, heir to the earldom of Dunraven and Mountearl,
joined the First Life Guards as a subaltern (the rank below captain)
after leaving Oxford but resigned when he failed to get an appointment on the general's staff; he then joined the Abyssinian expedition of 1868 as a special correspondent, a ploy also used by Winston
Churchill during the Boer War. Dunraven fairly thirsted for military
action, and during the Franco-Prussian war was again at the scene
of action as a correspondent; he also had seen the Carlist rebellion
in Spain and the Crimean War of 1857.

Extensive and complex as the formal honors, schooling, and military service were, they did not in themselves serve to define what a
gentleman was. Some Americans watching from afar thought this
training process and background inhibited growth and improvement; Owen Wister observed: "The young Englishman of today is
not so different from his grandfather. For the Englishman is a con-
gealed specimen—a permanent pattern—while each generation of
us is a new experiment."[12]

Nor could the pattern be called into being at will. With the cre-
ations of so many new peerages (some of the early ones had been
acquired by purchase), it is impossible to think that those receiving
such an honor would be magically converted into gentleman. Certainly any distinction that may have justified the creation of a peerage or baronetcy would not necessarily manifest itself in future generations. Except for the initial recipient, the right to a title was a
function of birth, so that it could be said that the study of a group
of peers, such as dukes, might well produce a truly random sample

of humanity. There have been marvelously brilliant dukes, some who were certifiably mad, and a full spectrum of variations in between. Great commanders do not necessarily pass their brilliance to their progeny, particularly in a system where the title may pass sideways on the genealogical chart to distant heirs.[13]

But the dignity of a peerage often did have the effect of fostering an appetite for excellence, and this appetite animated whole generations of upper-class young men. There was something in the character and training of British gentlemen that made it imperative for them to take the next ship to defend the Empire—as Lyulph Ogilvy did—even if it was a horse transport. A "noble" way of thinking and behaving was said to accompany the possession of power, by virtue of the high responsibility of such a station and of habitually dealing with great matters and being placed "above the necessity of constantly struggling for little things."

It all sounded terribly arrogant to American ears, but aristocracy was not a matter of the moneyed classes arrayed against the poor; indeed, as in the United States, the English gentleman was typically suspicious of the inroads on society being made by men of business. Matthew Arnold, the English poet and critic, deplored this tendency, asking rhetorically, "Who or what will give a high tone to the nation?" A merchant or manufacturer should be excluded from the world of fashion, according to Arnold, not because of his lack of manners but for his lack of the moral sentiments of a gentleman.[14]

Moreton Frewen met the young Rudyard Kipling in India and resolved to help the aspiring journalist get his work published in England. Kipling, who had also received a gentleman's education, invented the phrase "the white man's burden" to describe the duties and responsibilities of Empire; and although there were racist undertones in the concept, it also conveyed a sense of the obligation of gentlemen to make the lot of the queen's subjects better than they found it.

The conviction that British institutions and principles of behavior were the best in the world was almost a matter of religion. Indeed, on a rare occasion when a British cavalry regiment in India was fleeing from the Sikhs, a chaplain halted them with the assertion that Almighty God would never permit a Christian army to be cut up by pagans. Of course, this attitude served to justify a great deal of martial activity. It is ironic that historians have used the term *Pax Britannica* to identify the long period of war presided over by Victoria's Empire; one writer at least has taken the trouble to list a number of the military engagements fought during her long reign: They average nearly two per year.[15]

Nevertheless, the principles that were pursued so relentlessly were not trivial. In 1833, Britain abolished slavery in her territories and therafter used her considerable power to make war on the peculiar institution wherever it still flourished. If the slavery practiced by white men did not escape British condemnation, one would expect cruel native customs to fare no better, and that was so. In India the British abolished suttee, the ritual immolation of the widow on the death of her husband; General Sir Charles Napier, who issued the order, was a gentleman descended from Charles II and from the inventor of logarithms. When the Indians protested that suttee was a national custom, Napier haughtily replied that the British also had a national custom, which was to hang those who burned women alive. "Let us all act according to national custom," he said. Napier freely admitted that he was on occasion unjust, saying, ". . . against all evidence I decided in favour of the poor; and argue against the arguments of the government so long as I can." He was a tyrant, but a refreshing breed of tyrant.[16]

Rudyard Kipling wrote stirring poetry that expresses the Victorian idea of the gentlemen. In "The Ballad of East and West" he tells the story of an English colonel's son who goes off alone to apprehend the border thief who stole his father's favorite mare. Riding into the thief's stronghold across twenty miles of rough country guarded by the outlaw's men, he at last comes face to face with the thief, who says in wonderment, "What dam of lances brought thee forth to jest at the dawn with Death?" When he reminds the rash young man that at any point in the past twenty miles he could have had him killed and left as carrion for the jackels and vultures, the colonel's son answers that if "a thousand swords" should follow to retrieve his bones the price of his father's favorite mare would be too high for a thief to pay. It was Kipling's idea of a gentleman's answer.

Although the episode was fictional, plenty of examples from life underlay its authenticity. When Captain Scott's party was pinned down by an Antarctic blizzard on the way back from the South Pole in 1912, Captain Lawrence Edward Grace Oates, knowing that his own infirmity reduced their chances of survival, deliberately walked out in the storm, saying, "I am just going outside and may be some time"; he was not seen again. The entire party perished, but the Oates' story, was preserved in their papers. It was the action of a gentleman.

Composure in the face of mortal danger was also a hallmark of the gentleman. When Major Lewis Lovatt Ashford Wise as a guest at Frewen's ranch in Wyoming, he and his guide, Oliver P. Hanna, were charged by a wounded bear in the Bighorn Mountains. Not losing his head, Wise calmly reloaded and fired, driving the maddened animal away (it soon died from the wounds), and thus saving the life of the badly mauled Hanna. He then carried Hanna back to camp and medical attention (although he stopped to blaze a nearby tree to mark the location of the trophy represented by the 1,100-pound bear). Hearing of the episode, Moreton Frewen remarked with satisfaction that Wise had reacted "quite as he should."[17]

Even when unpleasant tasks were at hand, the gentleman was expected to meet them with style. When word of the outbreak of the War of 1812 reached the British garrison at Fort George on the Niagara border, the officers were at dinner with their American counterparts. All agreed the dinner must continue, and the guests were afterward conducted to their boats with expressions of regret. Amid the moral imperatives and the public duties was also the duty to be gentlemanly.

The system did not try to produce an intellectual elite, and other qualities, if not of first importance, were at least closely observed. The earl of Lonsdale, who loved horses with the same enthusiasm as did his friend Frewen, said, "I can always tell all I want to know about a man by the way he sits on a horse." Doubtless an overstatement, it is made tolerable by the fact that the world of the Victorian gentleman also involved a leveling inconsistency in its distinction: The poor of "good breeding" could be received alongside one of the richest men in the realm who had only recently been raised to a dukedom, and they had in common only the fact that both were gentlemen—a quality that none could define but all could identify.[18]

On the western shores of the Atlantic, Americans (then as now) were both attracted and repelled by the idea of the gentleman. The rich engaged in outrageously exaggerated imitations of much that was least notable among the aristocracy, holding dinners to honor pet dogs and smoking cigarettes wrapped in hundred dollar bills—a phenomenon that sociologist Thorstein Veblen would later explain as a way for those in a capitalist democracy to achieve a sense of status. Yet, the efforts of the nouveau riche missed the fact that the style they sought was not solely a function of wealth. Lady Clodagh Anson, daughter of the marquess of Waterford, remarked on this paradox. "What struck me most about the towns in Texas in those days," she said, "was that they had all sorts of things we

should have called luxuries over here, like ice, electric light and tele-
phones, as a matter of course, but none of the *ordinary comforts* of
life" (emphasis supplied).[19]

To many the conspicuous consumption of the wealthy Americans
came to represent much that was wrong in the new industrial society, and the reaction against it made if difficult to give credit to
those with better motives; thus, even so unusual a millionaire as
Andrew Carnegie could give away $300 million in his lifetime, and
still not escape criticism for dying with some $30 million left.[20]

To be sure, sometimes the burdens of position were more than
the gentleman could cope with. Cast off by his parents, Harry
Thynne shot himself in Wyoming, after trying cowpunching for
Moreton Frewen's operation and then eking out a precarious existence by writing, all the while spending his meager earnings on
whiskey. Plunkett, never noted for tolerance, called young Harry
the "bibulous son of a bibulous father." His blood was blue, for his
father's brother was the marquess of Bath and his mother's father
was the duke of Somerset; Plunkett opined that he might have
ended differently had he been blessed with kind parents.[21]

Although not trained for business, the gentlemen often found
opportunity for them to learn of it in family enterprises. If the family
had extensive property, there was good training in management,
which some accomplished very well. Edward Montagu Stuart Granville Montagu-Stuart-Wortley-Mackenzie, by hard work and the
good luck of finding coal deposits on his Yorkshire estates, restored
the family fortunes, and Victoria raised him from Baron Wharncliffe
of Wortley to earl of Wharncliffe and Viscount Carlton of Carlton.
While Wharncliffe, who later chaired the Powder River Company,
had interests in the world of finance, he was also complimented by
Lillie Langtry for using his new fortunes to collect art and to encour-
age its appreciation.[22]

The gentleman inherited, along with his estates, what have been
called the "duties of land." Thus, there were penny clothing funds
to be formed, and the building of good cottages and schools. Some
landlords discounted rents for the poor, and a few, such as the earl
of Scarborough, provided nearly all the facilities for a new town,
including roads, a cattle market, a cricket ground and the water supply. While some might point out that such largess also gave him a
measure of social control, the facilities *were* a boon to the lower
classes. And there were other cultural advantages. Sponsorship of
sporting events by the aristocracy produced some of the traditional

horse races in England, including two by the earl of Derby—the Oaks, established in 1778, and two years later the famous Derby itself.[23]

Another aspect of the British gentleman's education that encouraged travel was the so-called sporting instinct. Moreton Frewen tried to explain it to Clara Jerome in this fashion: "You know, the sporting instinct implies a great deal beyond *killing*. The love of new & wild experiences, the artist soul, the love of untutored nature . . . ." The British gentleman was passionately devoted to the hunt, however it might be defined, and it was this devotion that brought him early to the western United States.[24]

The adventures of the sportsmen are not the centerpiece of our story, but it is impossible to ignore their extravagant expeditions, each of which became a major media event in the country. They did play a useful role in attracting the British investor to the United States, for some of those who joined the earl of Dunraven to hunt in Estes Park stayed on to invest in the Colorado cattle business; and after Lord St. Oswald's son came to hunt with his good friend Moreton Frewen, the young man organized the Big Horn Cattle Company.

There had been many noble hunters on the American plains before Frewen arrived and, unfortunately, they left behind an image of the hunter so well known that it tended to overshadow the more serious business the other gentlemen had to dispose of; it is for that reason we acknowledge them, if only as a contrast.

The sportsman was often portrayed as someone with more money than he could usefully spend and more time than he could usefully occupy, leaving him no alternative but to indulge himself. Of this type was Captain William Drummond Stewart, second son of a Scottish baronet; his father bought William a commission when he was seventeen, in time for him to serve under Wellington and to be decorated for bravery at Waterloo. The family estates in Perthshire included Birnam Wood, that movable forest made famous in Shakespeare's *Macbeth*. In 1832, after a bitter quarrel with his brother (who had trusteeship over the inheritance from his father), William then thirty-six, left Murthly Castle on the Tay and the following spring brought a party of 40 men (and 120 mules) to the high plains to hunt; William Sublette and Robert Campbell, outfitters for the Rocky Mountain Fur Company, had accepted five hundred dollars from Stewart to let him tag along with their annual supply expedition to the West. With the expedition was young Dr. Benjamin Harrison, son of General William Henry Harrison; young Ben (who had paid a thousand dollars for his "passage") had a drinking problem his father hoped would be cured by the long separation from civilization.

Stewart met that legendary mountain man and storyteller James Bridger, who could readily prove the truth of at least one tale of courage and daring, since he carried embedded in his hip an arrowhead, the souvenir of a struggle the previous year with a Blackfoot chief. Stewart and Bridger remained together after the annual fur trapper rendezvous broke up and saw much of the West together. Stewart went on to hunt in the Crow country north and east of the Bighorn mountains. A thief stole his best horse and, in a range, Stewart vowed to pay five hundred dollars for the thief's scalp; to his chagrin, a trapper took him at his word, returning with the horse and the bloody trophy. Stewart reluctantly paid his foolish bounty.

Stewart's group spent a number of years in the West, and it was on his 1837 journey to that region that William received the momentous news that his brother, the baronet, was dying, and that he was to become Sir William Drummond Stewart, baronet of Grantully. William returned home, bringing with him to Scotland two Indians, a pair of buffalo, a young grizzly, and assorted seedlings of western trees.

On the 1837 trip, too, Stewart (perhaps inspired by the example of the German Prince Maximilian of Wied-Neuwied, who had traveled the West with the artist Karl Bodmer to make a visual record), engaged the young artist Alfred Jacob Miller to record his travels in pictures. After their return to the East, Stewart invited Miller to continue his work at Murthly Castle, where the artist labored over a number of works that record their western adventures and was astounded by the trappings of riches. Yet Stewart's new wealth could not blot out the western years. He surrounded himself with Miller's paintings and preferred to sleep on buffalo robes, shunning the featherbeds in the castle.[25]

Although Stewart first came to the West nearly fifty years before Frewen and the other gentlemen came to ranch there, it is worth spending a moment contemplating this remarkable man. His early life in Scotland had been unhappy, including a bitter argument with his older brother as well as an awkward marriage to a pregnant servant. When he came to the West, that land of endless vistas and primitive people (both native and white) caught his imagination—much as it would captivate Moreton Frewen—and he brought back to Murthly Castle not only samples of the flora and fauna of the area he had visited but also the young half-breed Canadian he had hired, Antoine Clement. Clement was a sort of "child of nature" whom Stewart dressed in black livery to serve table, in a vain effort to mold the *voyageur* spirit that had so willingly served him on his western journeys to the life of service to a Scottish baronet (Clement later went back to America).[26]

Those finicky judges of character, the mountain men, complimented the Scotsman in their own idiom, saying that Stewart was "almost as good a mountaineer as any" and that there was the hair of the grizzly bear in him. In those settings he sometimes cut a strange figure when he unpacked his white leather hunting jacket and plaid trousers, but he also proved to have a better insight into the Indian character than his teachers; when a Crow stole a favorite tomahawk from him, Stewart made no effort to retrieve it. The Indian had warned him he would steal it if Stewart persisted in refusing to be traded out of it.[27]

Perhaps the most spectacular of the foreign hunting groups was that of St. George Gore, an Irish baronet whose annual income amounted to two hundred thousand dollars; he came to the West in 1854 and spent three years hunting. His entourage included twenty-seven wagons, four requiring six mules apiece; one was entirely devoted to firearms, including seventy-five rifles, and two others held the fishing tackle (a professional fly dresser was in the party). When the party paused for the night it must have been a striking sight, for Gore's personal tent was green-and-white striped linen and came equipped with a washstand and a brass bed. Among the numerous animals were 112 horses, 18 oxen, 3 milk cows, and 50 Irish staghounds and greyhounds, whose descendants enlivened the American countryside for some years afterward.

Like Stewart before him, Gore met Jim Bridger, who got along well with the baronet, but was not overawed by him; in the evening, the aristocrat would read selections from books to the old mountain man, and listened to Bridger's comments. The trip cost five hundred thousand dollars, and the slaughter accounted for two thousand buffalo and sixteen hundred deer and elk; there was some little permanence to all of this expenditure: Gore's name graces a number of places near Steamboat Springs, Colorado, as a memento of this journey.[28]

Despite the grandeur of the foreigners, the locals were no slouches at arranging hunts, as the army demonstrated in 1870, when a distinguished group came west to try their hand at the slaughter of buffalo and other game. Host of the expedition was Lieutenant General Philip Henry Sheridan, the Civil War hero, who had directed Reconstruction in Texas and Louisiana with a vigor that did nothing to endear him to the citizens of those states. In 1870 he was commander of the division of the Missouri, headquartered in Chicago and responsible for the sprawling territory from the Great Lakes to the Rocky Mountains.[29]

Transportation for the hunting party was provided in a spacious palace car furnished by the Northwestern Railroad. The presence of two newspaper editors ensured adequate attention from the media. Also prominent in the group were the two Jerome brothers from New York. Lawrence was a close friend of Chester A. Arthur (the future president) and the Prince of Wales, and he was famous as a high-stakes gambler. His brother, Leonard, who was to be Moreton Frewen's father-in-law, was even more distinguished and had amassed a fortune in Wall Street. A strong supporter of the Union side in the Civil War, he had contributed thirty-five thousand dollars to the construction of the vessel *Meteor,* built to hunt down and destroy the rebel raider *Alabama,* and he was a part owner of the *New York Times* (whose the offices he helped defend with a Gatling gun during the draft riots of 1863). Jerome had been American consul in Trieste in 1851–52, a tour of duty that instilled in Mrs. Jerome and her daughters a love of things European that would last throughout their lives, at some considerable financial cost to Leonard. His three daughters all married into the British aristocracy, and history remembers him best as the father of the dark-haired beauty who won the heart and hand of Lord Randolph Churchill, the second son of the seventh duke of Marlborough, making Jerome grandfather of the future prime minister of Great Britain, Winston Leonard Spencer Churchill.

The gathering was treated to a dress review of five companies of Fifth Cavalry, and there was a lavish ball at the North Platte depot before they took to the field. The hunt itself lasted ten days, and the celebrities were accompanied by a hundred troops and a sixteen-wagon train—one wagon devoted entirely to ice and three others to carry the guns for the party, and to convey the five greyhounds when they tired of the chase. All of this was ministered to by French chefs, who had linen, china, and glassware available to aid in a proper performance of their duties. The kill was extensive enough to cause one editor to question whether the upcoming royal hunt would find any game.

The next year was the year of the royal hunt. Clara Frewen's friend, noted artist Albert Bierstadt, had written to General William Tecumseh Sherman to tell him that the Russian Grand Duke Alexis was interested in a buffalo hunt; Bierstadt also suggested that assembling some Indians for the affair would add to the excitement of the trip. To make certain he was being heard, Bierstadt repeated his request to the secretary of war, who responded that the matter could be handled with "no difficulty." (Bierstadt later received the Russian order of Saint Stanislaus for his solicitude in the matter.)[30]

It was late in 1871 when the grand duke came. To set him apart from some of the aristocrats before him, Alexis was not only of royal blood but was also blue-eyed, blond, tall, certifiably handsome, and young—he would pass his twenty-second birthday on the plains. Although the grand duke was not particularly high in the line of succession to his father, Tsar Alexander II (he was the third son), Russian support for the North in the Civil War, the purchase of Alaska in 1867, and the pro-Russian attitude of the United States during the Crimean War had warmed relations between the two countries, causing the U. S. government to roll out the red carpet for the young Romanov. After a meeting with president Grant, the grand duke was placed in the charge of General Phil Sheridan to direct the planned hunt, and Sheridan in turn detailed Bill Cody to escort Alexis.

The army did not leave to chance the matter of providing an adequate supply of buffalo, and General John Pope sent an army unit to track the southern buffalo herd; General Ord set up a supply base in Omaha for the group. Although the party camped in tents and Sheridan had warned that the grand duke would have to be prepared to "rough it a little," it was hardly spartan; the grand duke's tent was heated and had a floor carpeted in royal red. To give the proper flair to the military escort, Sheridan assigned brevet Brigadier General George Armstrong Custer to accompany the grand duke, a task to the liking of the flamboyant young officer, then only four years from his spectacular end on a barren Montana hillside.

The Americans were much impressed by the Russian custom of breaking out a basket of champagne whenever the grand duke made a kill. The Sioux chief Spotted Tail arranged for a program of Indian sham battles and games of skill to amuse the Russians and only caused minor unrest when he lectured the party for the contrast of great luxury with the poverty of the Sioux (his speech was not translated for the royal guest). The hunt was a success from the grand

duke's viewpoint, although he was disappointed that the kill was
not a record number (only fifty-six). A certain Mrs. Raymond, who
was also an accomplished hunter (of game), joined the party for a
time, and the young Russian was happy to be one of the few aware
of her presence and the fact that she spoke French (as did he). After
a visit to Denver that included the grandest ball of the season, the
grand duke returned to Russia.[31]

Although the great hunting expeditions of Gore and others resulted in the naming of some places in the West, otherwise such
characters as Captain Stewart, St. George Gore, and the Grand
Duke Alexis left little save newspaper clippings in the wake of their
travels in the United States. If we merely mention the trappings of
luxury that accompanied these gentlemen sportsmen, we run the
risk of emphasizing only the sensational. While they were admittedly indulging in sport, there was little that was soft about them;
the earl of Caledon later assured Clara Frewen that when training
for his hunting trip to the American West, he had slept outside his
mansion and told his footmen to keep his blankets damp.

On the heels of the noble sportsmen came a new crop of "nobs"
who were intent not merely on hunting (although they would take
their ease in that sport as well) but to engage in the serious business
of raising cattle on the western plains. The great appeal of those
plains was the grass—countless square miles of it. The paradox of
this marvelous feedstuff was the fact that it actually nourished the
cattle better in those years when moisture was scarce; after a wet
summer, Frewen complained, "none of our beeves are fit to market,
grass after those awful wet months is green & weak in nutrition."
Consequently, in that part of the Powder River Basin south of Clear
Creek, where the winter snows seldom were deep enough to cover
the grass beyond the reach of the foraging cows and steers, the
herds could fend for themselves, growing fat in the winter months.
It was a region ready-made for such an enterprise as they had in
mind.[32]

The United States was also ready for the social infusion the
gentlemen represented. Then as now, the curiosity of titles that
were conferred most often only by birth (and occasionally by a willing sovereign) fascinated the Americans, perhaps because so few
members of the noble classes ever settled in the original thirteen
colonies. For the most part, the upper class was entirely missing
from the Atlantic shores; except for an occasional resident landlord
such as Lord Fairfax in the Northern Neck of Virginia, there were

no dukes, no marquesses, earls, viscounts, or barons; and very few knights. One historian, trying to discover the roots of nobility among the colonists of South Carolina, was finally able to find the names of "at least" eleven people who were entitled to coats of arms. While he doubtless thought the discovery important—and indeed, the South Carolina colony probably fared better than most in this regard—it was a meager representation of the upper classes from the old country.[33]

Moreover, the trappings of gentle society were entirely missing. While Frewen could reminisce about royal visits to his ancestral home, showing off a pair of slippers once owned by Elizabeth I herself, such opportunities did not occur in the colonies. As another historian commented, "New York had no royal towns like Windsor, no episcopal cities like York, no university towns like Oxford, and no pilgrimage towns like Cambridge. Its urban centers were . . . nurseries for a nation of shopkeepers." And Denver and Cheyenne were not New York. Even the language was changed by the lack of settled order at the top of society. As the redoubtable H. L. Mencken later remarked, the few men of education, culture, and gentle birth among the first settlers "were soon swamped by hordes of the ignorant and illiterate, and the latter, cut off from the corrective influence of books, soon laid hands upon the language," so that the American version of English quickly adopted words that would have been unthinkable in England.[34]

Nevertheless, the absence of titled people did not mean an absence of wealth or of class distinction, for that matter. The Americans immediately set about creating their own class distinctions, based on wealth, not birth. By the 1880s there was a long list of socially acceptable families in New York and elsewhere on the East Coast, and they were busily constructing the tangible evidence of their achievements. The wealth of the Rockefellers, Morgans, Vanderbilts, and Astors was familiar to every schoolchild, but there was not a title among them until they began sending their daughters eastward across the ocean to collect them.

In 1876, Consuelo Yznaga del Valle journeyed from the United States to win the hand of Lord Mandeville, heir of the duke of Manchester, and in 1896 her namesake, Consuelo Vanderbilt, was wed to the ninth duke of Marlborough, to the great satisfaction of old Mrs. Vanderbilt, Another American, Lilian Warren, had earlier been the second wife of the eighth duke after his first wife (the daughter of the duke of Abercorn) divorced him over his affair with the countess of Aylesford. Louisa Caton, daughter of a Baltimore merchant, married the duke of Leeds, and just after the turn of the century, May Goelet landed the duke of Roxburghe—and these were only the dukes; wealthy American girls had an even easier time among the lesser titles.

Of course, one must not leave out the second daughter of millionaire Leonard Jerome, Jennie Jerome, who married Randolph Churchill, the brilliant second son of the duke of Marlborough in 1874. She did not become a duchess, but before syphilis deranged his mind, her husband came close to being one of the younger prime ministers, and the political life of her son, Winston Leonard Spencer Churchill, was rich beyond any dreams she might have had, for he would in fact decline a dukedom preferred by a grateful queen. Jennie's older sister was Clara Jerome, and it was she who later married Moreton Frewen, the young man who had come to make his fortune in the land he called a "savage" country.

Frewen was by no means the only foreign gentleman on the range, and although the great majority of the noblemen and their sons were of British origins, a few came from other countries. The most famous of those others was Antoine Amédée Marie Vincent Amot Manca de Vallombrosa, the marquis de Mores (heir to the Duc de Vallombrosa), who came to a range on the western edge of the Dakota badlands, where he set up a ranch and built a slaughterhouse and a town; he also ran a stage line south to the Black Hills.

In Denver, a Prussian army officer and veteran of the Franco-Prussian war, Walter Baron von Richthofen (a relative of the so-called Red Baron of World War I) ran a dairy farm with purebred Holstein cows and a horse farm, and laid out and developed the town of Montrose, Colorado, while publishing a book on the range cattle business.

Most of the rest were British. A friend of Moreton Frewen's, Algernon James Winn, son of Lord St. Oswald, came to establish the Big Horn Cattle Company. Next to Frewen on the Powder River was Horace Curzon Plunkett, third son of Baron Dunsany, who first came to America in association with Alexis Charles Burke Roche and Edmund Burke Roche, sons of Baron Fermoy. Another of Plunkett's partners was Edward Shuckburgh Rouse Boughton, second son of a baronet, who later moved south to the Laramie Plains, where he ran the Ione Cattle Company, buying land from the Union Pacific Railroad, raising cattle, and also building windmills and breaking the prairie sod to grow crops by irrigation.[35]

Another rancher in the Powder River country was Oliver Henry Wallop, a younger son of the earl of Portsmouth, who had set up a ranch to sell horses; the outbreak of the Boer War created a ready market for them. His partner in the venture was Malcolm Moncrieffe, the son of Scottish baronet. Together they ran a 2,700-acre ranch, brought the first thoroughbreds to that part of the country, and built one of the first polo fields in the nation.[36]

While the ranges were thus being stocked in the north, other outfits were forming elsewhere. In Colorado, Frewen's friend the earl of Dunraven caused a great stir during this period by buying the heartland of Estes Park and running it as a ranch and resort. Others were present further south. In Texas the mighty Matador, Espuela (Spur), and XIT outfits were all controlled by British money and had British managers. These huge ranches operated on ranges the companies owned and fenced; they included some of the largest assemblages of deeded land the country had ever seen. In the same state was the famous Rocking Chair Ranche, headed by Dudley Coutts Marjoribanks, first baron Tweedmouth, and his brother-in-law, John Campbell Hamilton Gordon, seventh earl of Aberdeen; they were rumored to be representing the queen herself in the enterprise.

And the list goes on. Of course, there were also some truly unfortunate examples. Another of Moreton Frewen's friends, Heneage Finch, the earl of Aylesford, exiled himself to the United States following the scandal of his wife's affair with Lord Blandford, heir to the duke of Marlborough. Settling near Big Springs, Texas, the unfortunate earl bought some land and cattle and consumed truly heroic quantities of beer and spirits while vainly trying to establish a new fortune for his daughters. Further south, in northern Mexico, Lord Delaval James de la Poer Beresford, youngest son of the marquess of Waterford, took up ranching (he also had operations in New Mexico and Canada), and to the dismay of his family consorted with (some say married) a local woman who may or may not have managed the Mexican ranch—with fair success.

Even with the few bad apples, it was a remarkable collection. And these were only the ones who ventured out on the range. Back home, the boards of directors of the western cattle companies were filled with titles—a duke was by no means impossible (Manchester headed Frewen's Powder River Cattle Company), and there were earls and barons aplenty.

What was the attraction of the cattle business for such an aristocratic group? Certainly, it was more than an expensive game, and while they were concerned with creature comforts (many in those days would have called them luxuries), they also paid attention to the business. Although they did not lack experience with cattle raising in England and Scotland, where the world came to buy quality Hereford, Sussex, or Shorthorn breeding stock, none of these men had experience on the scale and under the conditions the range-cattle industry was developing on the western plains. Yet they were soon contributing to new conceptions of scale in the new land.

It was 1878 when Moreton Frewen first came to the American West, in the company of John George Adair, an Irishman who was then in the ranching business in Texas. On that trip (of which more later) the twenty-five-year old Frewen was immediately taken by ranching and began to make plans to launch himself into this industry. Moreover, things had not gone as well at home as he could have wished; his Uncle Charles, who had dangled an inheritance before Moreton's eyes and had at least partially cooled the young man's passion for gambling (Moreton thought this was the price of favorable mention in the will), had finally died, and Moreton waited anxiously until the word of his share became known: nothing. (Almost more painful than the pecuniary loss was the thought of the discipline he has imposed on himself to comport with the old man's ideas of proper behavior; but, alas, there was no way to reclaim those wasted hours.)

Then, too, matters of the heart were not measuring up to the standards he had set for himself. Not that there was a lack of female companionship for the tall, handsome man, but he was shooting high: His target was the Jersey Lily herself. Soon after Mrs. Langtry (born Emilie Charlotte Le Breton, she was now married to Edward Langtry) was introduced to London society by the earl of Wharn-cliffe (who later chaired Frewen's company), she came to the attention of the most eligible young aristocrats. Lord Randolph Churchill (who was to become Moreton's brother-in-law) thought her "a most beautiful creature" and added, "they say she has but one black dress"; in due course, Moreton found himself her dinner companion, on which occasion he is supposed to have been relatively speechless. Nonetheless, the friendship ripened, but unfortunately Lillie was attracted to titles, and Moreton found himself clearly outclassed.[37]

The final act of a fickle providence was delivered to the young man at the Doncaster races in Yorkshire, where at first he won a handy sum and then determined to risk all on the next race and thereby secure his financial future. To his intense chagrin, Lord Ellesmere's horse Hampton took the cup from Pageant, the horse Moreton had bet on, and ever after Moreton told people he had been sent to America by Lord Ellesmere's horse.

Hugh Lowther, future earl of Lonsdale, eased Moreton's cash-flow problem by buying some of his friend's horses (later resold at a loss), but Moreton could not bear to sell his favorite, Redskin, and this one he gave to Lillie Langtry, after he and John Leslie (Moreton's other future brother-in-law) had given her riding lessons. The transaction was later to cause trouble in his courtship of Clara Jerome, although he explained that it was all for the sake of Redskin, who deserved the love that Lillie could give him. Of that love there can be no doubt, for in her autobiography, Lillie calls Redskin "a perfect gentleman in appearance and manner." She says not a word about Moreton. In any case, Lillie was soon riding in Hyde Park with the Prince of Wales, while her former suitor was far to the west, learning about an entirely new venture.[38]

Moreton made his departure from England in style. There was a farewell dinner in London, at which his friends gave him an elephant rifle (there must be elephants in America, mustn't there?), and then he departed by sea from Queenstown in Ireland, but only after chartering a special train to overtake the departing ship. A fast tender put him aboard, and a new life opened up ahead of him.

# 3

# The Serious Business of Ranching

*Life and Work on the Western Range*

———◆———

In the summer of 1883, Dermot Robert Wyndham Bourke, seventh earl of Mayo, visited the Powder River country for a hunt. His host was Horace Curzon Plunkett, son of Baron Dunsany and a cattle rancher in the Powder River Basin. Lord Mayo, then thirty-two, was to journey to the ranch from the Rock Creek station on the Union Pacific Railroad, but the appointed time for his lordship's arrival came and went with "no telegram, no letter," as Plunkett said. However, the earl, whose father had been viceroy of India (he had been assassinated there in 1872), was well known, in part because of his eccentricities, and his progress was duly reported up the line by other drivers, so that Plunkett soon learned that the nobleman was indeed coming, with his valet, a gamekeeper, and six dogs. When he finally arrived (with an additional uninvited "hanger-on," of the "shopkeeping order"), the delay was explained by the fact Mayo had bought a wagon to complete the trip north to the ranch but had neglected to grease the axles, with the result that the horses soon became exhausted. "Such are globe trotters without niggers to wait on them," Plunkett sourly confided to his diary.[1]

The new breed of gentleman on the plains represented by the likes of Horace Plunkett and Moreton Frewen were not globe-trotters, however, except as they had to be to visit their western properties; and necessity and training soon made them aware that wagons had to be greased and horses cared for, whether servants were present to do the work or not.

Frewen himself was not among the first British investors in the United States, nor even among the first large ones. The railroad boom of the nineteenth century had attracted the interest of those with money in the British Isles, and American railroad securities were the object of much speculation. Later the opening of the Midwest to settlement attracted settlers from Europe, but it was the chance to assemble large tracts of land at low cost that brought the first large investments from across the ocean. One such investor was William Francis John Scully, an Irish member of the lesser gentry from County Tipperary, who in 1843 inherited 1,000 acres in Ireland. Scully came to the United States in 1850 and eventually acquired almost 225,000 acres in Illinois, Kansas, Missouri, and Nebraska; there were fifteen hundred tenants on his properties.[2]

Another large foreign-owned real estate venture was that of the Close brothers, in Iowa. Their father was a banker and business advisor to Ferdinand II of Naples, and the brothers had been educated in English schools; family connections with aristocratic society were cemented by the marriage of a cousin to the marquess of Huntly. In 1876, William and Fred Close came to the United States and began to invest in land, buying nearly 2,600 acres that year. In due course a company was organized to finance and operate the Close Colony. The company, the Iowa Land Company, owned at various times about 400,000 acres, chiefly in Iowa, Minnesota, Kansas, and Texas.

A feature of the Close Colony (as the settlement was called) was the apprentice, or pupil, system (pupils were called "pups"). For a fee of five hundred dollars per year, a young man could be apprenticed on one of the brothers' personal stock farms to learn the business of agriculture. The system worked well, and a number of British aristocrats sent their sons to try their hand at farming.

Horace Plunkett stopped at the Close Colony in 1881 (he was interested in a cattle-feeding collaboration in Iowa, using cattle from his western range). He was impressed with its financial promise, although he noted that compared with ranching "there is no romance except ploughing & c., and it is not as healthy." He spent some time with Captain Reynolds Moreton (the younger son of the earl of Ducie), who was managing the "pups." Plunkett was amused to see Lord Hobart, heir to the earldom of Buckinghamshire, barefoot and following the plow. "True, I never saw anyone more like a ploughboy & less like an Earl," Plunkett noted, "but the blood is there. . . ."[3]

These British landowners made impressive investments, but there would be no stampede of wealthy aristocrats in Britain to follow their example. Buying land was a capital-intensive business, and the return was no greater than the great moneyed families could make from investing in businesses they knew well at home. It required another incentive to attract them to American adventures.

The range-cattle business provided that incentive. With the first successful shipment of refrigerated meat to England in the summer of 1880, there was a sharp rise in British demand for American beef. In 1878–80 imports from all sources into the United Kingdom were fifteen times the 1876 level, and 80 percent of that total came from the United States. The increased supplies of low-cost meat excited great consumer interest, and in Liverpool and Dublin there were near riots by people seeking the cheaper product. This turn of events caused great consternation among the local stock raisers in Scotland and England, whose prices were thereby depressed.

The British stock raisers had sent their own emissary to the United States in 1877 to observe the situation, but he concluded that range cattle were of inferior quality to British stock and thus did not represent a threat to his clients; in 1879 a royal commission headed by the duke of Richmond, Lennox, and Gordon stirred awareness of the threat represented by the American herds and also suggested that there was money to be made from what was truly a revolution in agriculture: the grazing of cattle on the "self-made hay" of the free public domain. The blue-ribbon commission included Clare Sewell Read and Albert Pell, both members of parliament, and one of the members was John Clay, Sr., father of the John Clay who would later become one of the most influential figures in the American cattle industry. The younger Clay, then only twenty-eight, was appointed as a subcommissioner and spent three years in the service of the commission.

After conducting a wide-ranging investigation, the royal commission issued its preliminary report in 1881 and wound up its work the following year. A key conclusion was that capital invested in the American cattle industry in the previous ten years had earned over 33 percent annually. The statistic was a tantalizing one. While this information was being digested, the earl of Airlie visited the United States and on his return warned his countrymen not to start ranching on too small a scale. The warning acted as a powerful stimulus, and the rush was soon on.[4]

The mother of the British companies on the range was the Prairie Cattle Company, which would be chaired by Lord Airlie. The earl also bought a ranch for his younger son, Lyulph Gilchrist Stanley Ogilvy, a big, loose-jointed Etonian of "towering physique" with a sandy beard. The earl had a fine herd of Aberdeen Angus in Scotland, and Lyulph introduced that breed and Hereford stock to his farm near Greeley, Colorado, where he had nearly two thousand acres fenced and also developed irrigation projects. Airlie travelled extensively in the United States; he died in Denver in 1881, while on an inspection trip for the Prairie Company.

Even before the Prairie Company was organized, other investors had already entered the field; one was John George Adair, the man who introduced Moreton Frewen to ranching. The owner of a large estate at Rathdaire, Monasterevan, in Ireland, Adair was a man of means, looking for places to invest money in the United States. An interesting suggestion was made by a man who had borrowed money from Adair's agent in Denver; this was Charles Goodnight, a cattle rancher now famous for pioneering the cattle trails leading from Texas to the northern plains along the front of the Rockies. Goodnight was about to lay out a new ranch.[5]

The place Goodnight selected was a featureless plain in the Texas Panhandle called the Llano Estacado, or Staked Plain, which included a geographic anomaly for this region—a valley with abundant water, where cattle could graze and still be protected. On inspection, the strange area lived up to its early billing. Sweeping sandstone cliffs sheltered the valley so well that the party at first could not find a way down into it. This was the same place where Colonel Mackenzie had surprised and defeated the hostile Comanche, forever destroying their hegemony of the Staked Plain. Here, in the Palo Duro Canyon, named for its growth of the strong cedar used by the Indians for making arrows, Goodnight established the ranch, after first expelling a herd of buffalo he estimated at ten thousand.[6]

The canyon ranged up to fifteen miles wide and ran sixty miles along the river known as the Prairie Dog Town Fork of the Red River; its thousand-foot walls were a better fence than any man could build. When Adair saw it, the Irishman immediately took a half interest in the ranch, which Goodnight called the JA, after

Adair's initials. Thus was born one of the great Texas ranches, and the first to be established in the panhandle.[7]

From the beginning it was necessary to own the land, for the Palo Duro Canyon had already attracted the attention of land locaters, and Goodnight made the purchases. By agreement, the partnership was to last five years, with Goodnight managing the operation for an annual salary of twenty-five hundred dollars; Goodnight was to furnish the initial herd, and at the end Adair (who would withdraw nothing in the meantime) was to have his advances repaid with 10 percent interest, the remainder to be divided one-third to Goodnight, two-thirds to Adair. Eventually, the JA would run sixty thousand head of cattle on six hundred thousand acres.[8]

On their trip west in 1878, the Adairs brought Moreton Frewen with them, and the trip to the Palo Duro was an event that kindled a flame in him that would not be quenched for some years. Frewen was enthralled by the spaciousness of the Palo Duro and its savage history. He saw the buffalo jumps where the Comanche had run the great animals over cliffs to provide meat for the tribe, leaving countless dead and dying beyond what they needed for food. But the cattle business was the element that really caught Moreton's attention, and he determined to return to the West to try his own hand at capturing the riches he craved to finance the life he ought to live.[9]

The following fall he returned with some friends who were interested in a western hunt. With him was his brother Dick, who would finance much of the venture and serve and fight for him, and with him, as long as he lived. The party set out for the United States to hunt the Wyoming Territory and to select a ranch that should be even more profitable than John Adair's spread: After all, the land up here would be free.

With the Frewens were two companions from Cambridge—Gilbert Henry Chandos Leigh, heir to a barony, and James Boothby Burke Roche, son of Baron Fermoy—who were looking for a winter hunt. Originally, they had planned to hunt the Yellowstone Park region, but when they stopped in Chicago to visit with General Phil Sheridan, he discouraged them from that destination because of concern about the Indians. The group then took the train west to Rawlins, in Wyoming Territory, and proceeded northeastward. After the hunt, their friends returned to England, while the Frewen brothers, with a prospector named Jack Hargreaves and a Texas cowboy named Tate, set off on the serious mission to locate a ranch property on the Powder River.[10]

It was now late December, and the snow was deep in the mountain passes. They encountered a band of Shoshoni Indians and gained their instant friendship by shooting enough buffalo from a herd of two or three thousand to feed "twenty lodges," according to Moreton. But the situation became grim when Dick's horse gave out in the deep snow; moreover, Dick himself was decidedly unwell. They then conceived the novel idea of using the massive herd of buffalo as snowplows to make their way through the snow-filled pass and into the Powder River Basin. The huge beasts obligingly led the way, at times disappearing entirely beneath the heavy snow, so that it moved over them like ocean waves. The trail behind was beaten well enough for the weary horses to follow, and when they were safely on the other side of the mountains, the brothers rested while Dick recovered his health. It was an awesome beginning to their Powder River venture.

The two Frewen brothers were colorful figures. Both were tall (about six feet three inches) and physically vigorous; Richard was a year older than Moreton. It is unquestionably true that they loved each other, for when either was threatened the other did not hesitate to defend or help. Thus, Moreton nursed Dick back to health in an abandoned cabin on the Powder River that first winter of 1878–79, and Dick returned the favor in the fall of 1880, when Moreton was seriously ill with mountain fever and Dick was up at all hours to mix his quinine.

But it is also true that they could not long abide close association. Their arguments were so hot they sometimes came to blows, and their correspondence was often no less heated. Soon after Moreton married Clara, Dick wrote to Leonard Jerome that they should not have married, as he would now have to support them. "Be sure & stop [the letter]," Moreton told Clara, who was then at her father's house in New York. Those who chanced to come between them learned the lesson that their anger could be directed toward a common enemy even more readily than against each other; Dick swore a war "to the knife" with Horace Plunkett (who had once been their friend) when he fancied the Irishman had dealt unfairly with Moreton. It was a relationship that was totally unpredictable for so long as they both lived, and despite their many disagreements, when Dick died unexpectedly, his remaining estate went to Moreton.[11]

Moreton later would claim that he and Dick were the first to set-

tle in the vast Powder River Basin, but this is to take a very re-
stricted view of those who were already in the area. Guide and trapper Oliver Perry Hanna was already there and would settle the
following spring north of the range Frewen chose for himself, to
make his living supplying Fort McKinney with elk and deer meat;
he later guided for Frewen's noble guests. There were undoubtedly
others in the area, and of course Fort McKinney and its men could
scarcely be ignored. Nevertheless, Frewen was the first to do what
he had come to do, which was to set up a cattle-ranching business
in the Powder River Basin on a scale that was rare in that sparsely
settled territory.[12]

The Union Pacific was the only railroad that had then penetrated
the plains, as the Northern Pacific had been stalled at Bismarck, in
Dakota Territory, since 1873 and would not reach eastern Montana
until 1883. The Union Pacific's jumping-off place for the Powder
River range was the Rock Creek Station, at the point where the
railroad looped north to get around Elk Mountain, the highest of
the Medicine Bow peaks. Rock Creek station disappeared when the
main line of the railroad was moved in 1900, but in the 1880s it was
a busy place, with four saloons, a hotel, a blacksmith shop, and a
store. Most of these establishments were owned by G. D. Thayer,
son of the man who had been territorial governor in 1875. There,
in what Plunkett called "the most miserable place in the West," one
might sleep ten in a room with others of low and high breeding, and
some uncounted creatures of the lower orders among the bed-
clothes.[13]

The region where Moreton Frewen and his brother were to establish their range consisted of a great swatch of the Powder River
Basin in northeastern Wyoming and southern Montana, a region
Moreton expansively said was as large as Ireland. While it was actually considerably smaller than that country, it did run for eighty
miles north and south and fifty east and west—still a formidable
holding. From Rock Creek north to the ranch headquarters was two
hundred miles, and the roads were none too passable even in good
weather. Both in summer and winter the route was subject to inter-
diction by storms, for the summer rains could be violent; and winter
weather so often rendered travel impossible that the owners in the
north generally went home for that season. Thomas Willing Peters
was one who stayed on, and the cowhands then called him "Twice
Wintered" in recognition of his toughness.

Even today, one can feel the majesty of that long-past undertaking. When one crosses the Bighorn Mountains from west to east, one is suddenly struck by an expanse of land stretching as far as the eye can see. Dropping sharply from the mountains by several thousand feet, the basin slopes off gradually perhaps another thousand feet to where the Powder River makes its way northward at the bottom of its indented watercourse. We call this the High Plains, but the expression is in part a misnomer, for this is no flatland; small streams and dry gulches have creased its surface, creating innumerable hiding places where a steer or even a small herd could weather a sudden storm. Today the air is still redolent with the characteristic aroma of the salt sage, and it is easy to imagine that our English gentlemen may have paused to savor that smell.

Once the site had been selected, the brothers set out to buy the necessary materials to establish a headquarters and cattle to stock the ranch. There was no shortage of animals for sale, if one had the convertible currency to make the purchase, and in no time the brothers had a herd of some size. And for a time, at least, there was enough currency; they had a total of just over $100,000 to spend, of which $63,000 came from Dick and $39,000 from Moreton, who had already spent a good part of the £16,000 he inherited from his father.

One of the early purchases was from a man named Tim Foley, a rancher on a range west of old Fort Caspar; this purchase for $70,000 brought with it 4,500 head bearing the 76 brand. The origin of the brand and the herd have both disappeared into a welter of conflicting stories from which it is difficult to discern the truth. A persistent version is that Frewen bought the 76 herd more than once, as Foley's men drove the cattle round and round a hill. But the terms of the transaction make this a difficult story to accept, since Foley was obliged by the contract to make up any deficiency in the book count of 4,500. Frewen also denied it vociferously.[14]

The house had to be built, located with care to avoid the mosquitoes and to take advantage of an outcropping of coal that could be used for fuel. The main room was forty feet square, and twenty could dine there in comfort before going out on the "piazza" to watch "the great purple shadows stealing down over the prairie from the mountains." Getting the ranch house properly equipped took a bit more time. The walls were papered, and Moreton sent a sample off to his new bride so that she could plan complementary colors. The staircase and all the interior woodwork were imported from England, and the piano had to be shipped from Chicago, as did the materials for the telephone line that ran more than twenty miles from the ranch headquarters to the store Frewen ran at the Powder River Crossing of the old Bozeman Trail. The telephone, rare enough in western homes in 1882, was downright supernatural to the Indians; when Chief Plenty Bear at the ranch and Chief Wolf's Tooth at the store were treated to the sound of each others' voices over the line, they pronounced it "mighty medicine."[15]

Although the cowboys called the house on the Powder River "Frewen's Castle," he told Clara that it was a mere "shooting box," patterned after similar dwellings in England. To be sure, the place soon hosted many friends who came to hunt the Bighorn Mountains behind the ranch, and their kill was not insignificant; Moreton reported seeing nine bears in a single day and taking "bushels" of trout from a stream aptly named Trout Creek. Despite the remoteness of the ranch, the names in the guest book are impressive, although some were shareholders of the company Moreton was by then managing for them; thus, F. A. K. Bennet and Andrew Whitton could combine business with the pleasure of the hunt. Frewen's friend Hugh Cecil Lowther, second son of the third earl of Lonsdale, was in the very first hunting party at the ranch and would return more than once; their party accounted for twenty-six bears the first fall that the Frewens were on the Powder River. Another sporting visitor to the ranch was Clement Finch, the brother of Moreton's good friend, the ill-fated Lord Aylesford ("Sporting Joe"); Aylesford was soon to be in self-imposed exile in Texas, where he would ranch (and drink) until he died.[16]

Moreton's vision of the sporting life is well illustrated by an incident that occurred during an 1880 hunt arranged for Sam Ashton, another friend. Moreton convinced the men to leave their heavy rifles at camp and hunt buffalo with only their revolvers, trusting the speed and stamina of their horses to avoid any serious trouble. Moreton loaned his horse Walnut to his older brother Ted, and Ted had great sport bringing down a bull with four shots. But Sam got into trouble with a wounded bull and emptied his pistol in vain; Moreton had to bring up a rifle to finish off the beast.

Moreton had more than hunting and cattle ranching on his mind during this period. On his journeys through New York, he had met Clara Jerome, Leonard Jerome's oldest daughter (the blond one; he was not so taken with the dark variety represented by sister Jennie). He thereupon embarked on a Victorian courtship, complete with tête-à-têtes on a red sofa, under the watchful eye of Mother Jerome, whose sternness caused Moreton to dub her "Sitting Bull" (it was said that she was part Cherokee). Mrs. Jerome—who had already turned away the pleadings of a Spanish duke (possessed of a fatal religious flaw—he was Catholic) and was now hoping for at least a British earl (Lord Essex had been mentioned)—was not thrilled by these attentions to Clara from an untitled gentleman.

Nevertheless, the courtship proceeded, in person when Moreton could visit New York and by letter when he could not. The correspondence still survives (except for some presumably steamier items under a black seal which Clara must have destroyed), and it was extensive—one could even say tiresome. Protestations of affection ("if you are at all anxious let us not delay") were interspersed with predictions of profit (six thousand pounds a year "clear"); "although the work is not light, it is pleasant work," he said, "& the day you determine you had rather be in England I'll give it up to some competent paid manager & we'll go back to the world."[17]

Finally, the objections of the mother and the reluctance of the father were overcome, and a date was set for a wedding to be held at Grace Church in Manhattan. One last cloud appeared, in the form of a dispute with Leonard Jerome over the dowry. Leonard had given Jennie a handsome dowry of nearly ten thousand dollars per year when she married Lord Randolph (although we cannot know how willingly, for the duke of Marlborough himself was involved in *that* haggling), but his fortunes had taken a turn for the worse since the earlier wedding. He now claimed that his consent to an early wedding for Clara had been in lieu of a dowry, an assertion that was hotly contested by Moreton ("there was no such folly on your side or on mine," he told Clara).[18]

It was June 1881 when the wedding took place, and there was no dowry, although Leonard gave his daughter a handsome diamond necklace (thirty diamonds that would later be a limited source of cash). The jewelry displayed at the wedding did not compare with that worn four years earlier when Mrs. Astor's daughter Helen married James Roosevelt Roosevelt in the same church—in a ceremony in which the bride's mother, "literally armored" with diamonds, outshone the bride. But Moreton's wedding was not shabby, and his side of the guest list at least helped make up in titles for the relative shortage of diamonds. As best man, Moreton got William Bagot (then twenty-four), later fourth Baron Bagot. Willy was then serving as aide to the marquess of Lorne, eldest son of the duke of Argyll, who had contracted a lucky marriage with the fourth daughter of

Queen Victoria and had been appointed governor-general of Canada, presumably to feed and clothe the bride. Also at the wedding was Cromartie Sutherland-Leveson-Gower, the marquess of Stafford, later duke of Sutherland and the greatest landowner of the realm.[19]

The day before the wedding was the date for the running of the English Derby. Entered in that race was a horse owned by Pierre Lorillard IV, scion of a great tobacco fortune and a legendary womanizer who had himself been courting the lovely Clara (a kind of complication that never troubled Moreton). There were few things in life that Moreton loved better than horses, and the Derby was at the top of the list for horse events. Lorillard, Jerome, and Frewen were at the Union Club watching the ticker when it began spelling the name of Lorillard's horse Iroquois. It was drinks for the house in a celebration that carried on into the night, leaving the groom in poor condition for the following day's ceremony.[20]

After the wedding it was westward, to show Clara her husband's enterprise. Although Sam Ashton had visited the house and pronounced his room to be the equal of those in England, the country was nevertheless still a relative wilderness, and when the new Mrs. Frewen and her maid arrived at Rock Creek for the long journey north to the ranch, the maid could only sob. To make matters worse, before the summer was over Clara had a miscarriage, and the combination of these disappointments drove her from the west her husband loved so fervently. After she returned to New York, a letter from Henry Wadsworth Longfellow followed her on its journey back from Wyoming; the poet, then in his last illness, wanted to see her when she returned from "the land of the sunset." She had indeed returned from that land, and for good.

Meanwhile, Moreton threw himself into the work with gusto. It was a regimen of brandings and twice-yearly roundups, totally unlike anything he had experienced before. We have a press report of one roundup for that period, for the first division of the 1881 spring roundup was near the city of Cheyenne by the middle of June, and the Cheyenne *Sun* thought that two-thirds of the 250 cowboys in that division were in town, seeking relief from the monotony and hard work of the range. The riders would careen down the street, heading full tilt for the saloon door as though to ride inside. Later, when the "inner man" had been satisfied, they would vault into the saddle without the aid of stirrups. It was a scene that could have appeared in many a Hollywood Western.[21]

In all, there were perhaps twenty-four hundred cowboys working the roundup that summer. Ever after celebrated in song and fiction, the real cowboy is now almost undiscernible behind the facade that Hollywood has erected. Yet he was real: He lived on the range in some numbers, and he sometimes died there, often while doing or trying to do the tasks set for him. He could play hard when in town, but most of the year he was on the lonely range, protecting his cantankerous charges from predators (both man and beast) or from storm or fire.

The same newspaper that reported the riotous behavior in Cheyenne also noted that the broken legs always associated with roundup activity were "coming in," and a couple of months later recounted the story of an unlucky hand who roped a steer only to have the angry animal gore his horse, while in the confusion the cowboy's hand became tangled in the rope. He was lucky to lose only thumb and forefinger before he was rescued. From such accounts we learn that riding the range was not romantic, did not pay well, and had very poor job security.

There was plenty of work during roundup time. The roundup was the heart of the range-cattle-industry governance system, and for roundup purposes the entire range was formed into divisions, in each of which the roundup was conducted at the same time. The first Wyoming roundup, in 1874, required only two divisions, but by 1884 there were thirty-one divisions to cover the ranges of the cattle industry; in one division alone, two hundred cowboys and two thousand horses "worked" four hundred thousand cattle over a period of six weeks. It was a big business. In an orderly manner the crews "circled" the territory assigned to them, bringing all of the cattle to a central place, where they could be collected for branding. In the fall, the same process gathered cattle for shipment to market.

The big outfits, like Frewen's 76 and Plunkett's EK, participated in the roundups on their own ranges and also sent representatives, or "reps," along on roundups in adjoining divisions, to identify and collect cattle that had strayed off the range since the last roundup. These men saw to it that the proper brands were applied to their animals and then cut them out for movement back to the home range after the roundup herd had been worked. If by chance an animal with the wrong brand was shipped to market, the proceeds would be remitted to the owner of the brand.

The cowboy of Hollywood legend has obscured a good deal of the real man and his life during the time that Moreton Frewen and his friends were in the West. It is therefore essential to sketch again the range life of that era. The cowboy is supposed to have been overly fond of his horse, but whatever license there may have been in that image, the true role of the well-trained horse was a large one. Frewen was no stranger to horseflesh, of course, and claimed that Walnut was the fastest in Wyoming. Average hands needed at least four horses apiece, and the heavy work of "cutting" required seven or eight for each man, who rose as long as there was daylight and two or three hours at night, covering fifty to seventy miles in the long workday. A well-trained "cutting" horse would follow a steer through a herd as though attached to the fleeing animal; he had to be able to wheel abruptly to counter the evasions of the Texas steer, and agile enough to avoid the terrible horns when they came too close.

A horse and an expert rider were a formidable pair. The man dropped the lasso over the steer's horns, letting the rope fall on the off side of the animal so that the running steer was now between the rope and the horse. The cowboy then looped the rope around his saddle horn (these were called "dally" loops), and the horse braced himself, letting the rope whip the steer's feet out from under him and drop him to the ground. The cowboy would now jump down and tie the steer's legs while the horse kept tension on the rope so that the animal could not move. A green hand or a poorly trained horse made such maneuvers impossible, or at least cause for derision from the gallery of cowhands waiting to brand the animals. Skill was much admired, and the crews competed to show which was the best; in 1879, Judge Carey's CY outfit branded 166 calves in just eighty minutes, using three ropers.[22]

The main purpose of the spring roundup was to brand the young animals. Branding of livestock had been practiced by the Egyptians as early as 2000 B.C. (branding of slaves and criminals was also practiced until the nineteenth century), and was introduced to North America by Hernando Cortés in the sixteenth century (he used three large crosses); when Texas became independent, the new nation declared unbranded cattle public property, a condition swiftly remedied by the Texans' timely use of their own branding irons. As the cattle industry moved north, so did branding. Although the Spanish government was registering brands in New Mexico in the eighteenth century, it was 1880 before the first brand was registered in Alberta, at the north end of the range country.[23]

The idea was simple: to create a readable pattern by the use of a hot iron to burn the animal's skin so that hair would not grow. This could be done using a rod with a curved hook on the end—the so-called "running iron"—to make the brand by tracing on the hide. Because of the ease of altering brands by this method, the carrying of a running iron became illegal (indeed, a hanging offense) in some regions; the usual method of branding in the roundup was with stamp irons. The brand might require the use of a single iron or more than one, depending on the design required.

The injunction to the cattleman was to select a simple brand, but after a time, there were few simple brands that had not already been registered, so that the brand books began to include many complex brands. By 1885 there were 12,000 brands registered in Colorado alone, of which 250 were built on the letter h and a further 150 each used the letters c and d, to say nothing of those in the shape of a cannon, boat, or scissors. One outfit, the giant Prairie Cattle Company, owned nearly 40 brands.[24]

Brands were originally large—"so they could be read by moonlight"—but cattlemen later adopted smaller marks (not for humanitarian reasons but because the hides would be less damaged). The customary spot for the brand was the left hip of the animal, some have said because cattle tend to drift toward their left sides, making the brand easier to read. The iron was to be hot, the color of ashes, not red hot (it would set the hair afire): Shake off the ashes, stamp it firmly on the hide, and rock it back and forth to ensure contact across the full area of the design. Properly executed, the iron will burn off the hair and the outer layer of skin; the new brand should be the color of a new saddle.

When a branded animal was sold to another cattleman, its brand was cancelled by a special mark (called "venting"), and the new owner's brand placed on it. The jest was heard that some animals had been transfered so many times that they weren't worth much, but had plenty of reading material on them.

Fortunately, the range cow was generally a good mother, and had a strong interest in her calf—sometimes to the point of defending it with considerable vigor against predators or against the unfortunate cowboy holding it down for branding or other necessary work. A charging longhorn cow would cause a coyote to pause in his quest for the fresh meat the calf represented. And if the cow was solicitous of her own calf, she could also be downright disagreeable to the offspring of another cow. If another calf chanced to try to steal a bit of additional milk, it risked getting kicked or gouged.

So it would seem that the most dependable way to determine whose calves were walking the range would be to watch what cows they were following and affix the same brand to the calf. And that is precisely what was done—for the most part—but the exceptions to this rule created the need for yet more regulations. Of course, there would be cases in which the mother died after the calf was big enough to care for itself, so there would simply be no mother for the calf to follow. Then, too, no roundup system was perfect, and there would always be some animals hiding out when the "circle" passed through to gather up the cattle for branding. Finally, there were more sinister reasons for lack of identification of a calf with its natural mother. Anyone wishing to augment the supply of motherless mavericks might split the calf's tongue so that it could not nurse and would therefore abandon its mother. For whatever reason, there had to be a way to deal with the motherless—or apparently motherless—maverick.

The strange word *maverick*, used to signify the motherless calf, was in fact the name of a real person, who was ironically a rather indifferent cattleman to have bequeathed such a lasting legacy to the industry. Samuel A. Maverick was a Texan who in 1845 bought a herd of four hundred head of cattle, which he consigned to the care of a somewhat lackadaisical family who made little use of the branding iron, perhaps because the cattle were pastured in the relative security of Matagorda Island, a thin sliver of land in the Gulf of Mexico, close in to the Texas shore. However, that security was mostly illusory, for at low tide it was no great task to wade ashore, and doubtless many of the Maverick cattle did, for cattlemen along the coast soon came to refer to any unbranded calf as a maverick. The word was properly to be spelled without the initial capital *M*, since it was not intended to signify a state of ownership; indeed, it was intended to suggest the opposite. So it was that many of the Maverick cattle progeny melted into that uncertain limbo where we must commingle the ravages of predation whether by the two- or four-footed variety, and when Mr. Maverick sold his herd after owning it eleven years, he was paid for exactly four hundred head (although he may have taken some comfort from the fact that he realized six dollars a head, twice his cost); the natural increase of the Maverick herd had all become mavericks.

In the early days of the industry, all unbranded animals received the "customary" brand of the range on which they were found (if there was more than one, the mavericks were prorated among them). This principle was established by law in Texas in 1866, when it became a crime to drive cattle off their accustomed range. Unfortunately, the drifting of herds (especially during bad storms), and the varying interpretations of what was indeed the customary range soon called for a different procedure. Later the stockgrowers' associations devised the practice of selling the mavericks at auction, using the proceeds to finance the inspection operation of the association.

But even that solution was not trouble free. In some areas few, if any, mavericks were identified; in 1884, only a single maverick was sold in Uinta County, Wyoming. While the herds in that county were not so large as elsewhere, it challenges credulity that the calves in that region could be so much more adept at identifying their mothers than their juvenile colleagues on the other ranges. The inference was that the mavericks had either been given a "customary" brand, or that dishonest cowhands were hiding the motherless waifs out in the hills, to be recovered later for a private branding session.

Then there were the cases in which the maverick auction yielded very low unit values—sometimes as little as fifty cents per animal. Under pressure from complaints about the latter, the Swan outfit "voluntarily" paid an additional sum to bring its cost of maverick purchases up to the territorial average for the year, which was over thirteen dollars. Here, it appeared that the low-cost purchases were made in roundups dominated by the Swan outfit, and there was an understandable reluctance to bid against the big company.

Occasionally the wrong brand was affixed to an animal. The error was balanced by branding an offsetting animal with the correct brand, and an additional brand on the jaw would testify to the correction. These were the honest mistakes. A criminal could also make a fair imitation of a brand by trimming the hair of an animal so that those riding by would think it had already been branded. At his leisure, the perpetrator could return and place his own brand over the "hair" brand, and in time the trimmed hair would grow back, leaving only the bogus brand in place.

It was the courtesy of the range that when a cattleman came upon a cow with an unbranded calf, he would place that cow's brand on the calf. Undoubtedly, this principle was followed by the big outfits, who had to be able to rely on the integrity and interdependence of the system, if it was to survive. But even here there were exceptions. A suspected cow thief might have all his calves summarily branded by the big outfit whose suspicions he had aroused, and there was little chance of appeal from this rough justice.

Then there were those who did not observe the customary courtesies. A heated saddle cinch might make a passable branding iron for a quick change of ownership out in the hills, and the so-called "running iron" was the favorite among those who had more than a few such encounters to contemplate. The running iron was fashioned with a short handle, so that it could be concealed on the saddle (the standard iron had a long handle to keep heat away from the hands).

Two men handled the actual branding, one holding the animal while the other wielded the hot iron. The calf would also be given the owner's earmark, by cropping the ear in some distinctive way—an additional identification device. Then, if the calf was male and had not been selected to become a range bull, he suffered the additional humiliation of castration. Afterward, the symbols of his maleness might grace a dish which in Texas was called son-of-a-gun stew, and in the northern plains went by the name of Rocky Mountain oysters.

The branding was recorded in the tally books, an important source of information about the herds. Since the mature animals were seldom counted, especially on the northern ranges, the only actual counts of animals were the number of calves branded and the number of animals sold. From these tallies the size of the herd could be estimated and compared with the "book count" kept by the companies for their shareholder reports.

During roundup, life centered around the chuck wagon, which was the source of food, as well as the social center. Originally only the supply wagon for the cook, it later came to be the handy place for the water barrel and for medicines (for the crew and for the animals), tools, and other items needed on the range. The wagon itself came to be customized, with a canvas flap to shelter the chuck box, which had a hinged worktable for the cook. Charles Goodnight had his chuck wagon specially built of heavy wood and equipped it with iron axles. Food was plentiful, and beef was killed to provide fresh meat, which was accompanied by sourdough biscuits, bacon, beans, and dried fruits. Cooks often vied for the reputation of the best in the roundup. In the evening after the meal was finished, the chuck wagon was the place for socializing until the hands rolled into their blankets to catch a few hours' sleep before the predawn rising.

There was plenty of work during roundups in the spring and fall; the short time between was taken up with the odd jobs every outfit had. After the fall roundup, most of the hands were laid off, for in winter even the big outfits maintained only a skeleton crew in remote "line shacks" to keep a general watch over the great herds. Here life was spartan at best, with furniture of rough boards and stools, a few tin plates and cups, and a "straw tick" mattress filled with prairie grass; still, it was better than nothing. Those not lucky enough to draw line duty were paid off in the fall, with little hope of work until a new crew would be hired in the spring. In those days before severance pay and unemployment compensation, the jobless were left to fend for themselves as best they could. It was unlikely that many could find work, since all the outfits were disgorging their excess hands, and to avoid the pangs of hunger during the long winter, the jobless would "ride the grub line," stopping by each outfit in turn to cadge a few free meals before moving on.

The roundup system provided the key data for the basic accounting system of the big ranches, the book count. The book count system kept meticulous track of the calves branded and the animals sold; then an estimate of losses was deducted, and the result was the book count for the herd. The system has been much criticized, and some few outfits did make actual counts, as when the big Texas outfits with fenced pastures ran herds from one pasture to another, counting the animals as they passed; but this was rare, and the success of actual counts was indifferent. The Hansford Company described the situation to its shareholders in the spring of 1887. Although it was general practice to buy on book count with a "confirmatory" inspection, "actual"count was now being insisted upon, but unfortunately there were only a few examples of a full count being carried out. Under open-range conditions an exact count was "all but impossible," so that only a careful comparison of several years would yield a trustworthy result.[25]

Francis E. Warren, who had a large ranching operation in Wyoming and once commented that he took "no stock" in the book tally of any herd that had been on the range for several years without being counted, explained why this was so. Warren believed the shrinkage was not so much a matter of a large loss in a single season as a reflection relatively small errors in accounting for the large number of animals handled in such a herd. Thus, for a herd that had been running seven years on the range and had a book count of ten thousand, the total number of animals that had been handled might have been on the order of one hundred thousand or so; thus, an error of say, 5 percent could actually cut the book count in half, although that would not be too unusual given the large numbers involved.[26]

The experiences of the Swan outfit provide an amusing example of an attempted count. The directors observed what they thought to be a large discrepancy between the calf brand and the book count for the herd and ordered the acting manager, Finlay Dun, to effect an accurate accounting. Mr. Dun, who was also the secretary of the company and noted for his comprehensive reports to shareholders, was nothing if not conscientious. He hit upon the system of marking all the cattle that were counted to eliminate the chance of a double count. The paint used was a mixture of lampblack, varnish, and turpentine, but it proved not to be "sufficiently adhesive." The cowhands celebrated this understatement in a ditty of their own: "Daddy Dun's a dandy / But his paint won't stick."[27] The result of this fiasco was that the Scottish directors learned little from the attempt to obtain an actual count under open-range conditions.

When Frewen's Powder River Company was liquidated, the balances on tally books were written off after the last general roundup of "76" cattle, but the animals themselves kept showing up year after year, and in 1889, foremen Fred G. S. Hesse reported that another five hundred had been sold. When the JA ranch of Goodnight and Adair was divided among the partners, the unexpected loss was only sixteen hundred head on a total of three hundred thousand handled in eleven years. Of course, the JA had more fences and was less conducive to drifting than the open ranges of the northern plains. To be sure, the book count system was flawed, since there was no way to be certain what proportion of a herd was being lost to rustling, winter deaths, or predators.

The big cattlemen certainly believed that they were losing some numbers by rustling, and from time to time the Indians undoubtedly took some, although some of the big outfits had a working arrangement with the Indians that gave them free beef and so limited the risk of uncounted loss from that source. The winter losses were fairly predictable in "normal" winters with seasoned stock, but when Texas herds were brought onto the northern range, they suffered larger-than-normal losses, particularly if the winter was harsh.[28]

And there were broad measures that helped to validate the book count. The fall roundup culled the herd and sold off the mature steers (three- or four-year-olds). It took no great skill to ascertain whether they were selling animals of approximately the right age. Then again, if the proportion of bulls to cows was adequate, the calf crop would be fairly predictable, so that the annual brand would give a fairly good indication of the number and health of the breeding stock.

So the system was imperfect, but if an outfit was running thirty or forty thousand head of cattle over an area of many square miles, it had little choice but to adopt some rule of thumb to measure the herd. Unfortunately, the open-range system never had a long sequence of "normal" years to validate results. When the losses were greater than the allowance on the books, board members in far-off London or Edinburgh or Dundee asked questions that could not be answered; yet this does not argue that the system was wrong or even that it could be substantially improved upon.

The unwritten law of hospitality on the range required that every outfit feed the hungry traveler; indeed, if no one was at the camp, a traveler was at liberty to help himself to food so long as he washed the dishes afterward. Sometimes only this system kept the jobless hands alive until green grass and sunshine created another post for them in the spring.

The hands were also quick to detect and exploit the embarrassing situation. Thus, when Plunkett camped out in the hills only three-quarters of a mile from a well-supplied roundup camp he had not been able to locate in the dark, he came in for some good-natured ribbing. When he rode into the camp the next morning, he was not anxious to expose the details of his night's discomfort, but the truth soon made the rounds of the hands, who asked whether his hotel the previous night had been on the American or European plan.[29]

The cowboy's life was also dangerous. When the herds were being moved, either on the trail or from one range to another, they had to be kept together at night, and night herding required special skills. Not only was the herd subject to raids by predators but it was also liable to stampede for insignificant reasons—the rustle of a cowboy's slicker or a clap of thunder might be enough. A night stampede was a frightening event, particularly during a rainstorm, for the utter blackness soon disoriented horse and rider, and gullies, thorny brush, and other obstacles were a great risk. Of course, the man on a horse was a lightning rod in a storm, and the remains of more than one unfortunate cowboy were reclaimed by his friends, the smell of scorched flesh still sharp in the air, his clothes riddled

by the force of the powerful bolt. Hailstones large enough to kill
calves and colts would still lie on the ground unmelted the next day.
The night herders believed that singing had a soothing effect on
the cattle, and they often sang (although not the songs that Hollywood later put in their mouths). Any soft, crooning sound would
suffice.[30]

Men and animals had to contend with swollen streams, especially
in the spring. While following the spring roundup in 1883, Plunkett
crossed Ten Sleep Creek and found the stream so high that his
horse was knocked down by the torrent and "very nearly drowned."
Two days later, the poor horse was called upon to swim the swollen
Nowood River and—still suffering from the trauma of the previous
experience, refused—rolling over and over in the stream. Plunkett
had to swim away and "leave him to drown," while the guide saved
the saddle and some of Plunkett's gear. This turn of events left
Plunkett on foot for six miles until they reached the roundup
camp.[31]

Out on the range, mishaps could be more than ordinarily dangerous. Snakebite was treated by sucking the wound and liberally
"medicating" the victim with whiskey. Plunkett came upon one
snakebite victim who was paralyzed; Plunkett decided that the bite
itself had apparently been treated expeditiously, since there was no
swelling, but the medication had been overgenerous; he said, "I fear
the snake less than the whiskey."[32]

Another incident involved Moreton Frewen, on an inspection
trip to the Canadian range he later acquired for expansion. Riding
in a snowstorm, he and another man lost their way and had to camp
overnight, only to find two and a half feet of snow on the ground
in the morning. When they broke camp, a rifle cartridge accidentally fell into the fire and exploded, the shrapnel lodging inside
Moreton's thigh. They were six hours making the next nine miles,
leaving them still fifty miles from the nearest doctor (at Calgary,
Alberta), so Moreton contrived to do his own surgery; to his delight,
he found the metal fragment only half an inch below the surface.
He removed it with much "labor & sorrow," as he told Clara, ending
with the prediction, "I shall be well in a few days." And so he was.[33]

The Indians had for the most part left the ranges, but occasionally
they still showed up; in 1880, there was what Moreton called "a
little brush" with them. A raiding party swooped down on the
Frewen ranch and made off with eighty horses. The Frewen camp

turned out and pursued them: "Killed four & got all the horses," Moreton said, adding, "Powder River will be as safe as Broadway by the time you are ready to come [west]."[34]

Still other dangers lurked in the cowboy's world. The prairie fire, whether it occurred on the buffalo range or on the cattle range, was always a terrible thing to behold. When the grass was dry, it was particularly subject to fires caused by the careless, by lightning, or by those who had reason to want to see a fire. In 1879 a bad fire on the Powder River range was started by an emigrant party's campfire and destroyed extensive grasslands, killing many wild animals. A later fire in the Powder River country contributed to the demise of Plunkett's Frontier Company.

One of the worst prairie fires—which was thought to be arsonous—was the one that burned for three days on the Texas–New Mexico border, destroying the southern ranges of the XIT. This blaze started on the New Mexico side of the line and burned swiftly northward ahead of a south wind, until it had swept one hundred miles, leaving a slow fire behind the racing front. Then the wind changed and blew from the west, driving the fire front eastward toward the XIT. The XIT hands had plowed a seventy-five-foot firebreak along the New Mexico line, but the racing fire crossed it easily as dry, flaming "cow chips" dried cow manure skipped across the plowed land into the grassy range beyond.

A young cowhand from Chicago watched the progress of the blaze from the top of a windmill tower until he had to flee for his life. When the fire proved faster than a running horse, the boy and his mount had to spend the night in the relative safety of an old stone building while the flames passed around them. The young man emerged in the morning to a blackened world in which four thousand of the XIT's finest breeding stock had perished and thousands more were without feed as they shivered in the freezing March winds. The ranch has passed from a fiery hell to a wintry one, in which cows chased scraps of paper in their quest for something to eat. When the blaze burned out, its desolation stretched one hundred miles south to north and one hundred miles west to east.

The XIT would send its hands to fight any fire within one hundred miles; one desperate method was to drag the half-skinned carcass of a dead cow or bull between two horses to beat out the fire in the burned-over area. When the carcass became too charred to be effective, another was substituted. The hands fought fires without food or rest until the blaze was out.

In the dry country, the herds would head for water if they smelled it, defying efforts of man and horse to turn them. Harry Landers, a Wyoming cattleman, had brought a herd within a mile of the Green River when the wind came up from the direction of a big bend in the river twenty-five or thirty miles away. After the stampede in that direction was over, Landers and his men had to spend an extra day collecting the herd and getting it back on the trail. Some said a thirsty herd could smell water as far as forty miles away.[35]

There was never enough time to sleep. The summer days were long, and it would be nine in the evening before the herd was bedded down. Two hours of night herding fell to the lot of all except the trail boss, and rising at three-thirty finally ended the short night. Geoffrey William Millais, the son of the artist, Sir John Everett Millais, worked on the Peters and Alston spread near Frewen on the Powder River; he chronicled the hands' roundup day in a letter to his mother: "We have breakfast at 3 every morning & are out until one o'clock riding all over the country, so it is 10 hours before we get our dinner which we have scarcely time to eat before we are off again till six or seven when we come in to supper. You go to bed after supper & if there are any cattle to be held over you have to get up in the night & take your turn night herding for two hours. So you see out of the 24 hours you are working nearly all the time."[36]

It was a man's world, and the tenderfoot had to earn his place in the society of seasoned hands. It was fun for the old-timers to slip a prickly pear under his horse's tail and watch the bucking that almost always resulted. If the tenderfoot had the nerve for it, he might do something risky to earn the respect of his elders. A cowboy, Edgar Beecher Bronson, recounted how he traded a gentle horse to another hand for an unmanageable one, and then won the animal's confidence sufficiently to ride it. This act irritated the foreman (who saw it as bravado), and the next day the boy found his horse without the *jaquima* (or "hackamore," as the western cowboy anglicized the Spanish), the hair halter that could be tightened over the horse's nose and was used to subdue unruly mounts. Investigation revealed that the act was the work of the foreman, and an old hand advised Bronson to face the man down. This he did, in a scene out of the movies; his foolhardiness in taking this risk was not fatal only because the angry foreman saw that the old hand who had given

Bronson the advice was also obviously backing up the play. Bronson thereby earned his right to a full place with the crew.[37]

Until cutbacks after 1885, wages on the range increased over time from thirty a month to forty dollars a month for regular hands, and five dollars more for "old hands." The Swan outfit started nineteen-year olds at twenty dollars a month the first year, twenty-five the second (if work was satisfactory), and thirty the third; only in the fourth year was the forty-dollar level achieved.[38]

There were rules for the cowboy's employment, and sometimes they were even written down in some detail. The XIT had an extensive set of rules, including those prohibiting cardplaying and the carrying of guns on the ranch. Some owners complained about gambling during roundups, but the Wyoming Stock Growers Association tabled this complaint, and no prohibition was issued. After the problem of rustling became acute enough to command the attention of the managers, cowhands were prohibited from owning their own beef stock, although a few of the owners, such as Granville Stuart in Montana, took a more lenient view.

There was no rule prohibiting marriage, but on the northern ranges the married life was a difficult one for any except the senior hands. Some of the big Texas outfits encouraged hiring of married men for the additional stability thereby afforded, and at the Espuela Land and Cattle Company (familiarly called the Spur) married hands were favored for retention in the fall, when most of the roundup crew was laid off.

The girls the cowboys met in town may not always have been "nice" by the standards of more ordered society, but the cowhands were loyal to them and were proud they were a higher class than the women who consorted with the buffalo hunters; a girl would sometimes stake a broke cowhand to a new saddle or even a horse, and not a few marriages resulted from these relationships. Aside from the occasional foray into town, entertainment was scarce for the range hands. A dance held for the "76" outfit at the Crazy Woman headquarters was rare enough to warrant newspaper coverage. To be sure, the Denver *Daily Tribune* reported on an 1875 excusion to witness the roundup at the Wilson Ranch, where the mayor of Denver took along seventeen gallons of his best brandy and two barrels of whiskey, but these refreshments were intended for the excursionists (including prominent gentlemen and ladies), not the sweaty hands working the cattle. Down in Texas, dances were rare at the Spur, but not at the Matador Land and Cattle Company which set the social pace for the area.[39]

While the towns were glad of the dollars the cowhands brought with them on the occasional visits, the boys off the range had little clout with the authorities in these places, and justice had a certain arbitrariness about it. The story is told of one Bill, who was in town with his friends for a "little" drinking, when the sheriff appeared and summarily ordered the cowboys out of town. The hands took their time saddling up, and when the lawman had disappeared, they went back for one last drink. This irritated the sheriff, who promptly haled them before the judge on a drunk-and-disorderly charge. While awaiting the proceedings, Bill chanced to drag his spurs idly across the floor, an idiosyncracy that quickly caught the judge's attention and brought the threat of a contempt-of-court citation. The cowboy was attentive to the judge's admonition for a few minutes, but before long, habit intruded and he once again dragged the spurs across the floor; this earned him a ten-dollar contempt citation.

After all the fines were paid, the frustrated cowpunchers contrived to give the offensive judge a parting shot and agreed to ride their horses down the boardwalk in front of the courtroom. This they did, with great clatter of hooves, but poor Bill's horse was not shod in front and chanced to stumble and fall on the boards, spilling him before the judge and jury, who had come outside to investigate the clamor. The fine for this last infraction was twenty-five dollars, which exceeded Bill's meager resources, and he was obliged to endure the sheriff's hospitality until his friends could send the money to gain his release from jail. Even the little joys of life sometimes had a price.[40]

# Launching an Enterprise

*The Strange Career of Moreton Frewen*

The Frewen brothers were not alone in the ranching business in northern Wyoming for very long. In the fall of the first year, Horace Curzon Plunkett arrived. On doctor's orders to improve his health by seeking a drier climate than Ireland, he was given the choice of South Africa or Wyoming and chose to try his hand at ranching in the West. A younger son of Baron Dunsany, Plunkett sprang from a family who were among the largest landowners in Ireland.

Educated at Eton, Horace was twenty-five when he came to Wyoming; one biographer described him as a thin, spare man with a prominent nose and keen, kindly eyes but a limp handshake. He was five feet ten inches tall, and weighed only 130 pounds, making him both shorter and slighter than the Frewen brothers. His partner, Alexis Roche, stammered, "P-P-Plunkett is the s-s-strangest being you ever met." Roche's comment is significant, because Plunkett's opinions of other people were often highly critical; when he left Wyoming, he said he had no friends there. Although he started out as a close friend of the Frewens—so that at one time Moreton contemplated running their cattle together to cut costs—their relationship would later worsen drastically.[1]

Plunkett knew them both well, and his views were extraordinarily variable (not uncommon with Plunkett), two fairly typical negative comments being, "They have lots of ability but no ballast," and

"Dick is crotchety in business & Moreton regardless of the value of money." But Plunkett was also impressed with Dick Frewen's scheme to open a tourist service to Yellowstone Park and only failed to invest in it himself when his father expressed lack of interest. Similarly, Plunkett could say of Moreton, "What a lot of good there is in him. . . . In 5 years I think he will be a prominent Englishman," and when Moreton first broached his refrigeration scheme to be located atop Sherman Hill (between Laramie and Cheyenne), Plunkett thought it a "good" idea (although he later called it "the monument of Frewen's folly"). And when Moreton was hurrying off to England to promote his scheme for importation of live American cattle to that country, Plunkett said in amazement, "What wonderful energy that man has."[2]

Plunkett lived out his life as a bachelor, and the only woman who apparently seriously caught his attention was Elizabeth Burke, whom everyone called Daisy. Daisy played the role of the lively hostess for Horace whenever he threw a social event at Dunsany Castle, but she married his cousin, the earl of Fingall, whose great interest was the hunt, not the society and travel Daisy craved. Others also responded to Daisy's ready spirit, and one wonders whether the strong animus Horace displayed toward the earl of Dunraven did not stem from the earl's attentions to her.

Plunkett's partners in ranching were the Roche brothers, James Boothby Burke Roche and Alexis Charles Burke Roche, sons of Baron Fermoy, and Edward Shuckburgh Rouse Boughton, son of a baronet whose family had come to England with William the Conqueror. Alexis was then twenty-five, Boughton twenty-one. Plunkett's range was on Crazy Woman Creek, to the northwest of the Frewen range, and there was a good deal of contact among them as these gentlemen sought familiar faces on the lonely range.[3]

Plunkett's operations in the West expanded rapidly. He was shortly considering incorporating the original partnership, and in July 1884 the Frontier Land and Cattle Company was established, with a capitalization of $1.5 million and with participation from the original partners and Andrew Gilchrist, whom Plunkett liked, but described somewhat condescendingly as "a private in the Life Guards . . . who has built up a considerable fortune from nothing." Plunkett was president, with a three-thousand-dollar salary. He also took a share and leading management position in the Wyoming Development Company, a blue-ribbon group representing territorial leadership, including Governor Hoyt, Francis E. Warren, Judge Jo-

seph M. Carey and banker Morton E. Post. This company was spec-
ulating in irrigation projects, including an expensive venture that
involved drilling a 3,100-foot tunnel (7 by 8 feet) through the mountain to bring irrigation water to thirty-five thousand acres.[4]

Plunkett and his partners also tried their hand at speculation in
railroad land, buying about one hundred thirty-five thousand acres
from the Union Pacific, at one dollar per acre, payable in ten installments, plus interest at 6 percent. There was some difficulty with
other prospective purchasers (apparently the Swan Land and Cattle
Company, Limited), who attempted to thwart the deal. This was
not a cattle-ranching venture, as all of the land was apparently intended for resale, and Plunkett expected that the Swan outfit in
particular would soon be offering to buy. Commenting on one forty-
thousand-acre purchase, Plunkett said the chief merit was that it was
"Naboth's Vineyard to the Great Swan Co." This analogy proved
correct, and Plunkett soon learned that Swan wanted to buy fifty-
thousand acres at a profit to the partners of fifty cents per acre. A
further forty-eight thousand acres were sold to the new Ione Company, which was organized to take over these lands for an irrigation
project.[5]

In Nebraska, the Frontier Company established a cattle-feeding
operation, using corn grown in that area, and it was there they wintered some of their stock. The idea of feeding corn to range cattle
to fatten them before marketing was one that Frewen also tried
later, at a location farther east, on Lake Superior. Frewen wanted
the lake location for the access to shipping, while Plunkett and others (the Sturgis brothers, for example) preferred to be closer to the
cheap corn supplies.

There were more Plunkett ideas and investments, including a
ten-thousand-dollar investment in the Cheyenne electric light company and an abortive scheme to speculate on the expected terminus
of the Northern Pacific Railway, then building toward the West
Coast. These were enough to keep him busy with seemingly endless
correspondence and traveling, all the while complaining of diarrhea
and other symptoms of a weak constitution.[6]

A man well known to the Frewens and Horace Plunkett was both
a sportsman and a serious investor, with a different style than
the open range systems of their range. Born Windham Thomas
Wyndham-Quin in 1841, he later succeeded to the earldom of Dunraven and Mountearl; the estates he inherited included forty
thousand acres and four homes.[7]

In 1872, Dunraven, then thirty-one, was on his second trip to the United States, with Dr. George Henry Kingsley, his personal physician; they went west to Denver to spend Christmas, and there at the Corkscrew Club, an exclusive watering hole for foreigners (where women were not allowed), Dunraven learned of the beautiful area known as Estes Park.[8]

Dunraven wanted to see the place firsthand, so he set forth the day after Christmas with Kingsley and two men from the club for company, Sir William Cummings and Lord Fitzgerald. Fortunately, the weather was mild, and he was treated to the grandeur of the park in winter, presided over by the fourteen-thousand-foot Long's Peak, the highest in the park and visible for 150 miles out on the plains.[9]

On his way back to Ireland, Dunraven conceived the idea of acquiring the park, and he detailed young Theodore Whyte to begin the chore of assembling the property. Dunraven was able to buy five thousand acres in the name of the Estes Park Company, Ltd.[10]

Whyte took a lease on the land from the Dunraven company and for a time lived in the park with his second wife, the daughter of Lord Airlie (her brother, Lyulph Ogilvy, was ranching not far away); the Whytes lived in the cottage Dunraven had built for himself. By 1878 there were about fourteen hundred cattle on the ranch, branded with the cross and bar, which legal documents of the day called "half breed American" stock while other sources refer to Swiss breeds.[11]

Unfortunately, Dunraven's tenure as proprietor of Estes Park was not a happy one. The public outcry against the acquisition arose immediately, and his name was included in an 1882 Senate resolution calling on the secretary of the Interior to investigate land entries by the earl and his company. Finally, the earl departed the area in disgust, although he did lend his name to cattle ranching in the Dakotas, where he was chairman of the ill-fated Dakota Stock and Grazing Company, Ltd., a company organized by Moreton Frewen's brother Richard.[12]

Other friends and relatives of the Frewen brothers were eager to have Moreton and Dick manage cattle for them, and brother Edward soon placed a herd in their hands (financed by borrowed money, which later would be repaid only with difficulty). Pierre Lorillard IV, who had won the English Derby the year before and developed the seven-thousand-acre Tuxedo Park in New York, was looking for other investments for the profits of the tobacco business he had acquired from his brothers. He had met Moreton when Frewen was courting Clara Jerome, and Moreton had arranged a venture involving thoroughbred horses between Lorillard and Frewen's friend, Lord William Leslie de la Poer Beresford, brother of the marquess of Waterford. Lorillard's business instincts may have been reinforced in part by the attraction of Clara Frewen (Moreton warned her about being seen with Pierre when he was not with them), but in any case, Pierre decided to take a fling in the cattle business.[13]

His deal with Moreton involved the purchase of six thousand calves, which were to be left on the Frewen range and managed by them at a fee of $1.50 per head per year. Half the calves were to be delivered in 1883 and the remainder the following year; the price was to be set by two appraisers, one appointed by each party.

This deal soon became a key factor in the breakup of the Frewen partnership, which was not going smoothly. As has been noted, Moreton and Richard did not get along well, and on at least one occasion they came to blows; consequently, Moreton was soon casting about for ways to buy out Dick's share of the partnership. He briefly contemplated getting his older brother Edward to replace Dick, but Ted's finances were in poor shape, as tenants were scarce for his British holdings.

Moreton next hoped to use the proceeds of the Lorillard sale to buy out Dick's interest in the business. Dick was asking eighty-seven thousand dollars cash, plus the release of guarantees on borrowings of the partnership at the Post bank in Cheyenne, and in New York; Moreton also had to repay twenty-four thousand dollars they had borrowed from younger brother Stephen. Moreton expected to get fifteen dollars per head from Lorillard for the calves, which would cover the payments to Dick, although the timing of payments would still leave a cash-flow problem. Unfortunately, Lorillard's appraiser was Tom Sturgis, the powerful secretary of the Wyoming Stock Growers Association, and Moreton's appraiser was no match for Sturgis; the appriasers only awarded Frewen an average of thirteen dollars, leaving him short of his cash requirements.[14]

Then Moreton hatched a scheme to float a public company in England to take over the partnership ranch. It was near the end of May when Moreton got the bad news of the Lorillard proceeds, and he set off at once for London, crossing on the *Servia*. The time spent in crossing the ocean was not wasted, for Alfred Urban Sartoris, whose two sons would be ranchers in Wyoming, was on board and promised to take shares in the new company. In London, Lord

Wharncliffe came through with "sound advice" and another promise of participation. There were hopes of selling the stock to "millionaire Australians," and while the hope was not realized, there were plenty of others to fill the gap. The Powder River Cattle Company, Limited, was capitalized for one hundred thousand pounds of preferred stock and two hundred thousand pounds of common. Although the preferred shares were entitled to a 10 percent cumulative dividend, they were to be redeemed (at 120 percent of par). Moreton was so confident of success that he wanted to buy out the preferred shareholders and thus reserve *all* of the bright future for the common shares, where he held 20 percent of the total issue. As further confirmation of his confidence in the future, he agreed to be manager in America at no salary.

The investors and the board of directors were right out of *Burke's Peerage.* For chairman, Frewen got the very top of the nobility— William Drogo Montagu, seventh duke of Manchester, who had heard about the company from the marquess of Abergavenny. "They all love Dukes, here or elsewhere!" Frewen crowed in a letter to Clara. The duke held the additional titles Earl of Manchester, Viscount Mandeville, and Baron Montagu of Kimbolton; the dukedom had been created in 1719 and the earldom and barony a century earlier. When he came to the Powder River Company, the duke was fifty-nine and thoroughly enamoured of everything western.

After Lord Abergavenny told Moreton that the duke was interested, Frewen got his friend, Lady Mandeville (the American-born Consuelo Yznaga), to arrange the introduction. Lady Mandeville had married the heir to the Manchester title, and would herself one day be the duchess, all the white making colorful comments to enliven British drawing rooms. Even Lillie Langtry, who must have seen Lady Mandeville as competition, still found her to be "fair and ethereal"; she was also a favorite with the Prince and Princess of Wales.[15]

With his duchess and his daughter-in-law (Lady Mandeville) attracting so much attention, it is perhaps not surprising that relatively little is heard of the duke, whom Disraeli characterized as "silly, but not dull." Although Moreton exulted when Manchester agreed to be chairman, because of the prestigious name, even he remarked that the duke, although a "nice old gentleman," had little business aptitude. As chairman, his easygoing methods were no match for the aggressive tactics of the likes of Frewen and his opponents, and soon Moreton was fuming, "Stupid old Duke!" to Clara.

Also on the board of the Powder River Company was Manchester's nephew and Moreton's good friend, Frederick Augustus Ker Bennet, second son of the earl of Tankerville. The same age as Moreton, Bennet had been educated at Trinity College, Cambridge, and was a member of the Inner Temple Bar. He came west more than once to hunt and to observe the family investments at work.

Nor were the duke and his family the only good blood on that first board of directors. The Beckett family and their connections were also represented in the persons of Lord Henry Gilbert Ralph Nevill, son of the marquess of Abergavenny; Ernest William Beckett, who would later become Lord Grimthorpe; and Sir Frederick George Milner, a baronet. Lord Henry Nevill was a year younger than Moreton, and his wife was said to be the most celebrated hostess in London, in an era when such a distinction was very lofty, indeed, while Ernest William Beckett was said to be the most prominent member of the parliamentary bar (consisting of members of parliament who were barristers).[16]

Lord Wharncliffe, who carried the imposing name of Edward Montagu Stuart Granville Montagu-Stuart-Wortly-Mackenzie, sat on the Powder River Company board and became chairman after Manchester stepped down from that post. Born in 1827 and educated at Eton, he is entitled to the distinction of having been the first to introduce Lillie Langtry to society. For a time, Wharncliffe's relation with Moreton Frewen were cordial, although they would later deteriorate. Another Wharncliffe connection on the shareholder list was Andrew Whitton, a Scot who managed Wharncliffe's Scottish estates and was the largest preferred shareholder.

The shareholders in the Powder River Company also included Frewen's good friend, the earl of Rosslyn, of whom Plunkett remarked, "Ld is a poet & not a business man." The earl had been special ambassador to Spain at the wedding of King Alfonso in 1878, and his wife was a descendant of the dukes of Grafton. The Rosslyns were close to the court, and for a brief interval, the countess' daughter by her first marriage was being pressed by Victoria herself as a potential mate for Prince Leopold; the girl, however, refused the prince in favor of the earl of Warwick's son.[17]

Other shareholders were Hugh Lowther (who had bought Moreton's horses), and Rowland Winn, an old family friend of the Frewens, who would be created Baron St. Oswald; it was St. Oswald's son, Algernon James Winn, who had the nearby Big Horn Cattle Company.

What sort of information induced such a blue-ribbon group to invest in Moreton's company? He did not write a prospectus ("which probably no one will take the trouble to read"), but he did write a letter, which formed the only source of information the investors had to judge the potential profitability of the venture.

In the letter, Moreton quoted the report of the royal commission to the effect that the profits of cattle ranching in America had been at least 40 percent, adding, "This estimate at the time I considered excessive, but it falls below the mark for the last two years." Moreton did not try to predict profitability for the new company, except to say there would be a "fair" dividend out of income the next year, but he did give some little information about the profitability of the partnership just ended. According to his reckoning, the investment by the Frewen brothers was $114,000, and they had taken $125,000 out of the business; the remaining herd was valued at $192,000. This would imply a profit of nearly 60 percent per year, and although the young man had given only three figures in his analysis, who would quibble at a 60 percent return? The total subscriptions to the stock of the Powder River Cattle Company totaled nearly five hundred thousand pounds, for the three hundred thousand pounds of stock that were to be issued. The Cheyenne banker, Morton E. Post, wanted "40,000 of the common at par," but the stock was not available; "so you see he does not share that snob Frank [sic] Sturgis' view of my purchases," Moreton gloated to Clara.[18]

With the company organized and nearly $1,500,000 to spend on cattle and other necessities of life, Moreton took leave of his brother's partnership and hurried out to exercise his new role as American manager for the company. His mission was to expand the new operations for which the Frewen herds formed the nucleus. The transfer of the partnership assets to the corporation involved a total of just over $250,000, of which $206,000 was for the 6,797 head of cattle under the 76 brand, according to book count. Moreton bought 10,000 cattle and 10,000 sheep in a week after returning to Cheyenne; he even tried to buy Plunkett's EK outfit for $175,000, only to have Horace counter with $260,000, which Moreton thought "simply crazy." Others were not so difficult to deal with, and Moreton told Clara he found everyone "laying" for the Englishman with all those pounds sterling to spend. By September 1882, he had spent just over $1 million to buy 40,000 head (including the Frewen herds). "So strange that with Dick's exit, all real trouble seems to have disappeared," Moreton sighed.[19]

If 1882 was the year in which Moreton shrugged off the confining and confrontational partnership with his brother Dick and, by chartering the Powder River Company, widened his financial horizons as he had never been able to do before, the following year was the one brief interval in which his spirit could have full sway to express itself in all its bewildering diversity.

Though 1883 was not to be as happy as he would want it, at least it was to be eventful. Before leaving London for the West, Frewen met with his board of directors (with Lord Wharncliffe temporarily in the chair) and proclaimed the encounter "most harmonious." He even ventured the prediction that there was "no possibility" that he could be at odds with the board in the future. While this prediction was to prove false all too soon, for a time there was an almost unnatural tranquillity in his soul.

A stopover at the duke of Manchester's seat at Kimbolton Castle afforded a nice farewell touch before the voyage to New York aboard the *Fulda*. A visit to the Lorillard stud farm in New Jersey broke the trip before the long train ride to Cheyenne, where he arrived in May and found the city literally in the hands of the British. As a favor to his good friend Jim Winn, Moreton bought two trail herds to stock the ranges of Winn's Big Horn Cattle Company, one at $33 per head and another at $34 (in both cases the calves were included at the same price). One of these purchases took him to Denver, where he met Dunraven's manager, Theodore Whyte, and talked about the completion of the Northern Pacific railroad— a project that was then the talk of the entire West.

By the middle of May, Moreton was on his way to the Powder River country, a grueling forty-five-hour nonstop journey attended by rain and hail all the way. A few days later, he crossed over to Crazy Woman Creek and again encountered a hailstorm, this one so violent he was forced to unharness the horses and take refuge under the buggy; afterward, hailstones the size of filberts (hazelnuts) reached well above his ankles. It was on this trip that he bought a sheltered valley from rancher Bob Stewart, where he hoped to segregate five hundred Shorthorn and Sussex cattle for breeding purposes after erecting only two miles of fence to enclose an area that measured six miles by three.

Early in June, Jim Winn stopped at the home ranch on the way to his own ranch over on the Nowood, and Lord Aylesford's brother Clem was also there. The roundup was at the ranch on June 22, and everything appeared to be going smoothly.

Then it was off to the south to pick up the breeding stock from the Rawhide range for transfer to the new valley he had "bought" from Bob Stewart, where he expected to turn out eight hundred purebred calves a year. On this journey Moreton had the company of Horace Plunkett, who wanted to catch the stage at Fort Laramie, and the two men took advantage of a pause in the journey to bathe in Cottonwood creek and dry themselves in the sun. Unfortunately, while the men rested, the horses slipped their tether, and the two gentlemen were reduced to hiring two workhorses for the remaining journey to Fort Laramie, which they reached in pitch darkness over unfamiliar roads at two o'clock in the morning.

The roundup was not yet on the Rawhide range, so to fill the spare time, Moreton went on to Cheyenne for the Wyoming Stock Growers Association annual meeting. Expansion was in the air, and the association had added seventy-six new members in that year alone; one was Moreton Frewen. For Frewen, this act of joining the local association may have been somewhat symbolic; the following year he would file a desert land entry on Crazy Woman Creek, signifying in the application that he intended to become a United States citizen.

After the meeting in Cheyenne and dinner at Dick's house in that city, Moreton was off again to Fort Laramie and Rawhide, catching a night's sleep in a haystack. At the Rawhide range, he bought seventy "grand" bulls and four hundred heifers, recording in his diary his objective to make his herd the finest in America. The journey home involved a ride of forty hours to Fort Fetterman, a time when he did not catch sight of a single human being, even in the far distance, while subsisting on half a pound of cake.

Back home at the ranch, there was a message that Lord and Lady Onslow wanted to come for a hunt—as though there was plenty of time for entertaining. Moreton confided to his diary that having the lady was a "difficulty," since he wanted to return early to England, where his son and heir was soon to be born on a schedule that did not cater to Moreton's frenetic pace. Nevertheless, he agreed to meet the Onslows, and when the largest common shareholder of the company, his friend Charles E. Lyon, asked to come for a hunt, Frewen did not question the need to accommodate him. The same answer had to be given to Dunraven, who wanted to arrive about

Moreton Frewen, born the son of a Sussex gentleman in 1853, came to the United States after graduating from Cambridge. His visit to the Texas ranch of Goodnight and Adair awakened an interest in the range cattle business that led him to set up his own operation in Wyoming's Powder River basin. In the photograph above, taken in 1878 when Frewen was new to the West, he strikes a pose reminiscent of Colonel William F. Cody. (From the author's collection)

Moreton Frewen (*above left*) in New York in 1878, before his Western adventure began. Frewen married Clara Jerome (*above right*), daughter of New York financier Leonard Jerome. Clara's sister Jennie married Lord Randolph Churchill, whose son Winston would one day be prime minister. Clara came West with her husband after their marriage but soon decided that frontier life was unsuitable and returned to New York, where she kept up a lively correspondence with Frewen. (From the author's collection) Below, the so-called Frewen "Castle" that Moreton built as a home for himself and his wife when he managed the Powder River Cattle Company. The house featured a main room forty feet square where twenty guests could dine in comfort while musicians entertained them from the mezzanine. The house also boasted a grand piano and a telephone. (Courtesy of the American Heritage Center, University of Wyoming)

Horace Curzon Plunkett (*above*), a younger son of Lord Dunsany, came to Wyoming for his health and stayed to raise cattle. Plunkett was a close associate of Frewen; his Frontier Cattle Company had its range nearby, and the two Englishmen entered into many common projects. John Clay, Jr. (*left*) was another important figure in the American cattle industry. After serving on a British Commission appointed to investigate American investment opportunities, Clay came West himself, where he prepared reports for potential Scottish investors. The official study and Clay's reports led to a series of large-scale ventures, including a number of Scottish investments which were managed by Clay. (Courtesy of the American Heritage Center, University of Wyoming)

Lord Lonsdale. LOW

The foreign ranchers drew their capital from home-based corporations. Frewen energetically pursued a number of prominent peers for his board of directors, among them the first earl of Wharncliffe (*above left*) and the earl of Lonsdale (*above right*). Wharncliffe was director and then chairman of the Powder River Company. At first the earl and Frewen got on well, but they later fell out, and it was Wharncliffe's action in calling an outstanding loan that drove Frewen into bankruptcy. (Courtesy of the National Portrait Gallery, London) Lonsdale was a colorful man and a good friend of Frewen. It was he who bought Frewen's treasured stable of horses when the young man decided to leave England and devote himself to ranching. (Sketch by Sir David Low, courtesy of the National Portrait Gallery, London)

The seventh duke of Manchester (*above left*) was the first chairman of the Powder River Company. Frewen was delighted at securing such an elevated peer to head his board, but the relationship ended unhappily, with Frewen forced to sue the duke in British courts. (Sketch by L. Ward, courtesy of the National Portrait Gallery, London) Above right, the tenth marquess of Tweeddale, who headed the massive XIT in Texas, one of the largest cattle ranches in history. (Sketch by Carlo Pellegrini, courtesy of the National Portrait Gallery, London)

Not all the British who came West did so under happy circumstances. The seventh earl of Aylesford (*above left*) suffered greatly from the scandal of his wife's affair with Randolph Churchill's brother, Lord Blandford. Aylesford bought a ranch in 1883 in Big Spring, Texas, and lived there in self-imposed exile until his death. (Courtesy of the *San Angelo Standard Times* and the Institute of Texan Cultures at San Antonio) Above right, the fourth earl of Rosslyn, a close friend of Frewen and a shareholder in the Powder River Company. (Courtesy of the National Trust Photographic Library) Left, David Graham Ogilvy, ninth earl of Airlie, who chaired the Prairie Cattle Company. Airlie's son Lyulph managed a ranch north of Denver. (Courtesy of the National Galleries of Scotland)

The Cheyenne Club (*above*) was the symbolic center of the cattle industry in its heyday and served as headquarters for several large outfits nearby. Food and drink were the equal of any back East, and the house rules were as stringent as the most exclusive gentlemen's club in England. Many famous guests were entertained there, including Oscar Wilde and Lillie Langtry. (Courtesy of the American Heritage Center, University of Wyoming) A typical English dinner party, pictured below in A.E. Emslie's 1884 portrait of the earl and countess of Aberdeen entertaining at Haddo House in Scotland, illustrates the contrast of these opulent dinners with the harshness of old Cheyenne. Aberdeen was a major investor in the Rocking Chair Ranche in Texas and had another ranch in western Canada. (Courtesy of the National Portrait Gallery, London)

This is the real thing
painted the winter of 1886
at the OH ranch
C M Russell

This picture is Ch[arles]
Russell's reply to [my]
inquiry as to the
condition of my ca[ttle]
in 1886. L E Kau[fman]

"Waiting for a Chinook" or "Last of the 5,000" was the message returned by American artist Charles M. Russell in response to a query about the condition of herds during the disastrous winter of 1886–87. That winter marked the end of the free-range era in the American West, following a period of overcrowding that left many animals unprepared for the severity of that year's weather. Many British ranchers in the area were wiped out completely, and many more sold out at a considerable loss. (Courtesy of the Montana Stockgrowers' Association and the Montana Historical Society)

October 1, on his way to the Canadian Pacific. Moreton was never too busy to take on another task that he enjoyed or that he owed, always believing that his marvelous wellsprings of energy were boundless.

Yet he was not unaware of the risks. With all the appearances of permanence and the preparations Moreton made for his operations in the West, he never viewed them as more than a window of opportunity. He later wrote that he had hoped to be "let alone" on the range for a decade "or perhaps two," but he never said that the free range could last forever. Of course, his time estimate proved wildly optimistic, but in 1883 it still seemed possible.

Still, there were some dark spots. Even in 1883, there was concern about losses of cattle, and two groups of culprits were suspected by the cattlemen. By midyear Moreton was writing to Thomas Sturgis in his capacity as secretary of the stock growers association, to urge action against the Indians who were encamped on the Little Powder River and the Belle Fourche River; a band of Sioux were even given a pass by the Pine Ridge agent so they could go on a "hunting trip." The agent responded to criticism about these matters by asserting that such losses were risks of the cattle business, just as a bad winter might be.

The second group of suspects on the cattlemen's list were the rustlers. Moreton said that the owner of the 17 Mile Ranch had never bought more than four milk cows but had been able to sell a beef herd, acquired through the diligence of a hired hand who prudently occupied his leisure hours with the running iron.

On a ride back from the headwaters of the Nowood, Moreton noted that there was too little range for the cattle on it, and when he saw the cattle ready to be shipped from the Pine Bluffs station, he could see that the Rawhide herds were not fat (although the Powder River herds were in good shape). Up on the Powder River, another cattleman had turned a herd onto one of the Powder River Company ranges—Moreton thought to blackmail the company into buying them at a high price—but for whatever reason, there would be less grass for Powder River Company steers.

Although these signs were clear for him to read, he did not always seem to recognize the role he was playing in those developments. When he saw Cheyenne overrun with Britishers, he was pleased that cattle were selling at a 25 percent advance over the previous year; but that inflationary price was in part the result of the sudden infusion of all those pounds sterling.

Plunkett was involved with one of his partners in a new ranch down on the Laramie Plains by the Union Pacific Railroad. The Ione Land and Cattle Company was managed by E.S.R. Boughton, who moved down on the ranch to oversee it. Boughton was one of those owners (he then had two-thirds of the company) who was confident enough of the future to agree to take no salary, expecting to profit handsomely from the earnings of the enterprise (Moreton Frewen made a similar mistake). The company had a total of 54,000 acres purchased from the Union Pacific, and Boughton wanted to irrigate 6,000 acres, fence it, and improve it.[20]

Later in the fall, Moreton again met Alfred Sartoris, who had just returned from setting up his sons in another British-owned ranching company, the Douglas-Willan, Sartoris Company, which had its range on the Laramie plains. John H. Douglas-Willan was a stout, jolly Englishman who was well-liked in Wyoming. His partner was Lionel Sartoris, a very handsome young Englishman (born in 1863), and Lionel's brother Frank was also involved in the company. The Sartoris family had originally come from Savoy, and the boys' mother was the daughter of Viscount Barrington; their cousin had married the daughter of President Ulysses S. Grant in an 1874 White House ceremony. (It was this branch of the family who were related to the Wisters.) It was said that Lionel Sartoris had not taken to the West with good grace, but he built a ten-room house and conducted operations with considerable style; a number of servants were in attendance at the headquarters.[21]

Across the mountains to the northwest was the Wyoming range of the Big Horn Cattle Company, owned by Jim Winn; Milo Burke was the manager of the company, which used the Bar X Bar brand. To stay in touch, Winn was talking about building a telephone line to connect his ranch with Frewen's, a distance of some sixty miles.[22]

Nor was that the last of Frewen's friends to cast his eyes westward. Harold Lowther, first cousin of Hugh, was showing an "inclination" to settle in the West. Back in England that fall, Moreton was met on the first day of his return by a Reverend Bates, with five thousand pounds to set his son up in the western cattle industry, and Lord Wharncliffe was on the same mission for this nephew Ralph.

Ralph and another Wharncliffe connection found an investment with another ranch nearby in the Powder River Basin. Thomas Willing "Willy" Peters had set up a ranch about forty miles from the Frewens, and came nearly every weekend to visit. Moreton had been trying to get partners for him, because the young man wanted to get married and needed the additional capital to expand his operations. A partner soon appeared in the person of a burly Scot, Walter C. Alston, and together they ran the Bar C Ranch on the Middle Fork of the Powder River, in the famous Hole in the Wall country. Moreton drew up the partnership agreement. The two young aristocrats joined the operation as partners in their herds. Ralph Stuart-Wortley, nephew of the Lord Wharncliffe and Geoffrey William Millais both had a share, and both were active workers on the ranch. Geoffrey's sister was married to a first cousin of Lord Wharncliffe, and it is probable that the ranching idea came from that source. Young Millais noted that the 1884 results of the Bar C ranch would yield him about a thousand dollars, and that the increase of his share of the herd would amount to a total of about seventy-five hundred dollars.[23]

While Moreton was buying herds for Jim Winn, he did not often stop to contemplate the effect that the Winns of the world would have on the supply of grass. There would soon be too many herds owned by too many such investors. Others were helping to fill the formerly open spaces. On a trip north to arrange the sale of some Tongue River cattle, Moreton stopped by Sheridan, a town only six months old that already had thirty houses and a good store.

The 1883 roundup produced sobering evidence of losses—from whatever cause. There could not be a 20 percent dividend, but perhaps it might be half that large—still a handsome reward. Also, not all the news was bad, and Moreton's hope rose and fell with each fresh bit of evidence. The Tongue River gather was good, but the Rawhide was very bad; prices in Chicago were high, causing the prospect of 20 percent to rise again, only to fall when the numbers of animals failed to equal his hopes. His restless eye turned to the unspent capital (nearly a hundred thousand dollars) the board was hoarding in London, which might conceivably be spent to swell the dividend, but this idea produced nothing beyond a "civil" letter from the duke.[24]

At the end of August, Moreton was back at Rock Creek, where the only sleeping accommodation was the platform of the railroad station. After a stop at Pine Bluffs to see the cattle being shipped, he went on to Chicago, where the Powders brought fifty-five dollars per head, but the poorer Rawhides only forty-four. In early September he went to St. Paul for the fete opening the Northern Pacific, all the while giving interviews to newspaper reporters.

And he took some encouragement from his roots. In Chicago he met a young man he had last seen in 1878, just as the lad was matriculating at Trinity, and they talked about life at the university. Moreton was well pleased to hear, as he put it, "they still ride hard & still gamble," adding, "what a good sign the former & perhaps the latter is not without redeeming traits." Back in England for the winter, there was a continued whirl of social and sporting events, where Moreton met the Crown Prince of Portugal ("the most hideous royalty I have ever seen") and the hard-riding Austro-Hungarian Count Charles Kinsky ("the nicest little foreigner in the world").[25]

This busy year finally ended, closing out a succession of heady experiences such as Moreton had never known before, but he was not satisfied. Early in the following January, he wrote, "there are few people to regret that 83 had made room for 84. Financially & in some respects socially, the dreariest year of modern times is now hull down." It took a lot to excite Moreton Frewen.[26]

There were other ventures as well. Moreton had conceived the idea of increasing the profitability of the ranching business by extending the company's operations downstream into other functions of the beef industry. The shrinkage that occurred when live animals were shipped to Chicago could be avoided if they could be slaughtered in the West and the meat shipped east. Moreton's idea was to build a slaughtering plant designed for natural cold storage, to be located at the highest point on the Union Pacific: Sherman station (named for the Union general), between Laramie and Cheyenne. Frewen had learned that there was generally frost at this location every day of the year, so that there would be no need to supplement the natural refrigeration. The facility was really only an icehouse, with one building inside another; it was supposed to be large enough to handle a thousand head, but when it was finished Moreton thought it could accommodate five thousand. A ranch was laid out near the facility to receive the animals to be slaughtered. The plan was to hold the meat in cold storage until required by the eastern markets (presumably at good prices), when it could be shipped on the railroad in refrigerator cars. Moreton thought the return could be 75 percent or more. "Dear vulgar money," he wrote to Clara. "Don't laugh at my enthusiasm if I say the dream of diamonds may be near."[27]

Although construction was delayed by the same cold weather that had suggested the choice of location, the slaughterhouse was built and was ready to receive carcasses in October 1882. Unfortunately, the scheme did not succeed. Moreton found it impossible to buy enough fat cattle, and marketing proved more difficult than he had supposed. He also complained that he could not penetrate the barriers erected by the Chicago beef trust.[28]

Frewen's refrigeration and slaughtering idea was somewhat similar to that devised by another nobleman—a Frenchman—over in Dakota Territory. With the fulsome name, Antione Amedee Marie Vincent Amot Manca de Vallombrosa, he had been styled Marquis de Mores on attaining his majority. By April 1883 he was on the banks of the Little Missouri River, with his faithful family retainer and secretary, William F. van Driesche, where he broke a bottle of wine over a tent and christened his new business center Medora in honor of his wife, the daughter of a New York banker. The marquis built a dwelling at Medora for himself and his wife, but this French nobleman was not bringing his ancestral luxury to the western plains: Instead, he erected a comfortable house, furnished from sources readily available in that part of the country.[29]

The center of the town, and of his plans, was a slaughterhouse, owned by the Northern Pacific Refrigerator Car Company, of which the marquis was president. He had selected a point on the Northern Pacific railroad that gave him easy access to markets in the East while it lay close to the eastern edge of an immense cattle range. There was also adequate fuel available in the form of lignite, and there were the necessary water and ice to process and preserve the meat. Taking Frewen's refrigeration plan a step further, de Mores was going to ship meat direct to a central market in New York City, where it was to be distributed to retail markets in the city's tenement districts, underselling existing competition by nearly 30 percent.[30]

Problems soon developed. Much of the beef delivered for slaughter was not in prime condition (this was a problem Frewen also encountered), and although this caused the marquis to propose a plan to feed eighteen thousand cattle over the winter, it is doubtful that the plan went into full operation, since the Medora undertaking continued only until the fall of 1886. It appears that the basic problem of cattle quality was one that could not be solved. The only time fat cattle were available in quantity to the western slaughterhouse operations was in the fall, which created an impossible seasonal bulge. Moreover, consumer preference was for corn-fed beef, not range beef, and finally, there were intimations that the Chicago packers enjoyed freight rebates not available to their competitor de Mores.[31]

Frewen also devised a feeding plan, but he regarded it as an alternative—not an adjunct—to the refrigeration project. By the spring of 1884, Moreton had already concluded that the Sherman project would not succeed, and had told Frank Kemp (who kept the books for the company in Cheyenne) to try to sell the boiler (Kemp responded that the price might be better if the entire operation could be sold, and Frewen agreed, hoping to realize six thousand dollars for the facilities the company had bought from him for ten thousand).

For his feeding setup, Frewen selected a location at Superior, Wisconsin. His choice was based on transporation considerations, for Superior was to be the railhead of several rail systems and of course gave access to Great Lakes shipping. Frewen hired F. R. Lingham—who had been a leading exporter of live cattle from Boston to Canada—to build stables for five hundred head and set up the feeding operation. Some of the cattle Frewen fattened at Superior were sold to de Mores, after a brief negotiation in which Moreton haggled with the marquis for an additional quarter cent a pound.[32]

A second attraction at Superior was the prospect of making money from real estate development. Moreton was instantly enthralled by the place. "I somehow think our fortune will really date from this spot, not dear old Powder," he said. The railroad syndicate that held the townsite had agreed to let him in on the "ground floor"—almost. Moreton planned to build a hotel and a bank, and brother Richard was dispatched to conduct negotiations with the syndicate, who were "making noises" about requiring commitments for $1 million or so in improvements as the price of a deal with the Frewens. At the meeting Dick laughed heartily at them, an action that amused neither the syndicate nor Moreton (when he learned of it).[33]

Finally, the Superior location also positioned the company to exploit an even more audacious scheme. Live cattle could be shipped from the United States to Great Britain, but they had to be slaughtered on landing, a precaution required by the British government to protect British herds from the importation of diseases from across the ocean. But imperial policy protected the Canadians from such restrictions, and Moreton saw the opportunity to secure the importation privilege for western beef cattle by getting a similar dispensation.

To carry out this objective, he secured a handsome set of credentials from the Territory of Wyoming (over the governor's signature) and set out to lobby the Mother of Parliaments. The process was long and arduous and nearly succeeded. At first the signals were positive. Moreton met the Canadian minister of agriculture, who is supposed to have concluded that the project was "sound & of great benefit to Canada," but then there was a scare about the risk of infecting Canadian (and British) herds with Texas fever, and Moreton was soon abusing the Canadian prime minister as "that old villain." When the British appeared willing to act if the Canadians agreed, an equivocal answer from Ottawa was enough to stall the effort.[34]

It was not long before Moreton was in trouble with his board of directors. The initial purchases went smoothly, but when Moreton put together a deal to buy out Charles Oelrichs and two other ranchers on the Rawhide range (southeast of the Powder River range) for "some 600,000 dollars," the board balked. In October 1882, the corporate secretary cabled Moreton to say that the $225,000 they were sending would be the last until the following May. "I'll change their tune when I get home," he fumed, and two days later he was still upset about "those wretched people at home." Even more serious in tone was a cipher cable telling Frewen that the board was dissatisfied, and their confidence "much shaken," but this storm temporarily passed a few days later, with a conciliatory message that Moreton called "the *amende honorable*."[35]

It is true that his endless list of deals soon exhausted both the money and patience of the board, and his endless wandering may have left too little time for devotion to the details of running the business, but there was a more fundamental reason why the business was in trouble. The free-range system had fallen victim to its own success. The Frewen operation on the Powder River was being crowded by other herds, and it was apparent that something would have to be done.[36]

Wharncliffe tried to calm the situation, advising Moreton "in the most friendly spirit" to moderate his attacks on some members of the board (notably Lord Henry Nevill and Andrew Whitton). Soon there was a distinct cooling between them, as Frewen's active pen sent unguarded comments not only to friend and foe alike but also to the press, greatly irritating Wharncliffe. Finally, the situation worsened to the point that Wharncliffe called a five thousand pound loan, bringing Moreton to the verge of personal bankruptcy.[37]

Moreton's solution was to move north and obtain a lease on Mosquito Creek in Alberta, where he hoped to move the Powder River herds. Plunkett saw the lease later, when he was manager of the Powder River Company. Thin skinned in more than one sense, he sourly observed that the creek was aptly named, but eventually he also admitted that the logic of the move was sound when Moreton said that the range had "at least six times the grass to the average acre" as there was on the Powder River. Unfortunately, the Canadian government was in the process of imposing duty on such movements, and only the first seven thousand head could be got across the border before the deadline.[38]

For all of these reasons, profitability proved elusive, and the preferred shareholders, who were entitled to a 10 percent dividend, became restive. It was at this point that Moreton came into close contact with Wiliam J. Mackenzie, a man important in Dundee investment circles.

Mackenzie was not an aristocrat by birth; his father was the Reverend James Mackenzie, a minister who had also written a history of Scotland. Born in Donscore, Dumfriesshire, in 1847, young Mackenzie early had to assist with the support of his family, on the untimely death of his father. Nevertheless these circumstances in no way inhibited his rise in the business world. He became a stockbroker and was an original member of the Dundee Stock Exchange; he rose to the post of secretary of the Dundee Mortgage Company even before he had mastered double entry bookkeeping and company law. Mackenzie became an important preferred-stock shareholder of the Powder River Company and a member of its board. He was a good friend of Lord Airlie, and was with the earl in Denver when he died.

Moreton and Mackenzie got along well for a time. Mackenzie's letters seem genuinely warm to Moreton's interests, and Moreton told Clara, "he is an excellent fellow, very keen about Lingham & sizes Plunkett up about as I do, a thorough old woman & deceitful at that!" Mackenzie was the spokesman for the preferred shareholders, and in that role tried to make peace between Moreton and the board of the company. He tried to arrange the buyout of the preferred shareholders in exchange for debentures, and to do this a new corporation was to be chartered and the old Powder River Company liquidated into it. Mackenzie actually got 90 to 95 percent of the preferred shareholders to concur. Unfortunately, management disputes continued, over such questions as whether some of the herds should be moved to Canadian ranges, and the confrontation ended with Moreton's dismissal and his eventual replacement by Horace Plunkett. Moreton had considered giving up the management as early as the spring of 1885, when he wrote Wharncliffe and offered to pay someone a thousand pounds to take it off his hands (the money had to come from Moreton's pocket, since the company was not paying him a salary).[39]

As an outgrowth of this letter, Frewen first offered the job (with a thousand-pound salary) to Horace Plunkett, who refused the offer. Frewen then offered it to his old friend Willy Peters, who accepted on condition that Moreton would help. The friends soon fell out over the issue of winter feeding and moving the herds north (Peters was against winter feeding and thought the shift to the north would be stifled by Canadian red tape), and at an acrimonious meeting in London the following year, Peters threw up the job. The board then turned back to Horace Plunkett rather than contemplate putting Moreton in charge again.

Moreton explained to Clara the squeeze that had occurred. "I daresay Ted has told you that because they would neither send us money from London, nor send us permission to borrow out here, we were completely broke up," he said. Then London cabled that money could be raised on condition that Frewen resign: "[S]ooner than bring about a catastrophe, I have resigned."[40]

Horace took the management job, according to his own account, only to protect his own nearby operations from the chaos of a disorderly Powder River Company liquidation, but the result was a "war to the knife" with the Frewen brothers, who opposed nearly everything he did. Whatever his motive, Plunkett's insistence on the right to liquidate the company made it necessary for the board to make that step irrevocable if it was to have his services. Lawsuits were filed in England; when the company tried to have Moreton declared bankrupt (possibly to gain some leverage over his ever-active tongue and pen), his solicitor made a partial payment to creditors to avoid the action. Moreton then refused to turn over to the company the Crazy Woman and Tongue River filings he and Clara had made. He

arranged to have his friend Morton Post in Cheyenne sue him there
to create liens on the property and thus thwart the British court
actions. It was a fine stalemate.

It must have been particularly irritating for the duke of Manchester to be sued in the British courts by Moreton, whom he had
accommodated by going on the board in the first place. One day,
he stopped Frewen on the street to reprove him, saying, "There are
other ways of dealing with elderly men in responsible positions than
by running clean over them once a week." For once, Moreton accepted the criticism in good grace.[41]

Despite the conflict, some of Moreton's friendships proved dur-
able. Lord Rosslyn continued to try to mediate between Moreton
and the board, mostly without success. It was during this period that
he happened to wire his factor the instructions, "Buy all horned
beasts," and the transmission was garbled to read, "Bury all horrid
beasts." The harried earl used the incident to underscore his frustra-
tions with the cattle business, adding, "I wish we could."[42]

In spite of his family ties to Manchester, Bennet continued to
send Frewen information about conditions on the range; he even
lent the Powder River Company ten thousand dollars to help with
the stringent cash position. The real victim of all this dissension was
the old Powder River Company and its common shareholders, for
its liquidation now became not a reorganization step but a real liquidation. It was the end for the 76 outfit. The entire proceeds of liquidation went to satisfy the legal preference of the preferred shareholders, leaving nothing for those (including Moreton) who held the
common shares.[43]

In his efforts to liquidate the Powder River Cattle Company,
Plunkett succeeded in getting an offer for the Alberta herds from
Sir John Lister-Kaye, an English baronet whose family claimed de-
scent from Sir Kaye, a knight of the Round Table; Sir John was
another of those who courted Clara Jerome before she fell to Moreton's blandishments. Plunkett said that when he met the Lister-
Kayes, he discussed theology with Lady Lister-Kaye, the former
Natica Yznaga, American-born sister of Lady Mandeville, but it is
also likely that Natica already knew the Powder River Company
story from her family connections. In any case, Plunkett talked business with Sir John, who had a large fortune to invest in Canadian
properties. Plunkett made a typically acid assessment of Lister-
Kaye, calling him another Moreton Frewen, although not quite so
able and far more facile. "I feel he will be robbed." said Horace.[44]

As we have already noted, Dick Frewen did not leave the West after he was bought out of his partnership with Moreton but stayed on in Cheyenne and elsewhere to dabble in Powder River Company affairs; interestingly enough, now that he and Moreton were no longer business partners, they got along reasonably well. Then, in 1883, Dick organized his own public company in London, called the Dakota Stock & Grazing Company, Limited, with his friend Lord Dunraven as chairman and including as directors Baron Castletown and Greville Richard Vernon, brother of Baron Lyvedon. Lord Castletown had been a hunting guest on the Powder River in the first year of the Frewen partnership. Richard Frewen had forty-one hundred shares of the Dakota company, and siblings Edward and Stephen held another twelve-hundred shares.

This company bought the Hat Creek Ranch in Dakota Territory from N. Russell Davis for five hundred thousand dollars, payable in two installments a year apart. The range was described as "over 600 square miles," and was supposed to handle over seventeen thousand head of cattle. The next year the Dakota Company picked up a ranch on Chadron Creek; the deal was not completed, and the company finally recovered its downpayment in a lawsuit. Unfortunately, Dick's venture was soon in financial trouble, and he told Moreton in the fall of 1884 that he could pay no dividend and was too poor to go home for the winter. The Dakota Company went into liquidation in 1886, eventually paying nearly five dollars per share, which at least gave Dick something for his remaining three thousand shares. Nevertheless, within two years he was back in business raising horses.[45]

Moreton Frewen's adventure in corporate ranching in the English style was not a resounding success, to say the least. The Powder River Company was beset by the problems of the industry itself, which will be explored more fully later. But it was the English style—based solely on the availability of totally free "self-made" hay, promising a very high return if it succeeded and carrying a high risk if it failed—that was the fundamental problem, and it was only complicated further by Moreton's peripatetic style of operation and the difficulties in dealing with the company's London board.

# Kindred Spirits on the Range

## The Scots and Other Foreigners

———————◆———————

In the fall of 1882, when the Powder River Company was still expanding rapidly, the English board of directors cabled instructions to Frewen to cancel the purchase of the Rawhide range cattle he had negotiated for about $2 million dollars. Fuming, Moreton vented his frustration to Clara in a letter comparing his English bosses with the Scots: "I had a million times rather be accountable to a Board of Scotch businessmen." Unfortunately for him, the Scottish investors in the Powder River Company did come to have a strong voice in its operations. Accountability was very much their hallmark, and they proved not in the least easy to deal with.[1]

Not all the British investors in the range cattle industry had the same objectives as did the English aristocrats like Frewen on the northern plains. In spite of Moreton's initial enthusiasm for the Scottish businessmen, they in fact epitomized a style of operation very different from his own. Farther south, in Texas, others from the British Isles were ranching in the Texas style, which in many respects resembled the Scottish style. To complete the picture of this group of investors in this turbulent time, we now turn to the Scots and the Texas ranches.

The merchant and banking class of Scotland early saw the chance for profits in the American ranching business, and a number of companies were organized, some of them quite large. James S. Tait, a Scottish broker from Edinburgh, promised British investors 50 to

60 percent per annum, claiming it would be easy to compete with the Americans, as they were so short-sighted and had had their wealth virtually thrust upon them. The Scots were also confident that their management style was better than that of their London competitors.

While Frewen, Plunkett, and others were exploiting the free range, the Scots were following a different drumbeat. Because much of the criticism of the English companies and their operations comes from that source—and because any review of foreign investments in the American cattle business must ultimately fall under his long shadow—it is necessary to consider that different style, and to turn to John Clay, Jr.

Clay wrote a great deal about the cattle industry, and almost all that we know of his connection with it has been colored by his own prolific pen. By the time of his death in 1934, Clay had risen to the pinnacle of the industry, having served eight years as president of the Wyoming Stock Growers Association and operated the large livestock commission business of John Clay & Co., with headquarters in Chicago and branches in Omaha and eight other cities, to say nothing of his banking operations in the cattle regions.[2]

Nearly everything Clay wrote was from the vantage point of 1916 or 1917 or later, and these writings suffer from the benefits of hindsight; by then the range cattle industry of the eighties was no more: It had failed miserably. This man who knew as much as anyone about the reasons for that failure was not shy with his opinions, but he was also remarkably prejudiced.

Clay was born in 1851, the son of a Scottish farmer near the border town of Berwick-on-Tweed. Though the family was not of the aristocracy, it had served them. John Clay's sister married the commissioner of the duke of Richmond, Lennox, and Gordon; and his father was a tenant of a large farm owned by the duke of Roxburghe. When the cash lease expired in 1876, the duke raised the rent from seventeen hundred to twenty-three hundred pounds, and the elder Clay gave it up, losing the improvements he had made at his own cost. One wonders whether the elder Clay was galled at having to list his occupation as "tenant farmer" when subscribing to the shares of a public company, when others grandly wrote "peer of the realm."

Whether for these or other reasons, John Clay, Jr., was often critical of the gentlemen he met in the cattle business, and he was sensitive to the slights, real or imagined, that he received at their hands.

Thus, though Clay was high in his praise of the *business* acumen of Sir George Warrender, chairman of Western Ranches and the Scottish American Investment Co., he took pains to note that in his long association with Warrender, he was only invited to "break bread" with the baronet on one occasion, and then only because of a business deal of some importance. Moreover, the unceremonious way he was fired from the management of the Swan Company in 1896 remained a source of irritation for the rest of his life.[3]

There are some remarkably candid comments about Clay in an interview with Magnus Larson, a Swan employee from 1917, who had known John Clay during the Scotsman's years as manager of that company. Larson was thirty-three at the time. Clay had cut wages on the Swan during the hard times after World War I. Larson said he didn't have a good opinion of Clay and, when asked by the interviewer to expand on that statement, said, "He was a man, you know, he would cut everybody, you know to cut expenses, but he never cut himself." Larson was referring to the fact that Clay collected a commission through his Chicago operation on all the cattle the Swan sold. Larson also described Clay's trips to the ranch: "He would come out to the ranch and always brought a manservant with him to take care of himself: shave him and give him his bath, and give him his drinks, you know, when he wanted them." Eighty-eight years old at the time of the interview, Larson's memory may have been colored by events long after the fact, so perhaps we should make some allowances for this statement; nevertheless, it is obvious that Clay had made no great friend of him.[4]

For his part, too, John Clay held strong opinions of others. He described the English investors in the western cattle business: "The man that walked up and down Piccadilly in winter time or faced the dealer at Monte Carlo, or better still sailed across country astride a good horse in pursuit of the red fox knew little of what was taking place around Laramie Peak or the headwaters of the Cheyenne River as the drifting snow played pranks over level grassy divides or sagebrush flats." Although Clay was not above absenting himself from the range for long periods, or even visiting his native Scotland, somehow he did not associate this activity with those arguably similar pursuits of pleasure by the English gentlemen. It is ironically amusing that in later life, Clay even soured on relations with his Scottish masters. In 1907 he wrote that he had given up working for Scottish boards, because "their ideas of remuneration & mine were so far apart."[5]

The division of the companies considered here is not precise. A number of the big Scottish outfits are distinguished from their English counterparts because the Scots sometimes did not bother to adorn their boards of directors with titled aristocrats; instead they chose to give those positions to merchants and bankers. Thus, although the Scottish American Investment Company had Sir George Warrender, a baronet, as chairman, one of the most prominent investors was Thomas Nelson of the successful publishing company of Thomas Nelson & Sons. The Wyoming Cattle Ranche Company, another Edinburgh company, counted among its investors Thomas Nelson; Archibald Coats of J. & P. Coats; Henry Johnston, a lawyer; Andrew Thomson, a timber merchant; and the cashier of the National Bank of Scotland. The Hansford Land and Cattle Company, incorporated in 1882 with a capital of £210,000, had five Dundee merchants as its first board of directors. Yet some of the companies in the previous chapter were clearly in the real estate business, much as the Scots were, while the Prairie company, which we include here, had a huge open-range operation.[6]

The Scots came into the ranching business by a somewhat different route than their English colleagues. The Scottish American Mortgage Company and the Scottish American Investment Company, Ltd., were the two most powerful "money cliques" in Edinburgh. The mortgage company was looking for mortgage business in the United States and later set up the Prairie Company syndicate. The Prairie Cattle Company has been called the mother of British cattle companies, and we include its story here though its first chairman was a Scottish earl, because its style of management fits best with the companies managed by the Scottish businessmen.

The Prairie Company was promoted in Edinburgh by the Kansas City firm of Underwood, Clark & Company and was registered in late 1880 with a capitalization of about $1 million; it was a huge outfit operating in southern Colorado and northern Mexico and Texas, in three divisions. Its chairman was the eighth earl of Airlie. No figurehead chairman, Airlie was active in management and had extensive knowledge of the United States, arising from his travel there commencing in 1864, when he met President Lincoln, attended the Democratic convention in Chicago, and toured the Michigan iron ore country.

The earl had been involved in land speculation in the United States through the Dundee Land Investment Company, Limited, organized in 1878, which he also chaired, and where he worked with the able Scot, William J. Mackenzie, secretary of the Dundee Company, who later gave Moreton Frewen so much pain in the operation of the Powder River Cattle Company.[7]

The prospectus for the Prairie Company offered the simple proposition that a three-year-old steer cost only six to ten dollars to raise and would bring twenty-five to thirty dollars on the market. It noted that profits in the industry had been in the range of 25 to 40 percent per annum, and even 50 percent under favorable conditions. Nor were these empty promises; the dividend in 1882 was 19.5 percent, and in 1883 it was 20.5 percent on the £250,000 capital, but according to John Clay, this was possible only by partial liquidation of the herds. Nevertheless, 20.5 percent made a mighty impression in Edinburgh.[8]

The Prairie Company expanded rapidly, and by the end of 1883 it owned 139,000 acres in fee (that total would grow to 164,000 in the following year) in addition to nearly uncountable other acres of free range; it was a truly imperial spread, and some ranchers thought the company intended to own "all outdoors." The Northern, or Arkansas, Division had a range of 2,240,000 acres, according to Baron von Richthofen; the Cimarron, or Central, Division, 2,580,480 acres; and the Canadian, or Southern, Division, a mere 256,000 acres. The entire property had been acquired at sixty cents per acre, and the baron put a value of $4.3 million on it.[9]

According to the baron, the company started with 104,000 head of cattle, which increased in two years to 139,000, there having been sufficient sales in the meantime to pay all expenses and yield $50,000 of profit in 1881 and $250,000 in 1882. The calf brand in 1882 was 26,000.

The Prairie Company sent inspectors to the ranges in 1884; one was a Mr. Andrews of Texas and the other was Thomas Binnie, from the Scottish American Mortgage Company, but Clay thought their report produced no new information that was helpful. The company's report for the year 1884 did admit that the ranges were overstocked, and that the financial future was in doubt. The board thereupon dismissed Underwood, Clark & Co. as managers in the United States, in a settlement for $400,000, of which $300,000 was paid in cash and the balance in company shares. After this settlement, another deputation was sent to investigate the company affairs in the West; all three inspectors were from Scotland, and none had ever seen an American cattle ranch.

This inspection produced a report not much more helpful than before, if we take Clay's assessment, but the Prairie did turn its financial affairs over to Murdo Mackenzie in 1885. This able Scotsman, born in County Ross, came to the United States at the age of thirty-five; he became manager of the company in 1889 but only stayed a year, leaving to manage the Matador Company.[10]

Mackenzie's control of the Prairie apparently had little effect on the company's fortunes, for another report of inspection in 1888 noted that the Prairie herds were badly inbred, a factor that partially accounted for the lower realizations from sales, which had trended downward from $35.00 in 1882 to $17.90 in 1886. Moreover, it was discovered that one herd had been purchased twice from Underwood, Clark & Co., in 1881, for a total overpayment of nearly $101,000. This claim was finally settled with the American firm for a compromise of $65,000 in notes.

Despite these difficulties, the Prairie continued in business for a number of years, although its Cimarron Division became overrun by sheep operations and was finally abandoned to them. The company finally wound up its business in 1917 and went into liquidation in 1920.[11]

John Clay, Jr., never managed the Prairie, and he was consistently critical of its operations (as he was of many over which he had no management control). His own experiences in the American cattle business stemmed from the work of the Royal Commission of 1879, one of whose members was his father, John Clay, Sr. John Clay, Jr., who was then in Canada, was appointed a subcommissioner, which meant that he could draw a salary for his work (the members of parliament sitting on the commission worked without extra pay). Clay had come to North America on an extended pleasure trip in 1874 and while there had met George Brown, owner of the Canada West Farm Stock Association (the Bow Park Farm); two years later Brown engaged him to manage the property, and he was there when the Royal Commission was established. After his three years in the service of the commission, Clay was employed to investigate properties for investors who wanted a share of the 33 percent returns the commission found in the American cattle industry. His investigations and later work brought him to the same regions where Moreton Frewen was working, and by coincidence, both men joined the Wyoming Stock Growers Association in the fall of 1882.

The Cattle Ranch & Land Company, with a capital of four hundred thousand pounds, or nearly $2 million, was set up by Lord George Campbell, a younger son of the duke of Argyll; its herds were to be purchased from Rufus Hatch, a New York financier (who had taken a "flyer" in the cattle business), and two younger men who also sold herds to the Rocking Chair Ranche, another British company: Earl Winfield Spencer and Jacob John Drew. Clay disliked Drew, although he liked Spencer, who was cheery and had a good knowledge of the cattle business. John Clay, Jr., was hired to report on the properties, which were in Kansas, Indian Territory, and Texas, for a fee of $1,250 and expenses, plus $2,500 worth of stock if the company was successfully brought out on the stock market. Clay's father served on the board of the company, and the younger Clay later was hired by the company to manage the ranch.[12]

The Cattle Ranche and Land Company was supposed to have 26,000 head on hand at the end of 1882, and Spencer and Drew, as comanagers, sold $128,000 worth of cattle, which enabled the payment of a dividend of 15 percent on the preferred and deferred capital. The following year sales were $145,000 and the profits $101,000. The cattle totaled 28,197, apparently without any deduction for losses. By 1884 the company was in trouble, and in that year made sales of just $50,000, not enough to cover the expenses of operation; no dividend was paid, although the company reported a profit of $90,000, using the assumed increase of the herd to do so. No dividend was paid in 1885, and the American management was instructed to make a count of the herds; this count reduced the 31,762 book count of November 30, 1884, to 13,500 in October of the following year. The calf crop was only 2,224. The deferred, or common, shares were simply worthless. After these events, Drew resigned to take the comanager's job at the Rocking Chair Ranche, although it is doubtful that he could have held on to his $5,000 salary at the Cattle Ranche after the new austerity measures were put in operation by Clay.[13]

After reporting on the Cattle Ranche and Land Company in 1882, young Clay went to California to buy for the Scottish investors a property that was renamed the California Pastoral & Agricultural Company; it was located in Merced and Fresno counties, and Sir George Warrender was president.

In the summer of 1882, Clay was also ordered to report on the purchase of a herd under the Seventy-One Quarter Circle brand by the Wyoming Cattle Ranche Company, Limited, from John T. Stewart of Council Bluffs, Iowa. The company bought 4,000 acres of fenced meadowland and 2,560,000 acres of range; the prospectus estimated that there were 19,000 head of cattle, and all of this was

to be acquired for $400,000. The actual deal was not for 19,000
head, but 14,250. The herd was to be accepted on book count, but
with a guaranteed calf brand of 4,000. Clay arrived just as the
roundup was disbanding, and there was later confusion as to what
the owner told him, but it was clear that the brand was only 2,800,
and the directors asked Clay to recover from Stewart for the defi-
ciency; the matter was finally settled by a lawsuit in federal court,
whereby the company recovered $55,000 from Stewart. Clay later
was given the job as American manager for this company, the first
managers having been discharged as the result of the incident.[14]

Another 1882 purchase arranged by Clay was that of the VVV
brand from Dorr Clark and Duncan C. Plumb, which formed the
nucleus of Western Ranches, Limited, an operation promoted by
the Scottish firm of Gordon, Pringle, Dallas & Co., and headquartered in Belle Fourche, Dakota Territory, running cattle on the Belle
Fourche River. The first herd was two thousand head, and by the
end of 1884, eighteen thousand more had been purchased, at prices
ranging from seventeen to thirty dollars. The company included
the familiar names of Menzies and Thomas Nelson, and Sir George
Warrender was chairman. The Scottish investment was five hundred thousand dollars, mostly spent on cattle. The company was
successful, and passed through the 1886–87 winter in fair shape; it
was reorganized in 1911 to enter the land mortgage business before
it was finally liquidated in 1919.[15]

Clay had maintained his headquarters in Chicago beginning in
1882, where he was in partnership with his brother-in-law, W. H.
Forrest (by the time he died, the commission firm was called simply
John Clay & Co.). To manage the Western Ranches in the field,
Clay chose a boyhood friend from Scotland, James T. Craig. Craig
came to the United States in 1884, when he was only twenty-two,
and went to work at the Seventy-One Quarter Circle ranch; he later
became superintendent of Western Ranches, with headquarters at
Belle Fourche, in Dakota Territory. He also served on the executive
committee of the Swan company, and was involved in some of the
banks that Clay invested in. An important figure in the Western
South Dakota Stock Growers Association, where he helped direct
the work of the detectives and inspectors, Craig was also prominent
in Wyoming. It was Craig who tried to ship supplies to the besieged
cattlemen and their Texas gunmen at the time of the Johnson
County invasion in 1892, but unfortunately the load was inter-
cepted and captured by Johnson County sheriff Red Angus.[16]

His work on the range brought Clay into contact with Alexander Hamilton Swan and Joseph Frank, who were then partners in the Swan and Frank cattle operation in Wyoming. They wanted Clay to prepare a report on the Swan operations, so that they could float a large public stock issue in 1883. Clay says that he refused to make the report except on the basis of an actual count, and his services were not contracted for. He described Swan as a man with a Duke of Wellington nose, a keen eye, and gold teeth, and then added caustically that Cheyenne men "worshiped at his feet." We must not be too concerned about the accuracy of this word picture, as it was written years after Clay had good reason to dislike both Swan and his method of operation. We do know that Swan was born in Pennsylvania in 1831 and had speculated in Iowa farmland for some years before coming to Wyoming in the 1870s, when he was well past forty—a relative patriarch in that land of the young.[17]

In March 1883, the Scottish bankers and merchants organized the Swan Land and Cattle Company, Limited, in Edinburgh, to purchase the Swan and Frank Live Stock Company, the National Cattle Company, and the Swan, Frank and Anthony Cattle Company, all associated with Alec Swan, and all operating in Wyoming Territory. Original capitalization was about $3 million, and the original chairman was Colin J. Mackenzie, director of the British Linen Company Bank; the board included Lord Douglas Gordon, of London, but he resigned at the end of the first year, pleading the pressures of parliamentary business.[18]

The Swan operation started up in grand style, and Alec Swan was manager at the handsome salary of ten thousand dollars per year. The Swan shares initially traded at a premium, because of the confidence of investors in Swan's management and the thoroughness of the reports prepared by the secretary of the company, Finlay Dun. More than 89,000 head were involved in the initial purchase of the Swan companies, and a further 12,035 were bought during 1883. After adding the calf brand and deducting the year's sales, the book count at the end of the year stood at nearly 109,000. Of course, the only actual count was of the 19,000 branded and the 12,000 sold; soon the management began to worry about shortages, and a special reduction of 7,900 animals was made in the 1884 financial report. The following year a further 3,000 reduction was taken from the steer totals, and in 1886 a 10 percent loss was assessed against the bull herd and 8 percent against the remainder of the animals.[19]

These efforts to bring the herd book count into agreement with actuality, whatever that may have been, was impeded by the lack of information. Soon the intervention of the winter of 1886–87 created a dislocation of the normal loss percentages that overwhelmed any effort at bookkeeping based on normal trends. In the summer of 1887 the remainder of the Alec Swan properties (but not the Scottish public company) became insolvent, and Alexander Swan resigned as manager of the Scottish company, to be replaced by the corporate secretary, Finlay Dun. Dun now made an unsuccessful effort at counting the huge herds, and the directors finally took a $1.6 million write-down of the capital account, which reduced the herd (after the year's sales) by nearly 58,000 head; legal proceedings were also commenced against Swan to recover for alleged short count on the initial purchase. While there was testimony as to the "little Russia leather memorandum book" in which Alec Swan presumably kept the only original record of the calf brand, the book was not produced and the case failed on procedural grounds.[20]

It was at this point that John Clay entered the affairs of the Swan Company. He admitted that he was chosen to manage the Swan not because of skill but for the financial infusion he represented (which he did not particularize). Under Clay's leadership the Swan gradually returned to prosperity. He gave up 283,000 acres under contract of purchase with the Union Pacific, which then reverted to the railroad, and made severe cost reductions; all this had the effect of improving cash flow, but the ranges were also in better condition following the heavy die-off of the herds, and soon what passes for normal weather in Wyoming blessed the Swan with some relatively good years. However, Clay's style was simply to do things and only afterward tell the board what he had done. In the scary years after 1887, this was tolerable to Scotland, but a better cash balance restored confidence, and with confidence came the old management assertiveness of the directorate; by 1896 they had had enough of Clay and he was fired.[21]

A Scottish company not managed by John Clay was the Texas giant, the Matador Land and Cattle Company, Limited. Organized at the end of 1882, with headquarters in Dundee, the Matador took over the operations of the Fort Worth–based Matador Cattle Company of Texas. The capital was nearly $2.0 million, of which $1.2 million was paid in, and most of the British shares were held in the Dundee area; the first board had William Robertson of Dundee, an engineer, as chairman. Two of the former owners were brought on the board and received a quarter of the stock in partial payment for the ranch properties. The directors personally guaranteed some of the new debt and took such firm control as to cause one historian of the company to comment that the real headquarters was Dundee, not Ballard Springs, Texas.[22]

The company started business on a range south of the Staked Plain, with about 100,000 acres of land owned in fee, and additional grazing "privileges" on over 1.5 million acres. In due course, 216,000 acres of school lands were leased (the Texas public lands were devoted to support of education), although this total had shrunk to 146,000 by 1890, as settlement of the school lands continued. The company soon authorized the purchase of more than 200,000 acres of additional land to eliminate incursions on the range, using the proceeds of borrowings and an increase of five hundred thousand dollars in authorized equity capital. The company also exchanged land with its neighbors to block up its range, in one case swapping 11,000 acres with the Pitchfork Land and Cattle Company. Until 1884, the Matador operated on the open-range principle, but by 1887 there was much fencing of the company's Texas ranges. When the company learned that much of the land was unsurveyed, and those surveys that existed were unreliable, it hired surveyors to delineate the company lands, and these surveys were eventually accepted by the state land office in 1905.[23]

The company kept all the females during the first two years and sold only enough cattle each year to pay the American expenses and finance the dividend. This policy permitted the herds to grow rapidly and generated concerns of overstocking on the Texas ranges (which were also being shrunken by settlement activity). Accordingly, in 1884 the Matador began driving surplus cattle to ranges in Kansas, Wyoming, and Nebraska, using a northern movement policy strikingly like that proposed by Frewen for the Powder River Company. In 1894, Alexander Mackay of the Matador met John Clay, and this meeting resulted in a proposal to pasture two thousand head of Matador cattle on the range of Western Ranches in Dakota Territory, at a cost of one dollar per animal per year. Murdo Mackenzie, the manager of the Matador, was not initially very warm to the deal, because he would lose control over the stock; he eventually got the right to have the cattle sent to a commission firm of Matador's choice, although Clay's firm was to get the business if it remained financially strong.[24]

The deal with Western Ranches continued for a time, but finally broke down when the Dakota ranges also became too crowded; at about the same time, the lease on another pasture expired, and the Matador then bought additional Texas pastures from the XIT, consisting of the Rito Blanco pasture and some land in Alamasitos, for a total of nearly 199,000 acres, at a total cost of $397,000. With other acquisitions the new pastures totalled 214,000 acres, all in Oldham County, Texas. Further north, 50,000 acres were leased in Canada at two cents per acre, and 530,000 acres were leased on the Cheyenne River Indian Reservation at three and a half cents per acre. These acquisitions and leases permitted the company to replace its former deal with Western Ranches. The fee land total was 879,000 acres in the peak year of 1916, when total range was about 1.5 million acres. Initially, the company's fee lands were held in trust to avoid state restrictions on foreign ownership, but with the passage of time it became apparent that Texas would likely not take any action against direct ownership, and the trust was finally dissolved.[25]

The Matador was fortunate in the winter of 1886–87, as it suffered relatively low losses, and thereafter it continued to expand. The Texas ranges were well watered by comparison with those ranges on the Staked Plain, and the Matador did not have to rely solely on windmills to pump water for the cattle, as it could construct reservoirs (which it called "tank dams").

The company did not pay large dividends to its shareholders (8 percent was the peak, paid in 1883), and there were a number of years when nothing at all was paid. The board was very conservative and maintained a reserve fund for contingencies that reached about one hundred thousand dollars by 1890. Finally, in 1951, a syndicate headed by Lazard Brothers offered $23.70 a share for the Matador's eight hundred thousand shares of stock; the company then owned 795,000 acres in Texas and 4,600 acres in Montana and 46,746 head of cattle. It was eventually broken into fifteen separate corporations. The Matador was one of the few successful cattle ventures, although it was not so profitable as some of the other British ventures in Argentina and Uruguay. At the end, however, it was primarily a land company, not a cattle company, since the herds could not have accounted for more than a third of the liquidation values.[26]

If the English-controlled companies represented by the likes of Frewen and Plunkett and the Scottish-controlled companies managed by Clay formed the mainstream of foreign investment in the cattle regions, there were also other outfits in that broad territory along the front range of the Rockies, from Alberta in the north to Mexico in the south. Their style was sometimes a bit different from those we have seen so far, but the men who ran these ranches were often related in one way or another to the gentlemen on the free ranges.

In Collingsworth and Wheeler counties, at the southeastern corner of the Texas panhandle, was a British company that—although it was managed by British aristocrats—became involved with the capital-intensive ranching system practiced in that state. A syndicate headed by a Scottish baron had acquired 150,400 acres of the best-watered land for $1.25 per acre from Earl Winfield Spencer and Jacob John Drew, whose predecessors in title had received it from the Houston and Great Northern Railway. With the land came a herd of cattle and the Rocking Chair brand, which lent its name to the company formed by the British. The company was formed in the United Kingdom in 1883 with a capital of £150,000 in three thousand shares of £50 each; the largest shareholder was Sir Dudley Coutts Marjoribanks, first Baron Tweedmouth, whose father was the senior partner of the Coutts bank, and whose family estates included 20,000 acres in Inverness-shire. Tweedmouth, a man given to ungovernable rages, had taken his son-in-law and nephew into the venture. The son-in-law was John Campbell Hamilton Gordon, seventh earl of Aberdeen (later to be viceroy of Ireland and governor-general of Canada, for which service he was elevated to marquess), and the nephew was Henry Edward Fox-Strangeways, fifth earl of Ilchester. On that first shareholders' list of only fourteen names was Sir Geers Henry Cotterell, a baronet, and Sir John Clayton Cowell, private secretary to Prince Alfred, duke of Edinburgh, Queen Victoria's second son.[27]

Sir Dudley sent his youngest son, Archibald John Marjoribanks, then twenty-two, to be comanager of the ranch. The eldest son, Edward, who would later rise to be first lord of the admiralty, stayed on in London to manage the company's affairs there. Archie—who suffered, perhaps unjustly, from bad press and was supposedly "troublesome"—was six feet tall, flush-faced, and reputed never to look anyone squarely in the eye; he received a salary of fifteen hundred dollars per year. Another son, Coutts, also caught the ranching bug and went north to Dakota Territory, where he had a two-thousand-dollar allowance at the Horse Shoe Ranche, another of the family ventures, purchased for a mere thirty thousand dollars; his mother sent over from Scotland some purebred Aberdeen Angus cattle to assist with development of the herd. Unfortunately, bad luck dogged his heels, and he later left Dakota to manage Guisachan, a 480-acre farm on Lake Okanagan, in British Columbia, for Lord Aberdeen. Aberdeen later added nearby Coldstream Ranch to Coutts's responsibilities; it was irrigated and planted with fruit trees, the first such venture in that valley.[28]

The other comanager of the Rocking Chair was the Englishman, Jacob John Drew, who had been one of the sellers of the original herd and left a five-thousand-dollar salary with the Cattle Ranch and Land Company for twenty-five hundred dollars from the Rocking Chair. John Clay, who met Drew in connection with the Cattle Ranch and Land Company deal, had heartily disliked the man, calling him "a miserable specimen of mankind, a sort of adventurer with an evil tongue, with no sense of honor."[29]

The company took over the $188,000 purchase contract on 150,400 acres from Spencer and Drew and bought their herd of 14,745 head for a total consideration of $365,000, partly paid in the form of shares. The land was not in a solid block but was checkerboarded with Texas state lands; at the time, this seemed an advantage, because the school lands initially could be grazed free and could eventually be leased, giving the ranch a solid block of some 300,000 acres. Unfortunately, events proved less sanguine than this outlook. When the railroad was completed between Quanah and Wichita Falls, the proximity of rail transportation to Collingsworth County caused land prices to rise and brought in many new settlers.

In 1887 the company took leases on 237 sections of school lands, giving it control of a total of 300,800 acres, in a 600-square-mile block. The leases cost only four cents per acre per year, which was reasonable enough, but there was a joker in the leases: Actual settlers had the right to purchase the land. (Although the law apparently required the state to give lessees notice of intended sale of school lands, such notice was not given to the Rocking Chair.) There were forty families on the school lands, and many had lived there for four years; when the Rocking Chair tried to evict them, there were clashes, some involving firearms. Nevertheless, the company continued to develop the land, building one hundred miles of four-strand fence. When the settlers began buying the school land parcels within the ranch boundaries, there was no choice but to accept the resulting loss of the range and the improvements.[30]

The Rocking Chair Ranche fenced its west boundary in cooperation with a big ranch and completed the other boundary fences at its own expense at about $250 per mile. When the school sections began to be sold to settlers, the fences sometimes had to be moved, and the ranch vainly tried to secure payment of $100 per mile for them.

The surrounding counties had been organized, so that they could levy their own taxes and hire their own officials, and settlers to the south, as well as those on the school sections within the ranch itself, pressed for the organization of Collingsworth County. To no avail, the company at first opposed organization of the county; efforts were then directed toward securing the county seat for the town of Wellington rather than the competing Pearl City. The bargaining chip used with voters was the promise of free town lots in Wellington, if it were designated the county seat, and this effort resulted in the choice of Wellington. For a short time it appeared that the election would be invalidated, and the London office alloted a thousand dollars to lobby for the location of the county seat at Aberdeen, within the ranch boundaries. When the territorial legislature validated the original county election, however, the matter became moot.

Once Collingsworth County was organized, the Rocking Chair had a problem that was fairly common for the big ranch corporations. It was a tempting target for taxation. The new county government launched a program to build a thirty-thousand-dollar courthouse, rather than the twenty-five-hundred-dollar frame structure Archibald John would have preferred, and although many of the settlers also cooperated with the ranch to fight this potential source of tax increase, the building was constructed as planned.

How profitable was the ranch? We can't say for sure, because we don't have the British books. The ledgers so meticulously kept by Archibald John Marjoribanks did not include the financing of the land purchases under the original $188,000 contract, nor did they reflect any home office expenses. The home office sent fifteen thousand dollars every year for expenses of the American operation, and the proceeds of cattle sales were deposited in separate accounts to be drawn upon only by the home office.

Cattle sales in the year 1890, 1891, and 1892 averaged just over fifty thousand per year, but about a third of this total came from the sale of cows, since the company was in the process of liquidating its herds to make range land available for sale. Expenses were about $22,000 per year, and the increases from year to year centered in such uncontrollable areas as taxes and legal expenses; Archibald John's carping at suppliers held expenditures for provisions to a flat profile in the three years. There was thus left a margin of about

$28,000 to pay home-office expenses and contribute to the financ-
ing of the corporation. It was not a large return on the land investment of $188,000, but then the ranch did not lose cash money, as
did so many of the foreign ventures.[31]

There is clear evidence that the British management suspected
that its cattle were disappearing. At first they assumed the cattle
were being stolen by the settlers on the school sections, and Corpo-
ral W. J. L. Sullivan, a Texas ranger, was hired at forty dollars per
month to live on the ranch and investigate the situation; after a
time, Sullivan concluded that the culprit was in fact the comanager,
Drew. The London office abruptly suspended both Drew and
Archibald John, cutting off their authority so precipitately that
there was no time even to arrange for the payment of outstanding
checks bearing their signatures.

John Clay said that the herd that was carried on the books at
12,000 only proved to contain 2,500, but he does not give dates, and
in other respects his account is clearly flawed. The company's book
count for the herd was 19,251 at the beginning of 1890. In this period, the company was not branding all of its calves, so that the book
count became of less and less value as a management tool (in 1893,
although 729 calves were sold, only 37 were branded, 20 of them by
other outfits). Selling unbranded stock facilitated attracting buyers
from nearby ranges, who did not want to buy Rocking Chair–
branded animals when the same brand was still active on the adjoining ranges.

Moreover, the losses taken on the books were more than the normal deductions in the industry. In 1890 a 10 percent loss was taken
on calves because of the depredations of the "loafer" wolves, and
in 1891 a similar loss deduction was taken on the younger stock. In
1892 a special 15 percent loss was taken against female stock because of the severity of the winter snowstorms; the balance of the
herd was reduced by 10 percent. Thus, it would seem that natural
losses were adequately covered by the loss provisions. Finally, the
fact that no additions were posted for most of the calves produced
another hidden loss provision, which should have made the 8,914
final total for 1892 a much firmer number than would otherwise be
the case. Unfortunately, we do not know what sales were made in
1893; Archibald John recommended that all remaining animals be
sold in that year.

There was at least one lawsuit filed against Drew, but there was
apparently no conviction on the charge of mavericking. It would

have been doubly difficult to secure a conviction, since the brand had not been formally registered, so that no charges under the brand could be brought in the state courts. Moreover, as has been noted, it was ranch policy not to brand calves, and the unbranded animals were impossible to trace.

In short, London believed its herds were being systematically depleted by stealing and fired its managers because of that suspicion, although nothing was proved. Even though both comanagers lost their jobs with the ranch, suspicions apparently centered on Drew, for Archibald John went from the ranch job to a position as aide-de-camp for his brother-in-law, who had been appointed governor-general of Canada.

The new manager of the Rocking Chair was George W. Arrington, but the decline of the ranch was not arrested under his leadership; it was closed down in 1893, taking three years to liquidate. The remnant of the land and livestock was sold to the Continental Land and Cattle Company in 1896 and the company was wound up two years later. The remaining 238 sections of owned land was sold for $75,200, including improvements thereon. This was land for which $188,000 had been paid, and which Archie had valued at $450,000 just six years earlier. It was obviously not a great real estate investment, not the golden goose Archie envisioned, and not an auspicious end for the ranch that had been called the richest in the panhandle.[32]

The lack of extensive financial information of the Rocking Chair Ranche makes it impossible to form a definite opinion as to what was wrong with the strategy followed by this company. Archibald John Marjoribanks thought that the land was the company's best asset, which would ultimately provide a profit for the shareholders; to realize this profit, the cattle herds would have to be liquidated, and this was the course followed. Yet, the land was ultimately sold for less than half its acquisition price. Other companies who held on to the deeded lands in their Texas ranges did better, and it can at least be argued that if the British owners had been more patient, they might have fared better as well. That there may have been thefts is undeniable, and this factor may have impelled British management to cut its losses and divest the troublesome land so far away from the center of their other activities. But if that was the sense of reasoning, it does not thereby condemn everything that was being done on the range in Texas.

Across the Mexican border to the south was the site of another

British investment. The story of Lord Delaval James de la Poer Beresford is another of those shrouded in confusion, with sometimes colorful and conflicting stories. Born of a distinguished Irish family in 1862, Delaval was the youngest son of John Henry Beresford, fourth marquess of Waterford, and was called the "pet lamb" of the family by his niece, Lady Clodagh Anson, whose husband had a ranch near San Angelo, Texas. The family was colorful, and Delaval's brother Charles had a long, sometimes stormy career in the British navy, serving as aide-de-camp under four successive viceroys of India; Delaval served briefly in the army, then resigned his commission and traveled west to Haiti and Cuba, finally gravitating in the 1880s to northern Mexico, where he started ranching. He reportedly ran his stake of a few hundred pounds into a fortune by buying up ranch land for "practically nothing" and stocking it with blooded cattle.

The ranching enterprise did prosper, although the reasons are in dispute. The more sober story is that Delaval dressed simply and built up a business shipping Mexican beef to Canada for butchering. According to this account, he traveled only occasionally to El Paso for amusement and contented himself by "riding to the hounds" on his Mexican estate.

The more colorful rendition involves his dubious liaison with a black woman, whose name was apparently Flora Wolf but who is called "Lady Flo" and "Queen Flo" in news stories. In this account, Delaval was a hopeless drunk who knew "nothing" about the cattle business, while Flo skillfully managed the operation, so that the property was worth $250,000 at the time of Delaval's sudden death. A vital part of this interesting story is that "Lady Flo," who claimed to be his wife, wisely protected her interests by branding every second calf with her own personal brand, so that in time fully half the herd was legally hers.

There are some witnesses. His niece said that she often invited Delaval to come to visit her in Texas, but that each time he journeyed the one hundred miles from the ranch to Chihuahua to begin the trip north, he got "on the raggle" and "always forgot why he had come there and just went home again!" This sounds as though Delaval did drink, and probably to excess.[33]

Delaval died in late 1907, in a train wreck on the Soo line in Dakota, while en route to Canada to inspect his properties there. His will left ten thousand dollars to a "colored woman" (who must have been Flora Wolf) and the balance of an estate (in Mexico and Canada) said to be worth $1 million, to his three brothers, who included the marquess of Waterford and Admiral Charles Beresford. One of the ranches in Chihuahua was said to be 160,000 acres, and a second was 73,000 acres.

Even if we credit Flo with considerable business skills, it is difficult to see how she could have managed the Canadian estates as well, so at least part of the story may be exaggerated. From this point on, we are left with conjecture; the foreman in Mexico is supposed to have counseled brother Charles (who was sent out from England to settle the estate) that he would be well advised to buy off Flo's claim, and there are stories that he did just that; but then Charles is also supposed to have taken Delaval back to England to die, which is patently untrue. Perhaps all that can be said is that poor Delaval may have become the victim of the western propensity to hang onto a good story, even if it is untrue (in whole or in part).[34]

While these cattle operations were spreading out on the northern plains, Texas continued to enjoy more of the foreign investment craze. In the Texas style, these were capital-intensive operations that bought much of the range land they used. The Spur ranch, whose corporate name was the Espuela Land and Cattle Company, Limited, registered in London in 1885, to buy the ranch properties of the Espuela Land and Cattle Company of Fort Worth. The Fort Worth company had bought 378 sections of land from the Houston and Great Northern Railroad Company on a contract for $515,000, of which 10 percent was paid down. The range therefore consisted of 437,670 acres, plus the intervening school sections; about forty thousand head of cattle were included in the deal.

The first board of the London company was headed by Charles E. Lewis, a member of Parliament and bank director, who was created a baronet in 1887; and included Alexander Staveley Hill, the managing director of the Oxley Ranch in Alberta, and Sir Robert Burnett, another baronet, whose presence was a key source of confidence for investors. An important shareholder was Alexander Mc-Nab, who was also involved in the Matador company and the Cattle Ranche and Land Company; the early investors seem to have been mostly from the County of Surrey. The properties included 437,670 acres of land owned in fee, and about forty thousand head of cattle. The Spur range was to the east of the range of the Matador Land and Cattle Company, which we will describe in the next chapter. The two companies agreed on a plan to fence the boundaries of their ranges, generally splitting the cost between them. The Spur was able to cut its cost of fencing from $175 per mile in 1885, to only $136 per mile in 1901—the difference reflecting mainly the lowering of labor costs in the meantime. Of course, the fenced boundaries reflected the usage of the companies rather than an attempt to delineate the precise ownership of land, and these old fence lines would later spawn much trouble and litigation.[35]

The rapid changes in the pace of settlement and transportation were graphically illustrated by the changes in delivery point for shipment of cattle. In 1885 the Spur trailed its cattle to Ogallala, Nebraska, but the next year they could be delivered closer to the ranch, even though settlement had pushed the trails westward to Coolidge, Kansas, near the Colorado line; in 1887 the herds went to Colorado City. Beginning in 1888 and 1889, the deliveries were made at points in Texas, first at Amarillo (which briefly became a cattle town), and thereafter at nearer railroad stations in Texas. The range itself came under pressure as settlements to the south took up the area crossed by the customary cattle trails and brought pressure for a cattle trail across the Spur range itself; the Spur finally fenced a trail to keep the herds from the south off their pastures. This expensive project, which was purely defensive, was completed in 1886, but in spite of this friendly gesture to aid the drovers, the Spur had to keep three deputy sheriffs on the ranch to deal with those trying to go through the ranch rather than around it.[36]

The intervening school lands also were the cause of trouble to the Spur, as they were to all the big Texas outfits, except the XIT (which owned its range in a block). Since the settler had preference to buy the lands, despite the grazing leases, some settlers discovered they could file on the land, paying one-fortieth of the price (or about two and a half cents per acre) down, and holding it for a year. Since the lands were inside the range fences, the "settler" could then run his own cattle on the range, making use of the bulls provided by the big outfit and thereby have a very economical small ranch.

Moreover, Texas law prohibited the foreign companies from purchasing the school lands from the state or buying the rights from settlers before they had received a deed. To get around these restrictions, the Spur used a device also employed on the public domain in the north, whereby friendly "nesters" filed on the school lands; these people were customarily hired to work on the ranch until they received the deed for their land, at which time it would be purchased by the Spur. Some of these deals went awry, but eventually the Spur got good title to 212,000 acres of school lands and thus blocked up their pastures.[37]

The Spur was purchased in 1906 by a New York syndicate headed by E. P. and S. A. Swenson; the shareholders received five dollars per acre for the 437,670 acres, including improvements and about thirty thousand head of cattle and horses.[38]

The next company in our review involves a truly Texas-size operation, the XIT, whose range was to the west of the Spur range; this great ranch was born in a deal that could only have been struck in Texas. After the Civil War, the "Reconstructed" state of Texas was blessed with a lot of land and little money for public improvements, and the easy way to get a new capitol building in Austin without burdening the taxpayers was to give away enough land to induce the Yankees to build the necessary structure. That is exactly what was done, with 3,050,000 acres of unsurveyed and generally undesirable land, in a solid block beginning in the northwest corner of the Texas Panhandle and stretching southward along the New Mexico border for 197.4 miles, across parts of ten counties. The legislature implemented the constitutional authorization in 1879, with safeguards to ensure that the Yankees did not become too rich. The state was to keep for itself the best 50,000 acres in the block, to cover incidental costs of handling the transaction (this tract was finally sold for a bit over fifty-five cents per acre), and title on the rest was only to pass in proportion to progress on the capitol. The project proceeded slowly, but it did receive some forward impetus when the old capitol burned down in 1881. The Chicago syndicate of Taylor, Babcock and Company won the bid for the reservation, over only one other bidder.[39]

The Chicago syndicate soon realized that the land they were to receive was unsalable even at fifty cents per acre, and it was then that they turned to the British capital market for help to get their stalled project off the ground. It was a good time to go to London for this purpose, because the early enthusiasm about the establishment of the Rocking Chair and Matador companies created a receptive market in which to float what would become a $15 million issue.

The company, which was registered June 25, 1885, was called the Capitol Freehold Land and Investment Company, Limited. The chairman was the marquess of Tweeddale, governor of the Commercial Bank of Scotland at Edinburgh, and other shareholders included Lord Aberdeen; Baron Thurlow; Henry Seton-Karr, a member of Parliament; and Sir William Ewart, a baronet from Belfast. John V. Farwell, one of the original owners, was managing director, and his brother Congressman Charles B. Farwell was also a director. The prestige of the American participants was considerably enhanced in the eyes of the British shareholders when in 1887 Charles Farwell was elected to the Senate, and the following year, Abner Taylor, the head of the Chicago office, was also elected to the House of Representatives from Illinois. Although the British shareholders in total held a majority, the Farwells held effective control, a fact which gave the operating management in Texas not one, but two headquarters to answer to: Chicago and London.[40]

It was intended that the land would be ranched only until it could be broken up and sold, but the sheer size of the block of land meant that the ranching operation would have to be a fairly long term venture, and by 1886 nearly 111,000 head of cattle had been purchased for just over $1.3 million. The cattle were branded with the XIT brand, said to have been designed by Abner Blocker; a single 5" straight iron was applied five times to create the design. (Later, considerations of damage to hides caused the ranch to shrink the brand to a single X.)[41]

The XIT rapidly fenced its lands, and 781 miles of fence were built the first year; the fencing was not so much to keep other cattle out, as to keep the XIT cattle at home, because the policy from the beginning was to introduce Hereford, shorthorn, and Angus cattle to replace the Texas stock in the original herds. The huge company also expanded outside Texas, and in 1888 leased a part of the Western Ranches range in Dakota to pasture fifteen thousand Texas steers; these were trailed north in spite of quarantines against Texas fever; none were brave enough to face down the Texas giant. Two years later, 2 million acres of Montana range were leased to add further muscle to the operations. The quality of its cattle was better than the common run; shorthorn and Hereford breeding stock made for heavier, more docile herds than the typical longhorns. By 1900 the XIT had seven divisions, with ninety-four separate pastures.[42]

The capitol eventually cost the company $3.25 million, which made the cost of the 3 million acres just over a dollar per acre. While this was not a high cost, the huge range needed a great deal of development to provide water for the herds, and there was no money to pay bondholders or shareholders. Moreover, there was trouble on the political front. When James Stephen Hogg became governor of Texas, he threatened to limit the company to fifteen years in which to sell its land and leave the state. If there was trouble in Texas, at least the big ranch did attract considerable support elsewhere, and in 1911 Congress settled the dispute over the Texas–New Mexico boundary, setting it on the XIT fenceline; New Mexico was forced to accept the result.[43]

Of course, the destiny of the company had always been to shut down when the land could be sold; in 1901 the bondholders, who had patiently watched their investment without return, forced the company to begin sale of the land. The first large sale was made to Major George W. Littlefield, who bought the nearly 236,000 acres included in the Yellow Houses Division of the XIT, and by 1912 so much land had been sold that the company was no longer in the cattle business. These and other sales easily paid off the bondholders, and the original syndicate was dissolved in 1915.[44]

Other English investors merit passing mention. Cecil Talbot Clifton, born in 1862, was called a "cowboy peer" when he made his home at Northfield ranch near Roundup, Montana; although he would one day succeed as twenty-fifth Baron Grey de Ruthyn, a fourteenth-century title that brought with it the honor of bearing the sovereign's gold spurs at coronations, while in Montana he went by the name Cecil Clifton. On the west slope of Colorado, Sir Genille Cave-Brown-Cave, a baronet, followed the roundup and broke broncos on the range. When he succeeded to the title, he left the ranch to an ovation from the cowboys. Then there was Edward Stachen Carey, grandson of a Scottish earl, who came to Colorado with the Dunraven party after a disappointment in love and there lived a reclusive life on the range, avoiding feminine contact so assiduously that one cold winter night he denied hospitality to a family because it included a woman. His hundred-thousand-dollar estate was bequeathed to a local sheepman (although a relative contested the will).[45]

The companies considered in this review are by no means all of the British companies chartered during this era, nor even all of the most important ones. While the early syndicates were dominated by wealthy investors who took good-size holdings, the cattle mania later attracted a number of relatively small shareholders, many from the military, and there were not a few "spinsters" among their number.

Although the description of a company's intentions did not have to be too precise for the stock to be salable, perhaps a prize for vagueness should go to an 1883 syndicate—that of the Sand Creek Land and Cattle Company, Limited, headed by the barrister and member of Parliament, Henry Seton-Karr, who was also a shareholder in the XIT ranch. The company bought the ranch of one Frank Ernest in Carbon County, Wyoming, and its prospectus described the property as consisting of "a good log house," grazing rights of 150,000 acres, "more or less"; 2,800 head of cattle, "more or less"; "about 30 bulls"; and "upwards of" 50 horses, all for the round figure of $106,000.[46]

# A Style of Business
## *Management Problems and Practices*

———◆———

**J**ohn Roderick Craig first met Alexander Staveley Hill, barrister and member of Parliament, when he was seeking financing in London for what would become the Oxley Ranche, in Alberta. Mr. Hill looked at the prospectus and said he was satisfied with the venture, but he refused to participate because he didn't want to associate in the venture with Craig's business friends (who were all ordinary Canadian businessmen). Hill said, "I don't doubt the standing of your friends, but I will not go in with business men. I would undertake it only with my own acquaintances—noblemen and gentlemen." There was a certain comfort factor in dealing with one's countrymen and class, and this factor was evident in many of the British cattle ventures.[1]

One might have supposed that the presence of so many kindred spirits from the homeland would guarantee congenial relationships, but this was not the case. As we have already noted, the Frewen brothers could wax so passionate at times that there was physical combat, and Plunkett harbored a low opinion, indeed, of many of his countrymen in the West. Of the Frewens: "Things never will go right with the Frewens, I fear." Of his partners: "Boughton is useless. . . . I don't altogether approve of Alexis' character. . . ." Yet Plunkett was pleased when a quarrel with his fellow shareholder Andrew Gilchrist was resolved by Gilchrist's gracious letter owning up to being "the vanquished foe." "This is manly," said Plunkett.

123

On one occasion, Frewen complained to Clara Jerome that he had been sent a parson's son to work on the range. "A man must have capital, strength & energy," wrote Moreton, "& here is one poor fellow who is devoid of all three."[2]

Although he sometimes made mistakes when doing favors for other gentlemen, for the most part Frewen seemed able to pick good men as employees, and he often elicited extremely loyal responses from them. E. W. Murphy, whom Moreton once called his "most valuable employee," was hired as one of the foremen and followed Frewen's bidding wherever he was needed, showering Moreton with letters full of news about the business and sometimes making unfavorable comparisons of other bosses with his treatment under Frewen. F. R. Lingham, the great, blond ex-lumberjack whom Moreton had recruited for the cattle-fattening operation he set up at Superior, Wisconsin, could surely have found someone who would have done more to advance his career. But he doggedly stuck to Frewen for as long as he could. And there was dear old Mack, Frewen's personal valet, who was often unpaid but stayed on to live and die with Moreton.

Frewen's Powder River Cattle Company had a chief foreman on the range at the home ranch (Fred G. S. Hesse). There were also subsidiary foremen at some of the other locations (E. W. Murphy was at the Rawhide Ranch), because of the distances involved. The company maintained an office in Cheyenne, where Frank Kemp kept his meticulous tallies of the company's assets, including the important book count of the cattle; and of course the London office was the workplace of the company secretary, another of the ubiquitous Kemp family, Charles W. Middleton Kemp (Frank's brother, Charles Fitch Kemp, also worked there).

Fred Hesse was a fairly typical manager for the British owners. Born in England in 1852, though he was for many years identified with the Frewen operations in the Powder River Basin, he was not actually brought over from England by them. He had gone to Texas in 1873, and came to Wyoming in 1876; when the Frewen brothers came to the Powder River country, Hesse went to work for them. When he was interviewed by Ashley Bancroft in 1885 (for the Hubert Howe Bancroft Western History series), Hesse was making $3,000 per year.[3]

A highly opinionated statement about the foreign gentlemen was made by John Clay. "The men from the other side of the Atlantic were young, mostly worthless in a business way, many of them dissolute, and when you rounded them up a very moderate lot. Very few of them have survived the ordeal of hard winters, over-stocked ranges, and other vicissitudes. A few have branched into other lines and won success. The ne'er-do-well at home was exported to the West, with generally disastrous results, not only to himself, but more especially to the friends who were asked to take him in charge."[4]

Thus spake Clay, in a piece written for the *Breeders Gazette* in 1916. Of course, he himself was from the "other side of the Atlantic" and had come over when he was still "young," but he was a man of hard opinions and sweeping generalities. (It was Clay who had said that Ella Watson—"Cattle Kate"—was "the common property of the cowboys for miles around," adding, "If they could not pay her the price of virtue in cash, they agreed to brand a maverick or two for her behoof," although one wonders how intimate was his knowledge of these assertions.) Clay was also quick to anger, and after the cattlemen's unsuccessful invasion of Johnson County, Wyoming, in 1892, he had *Northwestern Live Stock Journal* editor Asa Mercer incarcerated in Chicago for suggesting that Clay's absence from Wyoming at the time of the invasion was an act of personal cowardice in a venture he had helped to plan. So it is difficult to judge Clay's generalities. His hindsight had the benefit of knowledge that many of the big foreign outfits did fail—as did many domestic outfits, large and small. But the failure of the outfits they served—at a time when the whole industry was collapsing—hardly justifies Clay's blanket condemnation of all the young men from "the other side of the Atlantic." They brought with them an orderly style of business and not a little in the way of technical advancement—and, of course, they also brought ample funds to practice this style and put these advances into operation.[5]

The foreign owners were on the lookout for the best technology. Boughton wrote to Lyulph Ogilvy at Greeley, Colorado, to ask for a quote on the cost of breaking 640 acres and sowing it to alfalfa for hay, and the cost of preparing and planting another 1,000 acres in oats. Ever alert to technological progress, he wrote to one Henry Lee to ask about a machine Lee was supposed to have developed to sow alfalfa in unplowed land, and he contacted a chemistry professor in Boulder to learn how to get water samples analyzed. Later in the year, he was seeking analyses on iron ore from a professor at Boston's Technological College (Iron Mountain was partially on the Ione lands). The next year, a windmill was installed to harness the ubiquitous winds.[6]

The British tended to entrust the management of their ranches to their countrymen, but such assignments were no sinecure. Rouse Boughton offered jobs to the sons of investors in the Ione Land and Cattle Company, agreeing to pay each "what he is worth," provided the young man agreed to give "strict obedience." He then apologized for the "plain and curt" words, saying, "in matters of business it is best to say very plainly what one means." Later, Boughton wrote to a certain Major Peploc to tell him the arrangements for the winter he had made for the major's son (F. C. W. Peploc). "I am making him as comfortable as I can & am leaving a respectable married couple to work under his orders," he said. "He will have plenty of horses to ride & there is good antelope shooting." As the winter wore on, the lad found things "rather dull," and Corson, the bookkeeper, sent him some novels to read.[7]

The experience of such a disciplined life apparently wore on young Fitz Peploc, for by spring, he had hatched a scheme to invest in his own ranch property, and wanted Boughton's opinion of the idea. Boughton took the time to write a long letter, recommending against the investment, and cautioning young Fitz to be wary of a "put up job." "[B]elieve only 1/2 of what you see—& allow a discount upon that," he advised. To young Peploc's father, Boughton said, "I think that perhaps he finds that having to run about and do what he is told without question is more irksome to him than he thought it would be. . . ."[8]

The boy did not take Boughton's advice and went into business on his own; even though Boughton was opposed to the idea, he agreed to return the boy's investment in the Ione company, together with 7 percent interest. The new venture apparently produced only indifferent results, for late in the year, Boughton reported that he was back in England and commented, "I wonder how his venture is likely to terminate, or rather whether it has developed any more hopeful tendencies of late." Apparently the venture failed, as we hear no more about it.[9]

Charles Frederic Talbot Wyndham-Quin was another of the young men (he was born in 1864) sent to the West to learn the cattle business. A first cousin of Lord Dunraven, Charlie was the second son of a second son, forever doomed to miss the title by the nearest of margins (his brother, who became the fifth earl outlived Charlie). Charlie worked for Plunkett's EK outfit, but found the work not altogether to his liking, and Horace thought he was malingering at times to avoid roundup duty.

In contrast with Frewen, Plunkett had trouble selecting good employees, particularly foremen. He first hired Jack Donahue, and at the time thought he was the "best" in those parts, but soon there were signs that Donahue was insubordinate, and had hired as a cowhand "one of the worst thieves" in the country. Donahue was duly discharged, to be replaced by Phil du Fran, and Plunkett voiced his regret at having failed to hire Fred Hesse when that opportunity had been available. When du Fran was replaced by Roach Chapman, Plunkett again congratulated himself for a time, only to learn that Chapman had been arrested for horse stealing; worse still, Plunkett believed this charge was really a cover for a charge of murder. Nevertheless, Horace hired a lawyer to defend Chapman, only to hear a few days later that he had escaped from jail after betraying the confidence of a friendly sheriff. The last footnote to Plunkett's skill in selecting employees is Nate Champion, who had been with the EK during this period; later he would be singled out by the cattleman invaders of Johnson County as one of the first "confirmed" rustlers to be wiped out in that unfortunate foray.

But the work *was* hard, and sometimes marginal performance was not entirely the fault of the worker; Plunkett complained that another employee, a certain Mrs. Jennings, was not doing any work, but then said, as if by way of explanation, "There is however next to nothing to eat. Possibly when we feed her she will work." On a brighter note, Plunkett spent many hours teaching young Beau Watson, another of his employees, how to keep double-entry accounts, and was so impressed with the man's work that he brought Beau back to the British Isles when the cattle operations in the West were closed down.[10]

There were always some bad apples and, in exasperation, Moreton told Clara, "We claim that Americans sell us all their worthless securities, but it is free trade in return, we send them all our high class criminals." An English army captain, Egremont E. Shearburn, got the Frewens to introduce him at the Cheyenne Club and at the Stebbins and Post bank, and to endorse his notes; he then proceeded to gamble away the proceeds and default on the repayment. Chandos Pole, who was the kin of a baronet, likewise was trying to raise money by touting a bogus relationship with the Powder River Company, and another unidentified soul appeared at the Railroad Hotel in Cheyenne under the spurious name of Lord C. Beresford, much to Moreton's disgust.[11]

Yet these cases were not much worse than the actions of Clara's

American cousin, young Lawrence Jerome, who came to the West while "drinking, gambling, running into debt & being knocked down by a cowboy." He also for a time enhanced his attentions from certain females by posing as the notorious horse thief, Doc Middleton, until lawmen appeared to check the story; he then extricated himself from trouble by pleading his relationship with Frewen, to the latter's mortification.[12]

While discussing the activities of young men financed by foreign money, it may be useful to say a word about so-called "remittance men." This favorite pejorative of the Victorian era is supposed to refer to the younger sons—often the "troublesome" ones—who were sent to the West with an allowance to keep them out of harm's way at home. The stereotype is supposed to have been a spendthrift who had most of the social vices and squandered the allowance at least as fast as it arrived. But what of the sons of Americans who came to the West with some of their father's money in their pockets to try their hand at western enterprises? What of the Oelrichs brothers, Hubert E. Teschemacher, and Frederic de Biller, who came from the east coast to ranch and did not have to apologize for their education (although Harvard was not the same as Oxford or Cambridge), and also seemed to have plenty of money from home; were they remittance men? Apparently not, but why not?

The only identifying characteristic we have of the young remittance men was the fact they came blessed with an ability to pay their way. Gilbert Henry Chandos Leigh's only sin was to come more than once to the Big Horn Mountains where he hunted with Frewen, his host and schoolmate; Leigh accidentally walked off a sheer cliff and fell to his death on the rocks of the Ten Sleep Canyon above the creek now named for him. Well occupied with parliamentary and other duties in England, he never lived in the United States. Yet the historical marker erected by the state along the highway calls him a "remittance man." If one examines their behavior, the distinction between the remittance men and other men on a salary or funded by an allowance from home seem to blur, and we are left with the idea that the term was only intended to stigmatize the young men who had ample funds and perhaps enunciated their words in an unfamiliar manner.

Few of the owners of big outfits spent the winter on the range, but that did not mean the British owners were further from effective control on the range than their American counterparts. Cheyenne was a train ride and two hundred miles of nearly impassable roads away from the northern ranges, and the cattlemen living in Cheyenne might as well have spent the winter in London. In the fall of 1880, an early storm struck before the winter supplies had arrived at the ranch, and it was necessary to pack them in by mule. The same year brought eleven feet of drifted snow on the road between Fort Fetterman and Rock Creek. Indeed, Frewen commented that the British managers were often in closer touch with matters on the range, since "except for myself & just we few Britishers, not a boss ever comes near his range, let alone live on it."[13]

However, the practice of departing for home for the winter often produced unpleasant surprises in the spring. Plunkett lamented the "abuse of the property" and thefts that took place during the winter; things were "filthy" in the spring. Nevertheless, nearly everyone in authority still left in the fall. An exception was Thomas Willing ("Twice Wintered") Peters, who sometimes—as already noted—spent the winter on the Powder River range. The idea caught the fancy of the two young Britishers who came into the partnership with Peters, and Ralph Stuart-Wortley and Geoffrey Millais both decided to stay over as well. But Peters insisted that Millais return to England; one young man for the winter was enough.[14]

The degree of control exercised by the far-off board of directors varied with the operation and the temperament of the British boards. Frewen seems to have had considerable freedom to commit the company, even including the right to borrow money, but others were more tight-fisted. "Our people at home are very particular about getting vouchers for all transactions," wrote Frank Law, the Prairie Company manager in Denver. This attention to documentation was a regular feature of the British management style. Although the British companies commonly allowed their American managements some latitude in handling money without reference to the home office, the Spur required that all receipts of funds be sent to London, and that the American management draw on London for all expenses. This policy made it necessary to justify any unusual expenditure before funds were sent to cover it.[15]

The Victorian gentleman was a prolific writer, and those in management on both sides of the ocean kept up a steady stream of correspondence. Moreton Frewen bought a typewriter in 1882 and thereafter it went everywhere with him, spewing out letters in marvelous profusion. The new invention was a considerable improvement in legibility over his cursive style, but not everyone was impressed;

Clara was put off by it at first, and Moreton did try to send her some handwritten letters, but, as he put it, "It is positively a nuisance much as I love writing to my darling to take up the now unfamiliar pen." Soon she, too, fell before the onslaught of the new technology and handwritten letters became rare.[16]

For security reasons, the Matador required that every letter be acknowledged and that the sending or receipt of every cable be confirmed by letter, which added to the bulk of paperwork. The secretary of the company wrote to tell Murdo Mackenzie that the board met every Tuesday, and that it wanted to receive a letter from the United States at least once a week. No stranger to the operation of big companies, as he had also worked for the Prairie (where communications concerns were not conducted with such passion), Mackenzie was bold enough to suggest an unfavorable comparison. The secretary responded somewhat icily that he knew the Prairie "neither wrote nor sought letters very often," adding pointedly, "We are the other way." It does not appear that Mackenzie was overly attentive to the complaints he received, but then he was a giant in the industry and undoubtedly entitled to some special consideration by his London masters.[17]

The headquarters staffs of the British companies read the reports issued by their competitors and peppered the American management with questions when comparisons with their own operations were unfavorable. Thus, Dundee asked Murdo Mackenzie why the wage cost of the Matador was higher than the Spur; on this occasion, Mackenzie was delighted to be able to unearth the explanation that the Spur manager had devised a bit of creative accounting by netting the cost of his trail herds directly against the realization from sales, rather than showing the cost as an operating expense. The British management of the XIT also wanted to know why certain expense elements of their ranch were higher than those for the JA ranch of Goodnight and Adair.[18]

Sometimes the gathering of information in Britain produced recommendations for action in the United States, as when the home office urged Fred Horsburgh, the manager of the Spur, to buy horses cheaper, as they could be bought for fifteen dollars in Wyoming. The frustrated manager in Texas responded, "As to the price of horses in Wyoming, I am unable to regard that as having any bearing on horses down here . . . ," and in this case his view prevailed.[19]

For the range-cattle industry to work, cooperation was required among the ranchers, and this was accomplished through the stock growers' associations—powerful organizations, at times governments unto themselves. Richard Frewen was once bold enough to challenge the leadership of the Wyoming Stock Growers Association by proposing the formation of a committee to protect the rights of the nonresident members. (By 1885 the association represented a number of areas in surrounding states, but the rules were all set by Wyoming, where the legislature had made a number of its activities functions of state government.) While he was at it, Dick, who was anything but shy, also asked for a detailed accounting for fifty thousand dollars of expenditures. Judge Joseph Maull Carey, a prominent cattleman and later senator and governor, was in the chair; he turned this request aside with the comment that the money had been spent "in a secret way" and therefore could not be made public.[20]

Having failed in the accounting area, Dick pressed his question about assessment of nonresident members, and this time the judge opposed the motion from the chair (there was applause). Undaunted by this obvious snub, Frewen then asked what disposition was being made of his resolution, and Colonel A. T. Babbitt, manager of the Standard Cattle Company, resolved the controversy by moving to table, which passed handily. But Dick was not so easily muzzled, and in the evening he was back with the same resolution; this time the association bowed to his tenacity and gave him a favorable vote.

The incident is a distinct rarity, since almost no one had any success contesting the will of the leadership of the association, or of Thomas Sturgis, its secretary, who Moreton Frewen said was "about the most important personage here."[21]

At the peak of its powers, the association controlled the Wyoming legislature and dictated the terms of its relationship with the community. A butcher who bought an unbranded animal for resale was liable to be arrested, although cattlemen commonly sold unbranded calves to each other without a similar penalty; when the question of this enforcement discrimination was aired in the public press, Sturgis archly replied that the cattlemen knew their animals were not stolen.

When services were performed for the association, the bill submitted would be subject to the scrutiny of the executive committee and might well be reduced if found excessive. Most purveyors meekly accepted such action, but a Fort Collins, Colorado, law firm took umbrage when its $250 fee for representing the association was reduced to $100 by the executive committee. Sturgis responded that since the lawyers had rejected the $100, they would receive nothing. And so it was.

At the end of 1881 the leaders of the association decided to organize their own national bank in Cheyenne, and in only two months it had over three hundred thousand dollars in deposits, taken in part from the competing national bank; the Stock Growers National Bank quickly became the first federal depository in the territory. Although Judge Carey was the first president of the bank, he soon stepped down; the post did not thereby pass out of the hands of the association, for Carey's replacement was Tom Sturgis.

Moreton Frewen had a sometimes stormy relationship with Sturgis. When he first made the deal to sell six thousand calves to Pierre Lorillard, Tom Sturgis was the appraiser on Lorillard's side (Frewen had an appraiser, too, but he was overawed by Sturgis). The price Sturgis set fell some two dollars per head short of Moreton's expectations, and this caused a cash-flow crisis in the early stages of the Powder River venture. Nevertheless, Frewen had no choice but to deal with the powerful Sturgis. In fact, Moreton was later selected to represent Sturgis, the association, and the territory on a sort of diplomatic enterprise in Great Britain, in an effort to secure importation rights for live Wyoming cattle in that country. On this mission (which nearly succeeded) he carried authorization signed by the territorial governor, and issued under the seal of the territory, which Sturgis and Carey had secured for him and personally endorsed, saying, "no one could be better qualified" to carry out the job.

The stock growers' association was the organizational body that unified the range-cattle industry and enabled it to function. The one in Wyoming was organized first in Laramie County as the Laramie County Stock Association, at a meeting in the county clerk's office in Cheyenne on November 29, 1873; it took the name Laramie County Stock Association, which was subsequently changed in 1879 to the Wyoming Stock Growers Association. The Wyoming organization at times had members from Nebraska, Dakota, Colorado, and Montana, as the wide-ranging herds were no more impressed than the Indians had been by imaginary boundary lines drawn on the face of the earth by white men. A separate association was organized in Montana in 1883, and other states followed suit. But even among its members, the association was not a democracy, as Richard Frewen's experience at the 1885 annual meeting demonstrates.

The Wyoming association was a private organization, but it handled a number of cattle industry matters for the territorial government. As early as 1877, the cattlemen gained official control over the registration of brands, a key element in the discipline of the industry. Stock detectives were county employees chosen only on the recommendation of the association, and the 1882 legislature gave the association the same right to recommend the territorial veterinarian; at the next session the maverick bill gave control of the roundups to the association, together with the proceeds from the sale of mavericks (to be used to pay cattle inspectors). Once this law was in place, it was illegal for a cattleman to conduct a roundup except on the schedule set by the association, which by this time was in many ways a de facto territorial government.[22]

If a cowhand got into trouble serious enough to bring his name to the attention of the association, he ran the risk of being blacklisted throughout the territory. In Wyoming, for example, a formal blacklist was published by the stockgrowers' association; the printed list for 1885 contained twenty-seven names (ten from Johnson County), although three formerly blacklisted hands were "reinstated." No member of the association could hire a person whose name was on the list, and in 1884, Thomas Sturgis wrote to tell Fred Hesse that he must discharge one Bill Smith, whose only crime appeared to be that he was supporting three or four of his brothers, men of "notoriously bad" character. In this case Smith was not fired because of extenuating circumstances, but much negotiation was required to win that exemption.[23]

The enforcers of the industry rules were the stock detectives and inspectors, who were employed on the range and at the major shipping points. The Wyoming association employed its first detective, Billy Lykins, in 1875; by 1882, the association had thirteen inspectors. At the head of this group, as chief of detectives of the association, was Nathaniel Kimball Boswell, former sheriff of Albany County. The power of these association employees was nearly the same as that of a sheriff or constable (some actually held dual roles), and in some cases greater, for their pursuit of rustlers was not limited by state or territorial boundaries.[24]

The men who were hired as stock detectives were selected for their ability to accomplish the tasks they were sent to do, and this on occasion encouraged the use of those who had acquired their credentials on the other side of the law. At least two of the Wyoming detectives came to their jobs under assumed names; both later served other states in distinguished posts in government. The man known as Frank M. Canton started life as Joe Horner, in Virginia, in 1849, 1851, or 1854 (Canton was somewhat indifferent on the matter of dates). The incident that caused him to abandon the Horner name is clouded by confusion, but it apparently involved two or three black soldiers stationed at Fort Robertson, Texas; there is agreement that Horner shot and killed the soldiers, and that the soldiers' friends shot his horse from under him while he was escaping. Thereafter he became Frank M. Canton. It was also said that Horner was subsequently pardoned by the Texas governor—at the urging of one Frank M. Canton.[25]

Canton was good at his work, and his employers were high in their praise of him. Among others, he apprehended Teton Jackson, a notorious horse thief, and successfully pursued and brought to justice two reservation Indians suspected of cattle rustling; on more than one occasion he followed suspects into Nebraska. He was accused of murder in connection with a killing that followed the abortive Johnson County invasion of 1892, but this charge did not interfere with his ability to live out his life in Oklahoma as that state's well-respected adjutant general.

In Dakota the stockgrowers association also employed detectives. One of these, Joe Elliott, drew his salary of $125 per month and rendered good service until 1896, when he was met on the Wyoming range by some old enemies of the Johnson County invasion days; he was set afoot and warned to leave the state, which he promptly did. It was forty years before he finally dared seek compensation from the stockgrowers' association for past services: He was duly paid.[26]

In 1883 the stockmen got their own newspaper in Cheyenne, published by Asa S. Mercer—a man of some little rotundity, with a wealth of gold hair confined mostly to his face (to use the description of a rival Cheyenne editor)—and his partner, S. A. Marney. Their newspaper was called the *Northwestern Live Stock Journal,* and it was financed on credit, according to the sour comment of the *Democratic Leader.* It was soon claiming a weekly circulation of five thousand, and while the claim was probably inflated, the other Cheyenne papers were not amused and began writing stories about Mercer, some fairly wildly exaggerated.[27]

Neither the carping of the other newspapers nor actual dissension within the partnership served to dampen the *Journal*'s primary mission, which was to be enthusiastic about the cattle industry, and it poured out its optimism over the years and even through the winter of 1886–87, when cattle were dying by the thousands out on the plains. It was only in 1894 that Mercer turned against his old friends and wrote *The Banditti of the Plains, Or the Cattlemen's Invasion of Wyoming in 1892*, a highly damaging story of that notorious episode. In case anyone should be uncertain what his conclusion was, he subtitled the slim work, "The Crowning Infamy of the Ages."[28]

The ill-fated invasion still lay in the future in 1884, when the Wyoming Stock Growers Association secured the passage of the maverick bill. In that year the executive committee was expanded to include representation from Montana and Dakota, proving that the association was larger than Wyoming Territory, at least geographically. In gratitude for Tom Sturgis's service to the cause, he was given a bowl and candelabra from Tiffany's, for which five thousand dollars had been paid. The presentation was signed by the honor roll of the industry, including all of the key members and some of the titled shareholders who did not venture into the territory at all. It was the high tide of a sovereign body.

But Wyoming was not the only place where cattlemen wrote their own rules. Even in Oregon some of the same signs were apparent, in this case because of the common antipathy of the cattlemen toward sheep. A letter appeared in the Portland *Morning Oregonian* in 1904, purportedly from an organization called the Sheep Shooters of Crook County (Oregon). After warning sheep owners to keep their flocks off the cattle range, the letter noted that the "organization" had slaughtered between eight and ten thousand head of sheep during the last "shooting season," and expected to increase the total in the next season, "providing the sheep hold out, and the Governor and the *Oregonian* observe the customary laws of neutrality."[29]

A feature of the British investment style was the inspection visit. Soon after Moreton Frewen organized the Powder River Cattle Company, the board sent out an inspector to evaluate the price paid for the herd and improvements that were being acquired from the Frewen partnership. They chose for this task John McCulloch, a Scottish farmer from Dumfriesshire, who had experience in agricultural arbitrations. His credentials in Scotland were solid enough, but his knowledge of the American range-cattle industry seems to have been acquired in large part from a six-hundred-mile stage ride with one O. P. Johnson, who owned a small herd in the Powder River Country. Moreover, McCulloch started his journey late in the season and arrived at the ranch only on October 8, when the risk of a major storm was already high. With a worried eye on the cloudy firmament, McCulloch hurried his inspection; in four days he had seen all he would spare time for, considering the chance of being snowed in two hundred miles from the railroad. So it was back to Cheyenne for a stopover, with another stop in Chicago to observe beef shipments completed his tour. In due course he produced a report of twenty-four handwritten pages that was filled with so many generalities that Horace Plunkett sneeringly said McCulloch had only demonstrated that the English were a meat-eating people.

Of course, gaining even a limited understanding of what was going on in that vast region in just four days, while traveling in a coach or on horseback, was an undertaking doomed to failure. McCulloch estimated the range at fifty by eighty miles, but he gave it latitude and longitude bearings that were truly fanciful. His conclusion was that the open-range system was as sound an investment as "a first and ironclad mortgage," a comparison clearly calculated to attract the attention of the Scots, who knew in detail what could be done with mortgages. McCulloch also thought the company could pay a dividend of 12 percent on the common stock, after allowing the 10 percent preferred dividend. Later, McCulloch had trouble collecting his three-thousand-dollar fee for the inspection trip, so it is probable that his glowing assessment of the Wyoming range convinced almost no one.[30]

A more competent inspection occurred the following year. Since the first inspection, there had been a good deal of friction between the board and Frewen, including the disallowance of some purchases by the London office, and this time the board wanted something more than the view of a Scottish farmer. The board sent Andrew Whitton, their director from Dundee, who managed the estates of the earl of Wharncliffe and was also the largest preferred shareholder. When Moreton was first introduced to Whitton, he had been delighted by the Scot's philosophy of the proper role for the board: "The Board would do very ill to fetter you in any way," was the way Moreton remembered his comments. That view would later change radically. It was not to be Whitton's last trip to the range, and his growing knowledge of the company and its operations would later be a cause for conflict between him and Frewen.[31]

Moreton was in anguish while awaiting Whitton's arrival, since Clara was again pregnant and about to be delivered. The romantic Moreton would have rushed to her side for the occasion, but with Whitton coming he dared not leave the range. The Scot finally arrived in September, not so late in the season as McCulloch had been. Moreton reported to Clara that he was impressed by the range ("Wonderful, wonderful!" was the expression quoted), and although Moreton was almost always too optimistic, Plunkett also saw Whitton and wryly commented that Moreton had talked Whitton into "perfect confidence" in Frewen's management of the American operations of the company. Slyly, Whitton told Frewen that "he would not dare to put in any report how highly he thought of the business or no one would believe him." Moreton now could dash eastward to be with Clara, and on the way he received the news that his firstborn son had arrived—to be named Hugh Moreton, for Hugh Lowther, who had unexpectedly succeeded his brother as earl of Lonsdale.

Unfortunately, all was not as rosy with Whitton as Moreton supposed. When the canny old Scot returned to London to report to the board, there were some dark spots he had apparently not shared with Frewen; Whitton was not impressed by the small sheep operation Moreton had started, and he also correctly saw that the refrigerator project was a losing proposition.[32]

When the cowhands were exposed to an inspector, the results were sometimes amusing. John McNab of the Spur outfit visited Texas carrying an umbrella, which he used to shelter his head from the elements, to the dismay of the skittish range cattle and the contempt of the cowhands. Since he also violated the creed of the cowboy by walking everywhere rather than riding a horse, it is not clear which trait occasioned the most scorn. Mrs. McNab, who accompanied her husband, happened on to a group castrating calves, and chided the hands for treating the "cowlets" in this fashion; the reply by a ready wit was that they were not "cowlets" but "bullets."[33]

One would expect that British aristocrats would try to use the best animal husbandry money could buy from their homeland, and this was so. The tradition of British excellence in that science went all the way back to Roman times, for Caesar had commented that cattle constituted the true wealth of the Britons; the aristocracy of Great Britain lavished great attention on their prize animals. In Victoria's day the Prince Consort himself exhibited show cattle and won prizes for them, although the cost of the royal farms far exceeded the financial awards enjoyed by this man who was so well known for his business acumen. But this rare extravagance by Albert was not unusual among those who bred fancy cattle; the science absorbed the sort of funds only the wealthy landed gentry could devote to it, and aristocrats such as the duke of Bedford were always in the forefront. Bloodlines were followed with the same care that *Debrett's* gave to the human peerage, and it is said that Lord Althorp sat down every Monday morning to update the pedigrees of his cattle. Truly rarified names graced the top animals, and a herd auctioned in 1851 included bulls named for the third, fourth, fifth, and sixth dukes of York, to say nothing of the duchesses among the cows (since this royal dukedom had become extinct in 1827—though the royal title is still used today—it was perhaps only fair that other creatures of high breeding should succeed to it; apparently the real peers were not offended).[34]

There are numerous examples of the British operations improving the quality of the livestock on the American plains. Lyulph Ogilvy introduced blooded Aberdeen Angus and Herefords to his Weld County, Colorado, ranch, and Theodore Whyte experimented with Swiss cattle to test their adaptability to the Estes Park region. (Ogilvy also developed irrigation projects near Greeley). The JA ranch was the first in the Texas Panhandle to revolutionize cattle quality there, beginning in 1883; theirs were the first yearlings in the region to sell for as much as twenty dollars. When Murdo Mackenzie first took over the operations of the Matador, its sixty-five thousand head of cattle were all ordinary, and he set out at once to improve them by introducing blooded stock. The first registered Herefords were acquired in 1892, and thereafter the company won many prizes with its stock.[35]

Farther up north in Wyoming, Fred Hesse took up the effort to improve the Frewen herds, which originally were all native stock. Shorthorns of the Booth stock were imported, as were the Sussex—Hesse claimed they were the first to import the latter and considered it the best breed for that range, because of its hardiness. The small ranch Frewen bought on Crazy Woman Creek was easy to fence, so that the purebred shorthorn and Sussex stock could be segregated there. It was Pennsylvania-born Alexander H. Swan who brought the first substantial Hereford blood to the territory in 1878 (when he paid ten thousand dollars for forty bulls), but of course this stock came from Britain, anyway; Swan's policies were carried on and expanded after the Scots gained control of the ranch. It was his emphasis on stock quality that required so much fencing; the ranch was buying wire by the railroad carload. Alec Swan's Wyoming Hereford Cattle and Land Association had its own range of thirty thousand acres on Crow Creek, which was devoted to the blooded stock.[36]

The work could be grueling at times, and Plunkett continually complained about his weak constitution and overwork. In one twenty-two-day period, he logged 151 miles on horseback, 183 miles by stage, 262 by buggy, and 4,691 by train, for a total of 5,287 miles. If the normal difficulties of travel in this wild country were not enough, unexpected events could compound the problem. At Point of Rocks, Plunkett was sleeping in a room at night when a skunk came through the open window and the cook fired off a shotgun, causing a discharge that left the room "redolent of skunk."[37]

Nor was the route always well mapped. On one trip to the Ione ranch, he got off the Union Pacific at the Hutton station and found a pony tied to a telegraph post, with no other instructions. The station "master," who Plunkett estimated to be fifteen, gave him "directions" to the effect that he should ride straight toward a certain mountain peak in the distance, where he would come to the ranch. Fortunately, all was not lost, as Plunkett wrote in his diary: "Quite unnecessary. The pony knew the way."[38]

Nowhere was the management problem of distance and time more apparent than in the efforts to manage the Oxley Ranche. This curious story began in 1882, when John Roderick Craig, a Canadian-born breeder of blooded stock, secured a lease on one hundred thousand acres in Canada's Northwest Territories and sought financing for a cattle ranch. He raised about a hundred thousand dollars (another source says two hundred thousand) from some Canadian investors, and went to London to secure additional capital. There he met Alexander Staveley Hill, and as a result of their conversation (a portion of which was cited earlier), Craig abandoned his Canadian friends and threw in his lot with Hill and his fellow gentlemen. In due course a private company, the Oxley Ranche, Limited, was organized, named after the Hill family seat in Staffordshire, with the earl of Lathom, Hill, George Baird (Hill's brother-in-law), and their three wives as directors, plus Colonel George Patrick Hyde Villiers, brother-in-law of Lord Lathom (and also brother of the earl of Clarendon). It was distinctly a family affair, but this was not the most unusual aspect of this unusual company.

Craig returned to Alberta, and Hill shortly appeared on the scene;

together they inspected the lease thoroughly enough to conclude it was unsuited to cattle raising, and Hill directed Craig to secure nearby lands that looked ideal. Unfortunately, when Craig enquired in Ottawa, Hill's selection overlapped two large ranches in the area, but with the payment of some money he was able to secure the transfer of a total of eighty thousand additional acres.

Craig began buying cattle in Montana, but his requests for money often produced no response; he therefore borrowed fifteen thousand dollars locally and was able to stock the range with four thousand head. When the earl and Hill next appeared, Craig explained the financial situation, and the earl exploded at the idea of borrowing money from "shopkeepers"; he ordered that the debt be paid before he left town. Hill was supposed to handle this detail at the local bank, but when Craig appeared at the banking offices, he received a draft for only five hundred dollars to pay a fifteen-thousand-dollar loan.

Craig also had a conversation with the earl and Hill that he interpreted to be an authorization to buy more cattle, since the cost of raising eight thousand head was very little more than for four thousand head; he thereupon purchased sixty thousand dollars' worth of cattle on credit. When this news reached London, Hill refused to cable the 8 percent downpayment, and the Oxley herds were picked up by the sheriff.

There was a partial sale of herds before the financial situation was straightened out, and it is plain that someone was not communicating very clearly; Lord Lathom, who would later be Lord Chamberlain and had once paid $30,600 at auction in New York for a prize cow (a fact well known on the range), could easily afford the sums the company was spending. Craig finally journeyed to London to plead his case in person before the board, but he was then accused of mismanagement and fired. There is more—lawsuits, claims, and counterclaims—but the reader will get the general idea from this summary. Hill wrote a book describing his travels to Canada, but it throws no light on the controversy with Craig. And there the matter rests.[39]

What was different about the style of these men? The obvious differences, which were often remarked upon by editors (usually with an ironic twist), were an unfamiliar speech and a penchant for hiring others from their homeland, but these are surface matters of little importance. Though the rigorous management style they brought with them was little known on the plains and irritated the freewheeling Americans, it was also essential to the proper control of a large operation scattered over thousands of acres, all located more thousands of miles from the British board of directors. Their own experience with the breeding and raising of prize cattle made it easy for them to bring over with them the knowledge of cattle breeds that would change the nature of the American industry for decades to come. Finally, when these aristocrats came to the near wilderness that was then the Great Plains, they did not fail for lack of stamina or courage, even though there was little in their experience to prepare them for the trials they would face. Yet their background and training served them well as they rode the range and stood the hardship and even peril of the work.

# The Pearl of the Prairies

## The Cheyenne Club and Its Society

———◆———

The membership of the Cheyenne Club has been called a who's who of the livestock industry. In its gracious rooms the great cattlemen could discuss the harshness or mildness of the winter, the state of the range, and the different deals that had taken place since they last met, all lubricated by free-flowing wines and other spirits. Located on the transcontinental rail link, the club also often hosted great names from afar. The food was as good as any in New York, and the wines and cigars first-rate.

Although some cattlemen made their headquarters at the club during the heyday of the industry, the real work of the business was on the range, and Frewen was scornful of men like Willy Peters, who briefly tried to run the Powder River Ranch long distance from Cheyenne. (Ironically, as we have already noted, it was Peters who had earned the nickname Twice Wintered, for spending winters on the range.) Nevertheless, Frewen also maintained a modest house in Cheyenne; the club was a welcome respite from the rigors of the range and, time permitting, he entertained himself there whenever his unending travels brought him to its doorstep. Owen Wister called the Cheyenne Club "the pearl of the prairies"; and even John Clay, often so acerbic about the elegance that surrounded the aristocrats in the West, had a soft spot in his heart for the club, where he was one of the last permanent residents, in his "pink coat" beating time to the strains of "John Peel" played on the grand piano.[1]

143

Other clubs, notably the Corkscrew Club in Denver, which admitted only foreigners and no women, catered to the aristocracy. In
the 1880s and 1890s, the club was located upstairs in a downtown
Denver building and was said to resemble London, Cairo, or Bom-
bay more than it did Denver. The last president was Baron Walter
B. von Richthofen, and when he died the club passed out of existence.[2]

The Close Colony in Iowa also tried to import home culture to
amuse the homesick second sons and heirs of the nobility who had
spent the day following the plow; these amenities included fox
hunting and polo, and there were also taverns called the House of
Lords, the House of Commons, and Windsor Castle. The June
horse-racing meet was called "the Derby," complete with imported
thoroughbreds and colored silks for the jockeys, and on Sundays,
prayers for the Queen went up from St. George's Episcopal
Church.

The Prairie Club was another example of English culture said to
be even more important to the "pups" than St. George's. At first in
temporary quarters at Captain Moreton's and over a downtown
store in Le Mars, the club got its own separate quarters in the town
in December 1881, and there it performed the function of exercis-
ing moral control over the new arrivals from across the ocean. The
coatroom was attended by an "obsequious" porter, and the entertainment included a program of English ballads, violin solos, and
duets by violin and piano, while the kitchen could serve a "fairly
elaborate" menu. Admissions were managed by a selection committee, who apparently accommodated all Britons of the gentleman
class. This bastion of the aristocracy flourished in the colony for
two decades.[3]

At the Cheyenne Club, the incorporators included Richard
Frewen, but otherwise all were "locals." The first president was
Philip Dater, and the secretary was William Sturgis, Jr., whose
brother was the powerful Thomas, secretary of the Wyoming Stock
Growers Association. Despite the club's affinity for the livestock
industry, Dater, a Harvard graduate who had come from New York
City (where his father was a wholesale grocer), apparently never did
any range work, if we can believe John Clay. Dater was apparently
well liked, a fine, imposing man with a "streak of harmless sarcasm."
The board of governors appointed a three-man house committee,
and this committee was responsible for overseeing member conduct.[4]

The organization's first name was the Cactus Club, but that was soon changed to Cheyenne Club. The rules were designed to preserve a genteel atmosphere for the members, and they were enforced with vigor. Wagers of any kind were absolutely prohibited, and all games were shut down on Sundays; smoking was not permitted in the dining room until after 7:30 P.M., and pipe smoking was prohibited in all public rooms. J. H. Ford proposed that the card room be designated a private room, thus avoiding the no-gambling rule, but this motion lost; Ford then vainly argued that the house committee should be limited to keeping the house clean and in order and not be concerned with the conduct of the members. "Loud" or "boisterous" noise was proscribed, and members were "specially" urged to report violations of this rule. It was, withal, a society of laws, and it was certainly *not* a democracy.[5]

Even such important members as Frewen's friends, Charles M. Oelrichs and his brother Harry, ran afoul of these rules. Born in Baltimore, the Oelrichs brothers had come to Wyoming in 1878 to start up a herd on Rawhide Creek, which they subsequently sold to Moreton's Powder River Cattle Company. Harry then came back to Cheyenne, where he organized the Anglo-American Cattle Company, with a capitalization of $200,000. The company was American controlled, but had British investors, and Sir John Rae Reid, a baronet, was on the board. Oelrichs had an interesting salary arrangement: So long as the capital was under $150,000, his annual salary was to be $5,000, and it was to rise at 3 percent of any capital increase above $150,000.

Harry was a "character," having been associated in gossip with Sarah Bernhardt; but the brothers also got into trouble at the Club. When Charles struck a waiter, he was called before a special board meeting; the board suspended him and censured his brother Harry for language that was "emphatically condemned." The incident continued to fester, as Charles wrote a letter that further offended the board, and Harry tore down the notice that had been posted to advise members of the brothers' punishment; both subsequently resigned, but all was forgiven two years later and Harry was readmitted (although we do not know if he was penitent).[6]

When John Coble shot at an oil painting of a pastoral scene (he said it was a travesty on purebred stock), he was suspended for three months, leaving the punctured canvas behind; it now hangs in the Wyoming State Museum as mute testimony to a lively age when a man could take up arms against a painting of two bulls and other men could be incensed enough to censure him. A more important piece of art on the walls of the club was an engraving of Albert Bierstadt's painting *In the Heart of the Big Horns*, which had been presented by the painter himself.[7]

The bylaws prohibited drunkenness to an "offensive" degree, profanity or obscenity, cheating, or any act "so dishonorable in social life as to unfit the guilty person for the society of gentlemen." Persons not members who did not reside or do business within fifty miles of Cheyenne could be admitted as visitors for a seven-day period, which could be repeated not more than four times a year (military officers were exempted from this restriction, perhaps because they were gentlemen by definition), and guests could be admitted to the public rooms of the club for not more than one occasion per month, and no member could entertain more than two guests at one time. These strictures must have ensured that for the most part only the right sort would be on the premises, although another proviso of the house rules authorized members to take "persons" to their rooms "when so disposed" (the rule was not further elaborated).

The men at the organizational meeting suggested a total of twenty-three names for membership (in addition to their own), and that total included only one of the foreign aristocrats; indeed, the arbitrary cutoff on the list they were considering stopped just before the name of the second foreigner: Horace Curzon Plunkett. Nevertheless, Plunkett was soon received, together with a number of other Britishers. In the first of his letters inviting the new members, Sturgis explained that the choice of a limit of fifty was to "avoid black-balling too many 'natives.'" Since nearly everyone who was invited was a "native," it is obvious that the criterion was not residence but some sort of social selectivity. It also needs to be emphasized that the discrimination practiced in these early months of the club did not emanate from the foreign gentlemen.[8]

The invitations gave an insight into the intentions of the founders. They did not intend anything "extravagant," Sturgis said, but meant to establish something like the Somerset in Boston, with "a good restaurant for all, billiard room, reading room, etc." After failing to find a suitable existing building, the contractor James East was hired to build a three-story structure sixty-five by forty-six feet, with a mansard roof and a tower, at a cost of twenty-five thousand dollars, to which more than twelve thousand dollars was added for furnishings; a small cottage in the rear housed servants.

The dining room was paneled and there were hardwood floors throughout, with beautiful mantels for the fireplaces; the grates were decorated with blue-and-white and brown-and-white tiles, displaying Shakespearean quotations. In the six sleeping rooms upstairs were walnut wardrobes and dressers; the commodes had marble tops, and the beds were hand-carved walnut. The library table provided members with copies of the *Atlantic Monthly, Harper's,* the *New York Graphic,* and the *Boston Sunday Herald* to keep them abreast of the news of the world.[9]

The steward was a French Canadian named Francois de Prato, and the janitor was a New England sea captain. Members could dine in the main dining room or rent a private room for a more intimate function. Dress suits and evening gowns were worn to functions, and one cattleman, on seeing such an affair, called the men "Herefords," in reference to their broad white shirt fronts.[10]

Although one member said the club was operated "with the prodigality of a millionaire's country home during week-end parties," this "prodigality" was as much a reflection on the "local" members as the foreigners, since the foreign membership never controlled the club. Indeed, their function was rather like that of a social barometer.[11]

If the foreign gentlemen did not originally set the tone of the club, they soon found they could be very comfortable there. On his return to Cheyenne in 1884, Plunkett was pleasantly surprised at the improvement in Cheyenne society, where on one occasion he heard it questioned whether evening clothes or simply "Sunday clothes" should be worn. "A year or two ago, a flannel shirt would have been *de rigueur*," he said. He could even play lawn tennis before breakfast and found the ground "excellent." "Certainly Cheyenne has changed marvelously," he said. "It is a pleasant place enough in the summer." After six days on the road to cover the 280 miles from Frewen's ranch to Cheyenne, the club bath, bed, and table restored him, "almost by magic." Even when the mixture of wines was "horrible," Plunkett thought them no worse than in New York. Plunkett, who loved the game of chess, is said to have kept two tables in play, while calling his moves from the tennis courts.[12]

The location of the club in Cheyenne brought notables to its tables to a degree not possible in another site in the West. The Union Pacific was the link between the two American coasts, and those intent on making the journey often would break the long trek in Cheyenne. Consequently, the city was on occasion visited by people of an unusual level of distinction and culture. In late 1881, the marquess of Lorne, then governor-general of Canada, visited Cheyenne with his entourage; this was not the only such visit by Canadian officials during that period before the Canadian Pacific Railroad permitted direct access from Ottawa to the Pacific territories.[13]

Entertainers and artists also made their appearance, notably including Oscar Wilde, who passed through early in 1882. The *Sun* sent its reporter to interview him on the train and carried the story that Wilde was wearing a broad silk necktie of a color between burnt sienna and pink, with matching handkerchief, hosiery, and hat lining. This color coordination so impressed the man of the press that he began to wonder if the same rule had been followed in areas not subject to his scrutiny: "We did not investigate any further, but would bet a rusty horse pistol against a stone dwelling that his subterranean strati of apparel was of the same delicate shade." Wilde proved so sensitive to these jibes that he refused to lecture in the city, as had been planned.[14]

Two years later Moreton's old friend Lillie Langtry appeared in style, riding in the "Manitou Marble," a special excursion railroad coach placed at her disposal not by Moreton but by his father-in-law, Leonard Jerome. She appeared on the Cheyenne stage as "Galatea," and while there enjoyed the hospitality of Harry Oelrichs, who had run up florist bills of more than five hundred dollars for daily offerings to Lillie during her earlier visit to New York. Harry Oelrichs had a "drag" that cost four thousand dollars and weighed 4,200 pounds to carry guests to his Polo Ranch, just seven miles away on Crow Creek. This magnificent vehicle, said to be the only one west of the Mississippi, could seat twelve persons on top and four inside; it required four or six horses to pull it. Alas for Harry, who was broad, stout, bronze of face, and huge of hand (to use one editor's description), Lillie soon departed in the company of tall, slim Freddie Gebhart, whose money may have been more abundant.[15]

Later in 1883, a group of Britishers, including H. C. Plunkett, E. S. R. Boughton, Walter C. Alston, and Geoffrey Millais entertained a total of thirty-two members at the Cheyenne Club. "I never saw such a cordial drunk," Plunkett said. "Everyone was drunk, no one beastly drunk. The singing & speaking was humorous & good. The menu was altogether beyond what I thought the capacity of the club to manage." The affair consumed sixty-six bottles of champagne and twenty of red wine, which averaged a bit more than two bottles per guest. When the Americans tried to return the favor the following year, Plunkett pronounced it a failure, with the guests drunk before dinner began.[16]

When Frewen's good friend, Hugh Lowther, brother of Lord Lonsdale, visited Cheyenne in 1880, he invited William Robertson, the black waiter at the Railroad Hotel, to spend a year at Lowther Castle in England. The black man returned a year later, full of stories of his experiences in the strange land across the water. While there were people of wealth in the United States who could have afforded such a gesture, it would have been unusual, particularly in Wyoming, where racial prejudice hung heavy (the miscegenation statute was enacted along with the first territorial laws).[17]

Although it began solely as a social club, the Cheyenne Club was undoubtedly the center of the cattle industry during its heyday. The Board of Trade for Cheyenne had its headquarters in the club, where Chicago cattle market quotations were received. Moreover, the close ties of the cattle industry with the legislature made it a matter of course that the territorial treasurer (later governor and senator) Francis E. Warren should throw a party at the club for the entire legislative council during the 1884 session; this was the session at which the famous maverick law was passed by the legislature.[18]

Many cattlemen who otherwise would have lived elsewhere made Cheyenne their headquarters because of the club; some few actually preferred living at the club rather than on their ranches. The advantage to Cheyenne and its county (Laramie) was more than social; the custom in those days was to assess taxes on cattle in the county of the owner's residence, so that Laramie County enjoyed a considerable tax advantage for a time.[19]

The diversity of cultural backgrounds among the upper echelons of Cheyenne society at the time made for an interesting opportunity for the club. Clarence King, who had surveyed the fortieth parallel, was a partner of N. Russell Davis on a ranch in Colorado just south of Cheyenne. S. F. Emmons had been with the Wheeler expedition, of the area west of the hundredth meridian; and George D. Rainsford was an architect and an expert horse breeder (and was reputed to have the best command of profanity in Wyoming); Joseph Maull Carey had been justice of the Wyoming Territorial Supreme Court (and would later be United States senator); and Frank Wolcott had been United States marshal. Beyond that, there were bank presidents and, of course, the foreign investors; indeed, it is said that the Cheyenne of these days was the wealthiest city in the world on a per capita basis.[20]

In December 1882, a fire in the club's furnace room forced the guests into the street. The Cheyenne *Sun* noted that one guest fled with only the protection afforded by nature and "curtailed nocturnal garments," while Mr. Iselin and a clerk were wearing looks of alarm and a garment the size of a pillow case. Although the club was saved, the Turkish carpet in the reading room was ruined, amid other damage totaling three thousand dollars, but the management thereby also had an excuse to restore it to even greater elegance. The calamity gave the editor an opportunity to recount the advantages of the club, which had grown too small anyhow. The charges were not high—twenty-five cents for lunch and seventy-five cents for dinner—and the presence of the club in Cheyenne brought cattlemen to that city who would otherwise live elsewhere.[21]

Renovation of the club was under the direction of George D. Rainsford and cost ten thousand, not three thousand dollars; it included a completely new kitchen with three dumb waiters to the dining rooms. A servants' dining room was added in the basement, where there was also a wine cellar, a refrigerator for meats, a trunk room, and a large laundry. Under the staircase there was a post office for the convenience of the guests. On the third floor there were six large and eight small bedrooms and a new bathroom. All were lighted by the new electric lamps. The dining room, decorated in Japanese paper, could seat 75 in comfort, and guests could dine on pickled eels and other delicacies. The club's cellar offered a full range of rye, bourbon, gin, brandy, and ale, as well as Mumm's champagne, to say nothing of claret, burgundy, sherry, and port. When the taste of the sherry or the color of the cigars offended William Sturgis, the New York suppliers felt his ire. Of the 170 members, half were resident of Cheyenne.[22]

After the disastrous winter of 1886–87, the cattle industry that supported the Cheyenne Club was mortally wounded, and those who survived had little need and less inclination to preserve it. Those who figured large in its early years went on to other pursuits. Thomas Sturgis returned to New York City, where he served under Theodore Roosevelt for a time. William's son eventually became a vice president of the First National Bank of New York. The club itself was eventually unable to repay its debt and closed its doors. It was later reorganized as the Club of Cheyenne (with a much-expanded membership), and finally as the Industrial Club, the predecessor of the town's Chamber of Commerce. In 1936 its old home was razed to make room for a building to house the latter body.[23]

# Relations with the "Natives"

*The Foreign Gentleman and His American Cousin*

---

It is nearly impossible to gain a clear view of the real relationship of the British gentlemen with the American inhabitants of the range country, for the newspapers tended to concentrate on colorful stories, and there was little that could be directly traced to the men themselves, as they generally avoided press interviews. We therefore have a very incomplete picture of the situation, heavily weighted by the negative or the simply trivial.

Of the latter sort was a story carried by the Cheyenne *Sun*, which, on seeing the unaccustomed flood of titles in the city, suggested that the cattle industry create its own titles of nobility. Those having no cattle would be called mudsills, and distinction would rise with the number of head owned. Thus, with ten thousand, the cattleman would be entitled to be called viscount, and his children, "or any body else's children born as the result of his absence," would be the Honorable Bill, or the Honorable Susan, for instance. At fifty thousand head, one became a cattle king, and entitled to be styled "Your Mawgisty." Ironically, the Americans, who pretended to be so put off by titles, were continually conferring them on those who had no right to them; thus it was not uncommon for Frewen, who had no title of any sort, to be called Lord Frewen, or at least Sir Moreton, in press reports; and Lyulph Ogilvy, whose only proper courtesy was "The Honorable" was also often referred to as "Lord."[1]

Plunkett complained that the many aristocratic visitors to the Frewen ranch cost a lot of money and "make themselves & us unpopular in the country by their incapability to adapt themselves to the people & to interfere much with our business." After this brief jeremiad, he added more truthfully: "Still they are welcome over solitude." Moreton Frewen addressed the same thought when he complained that in spite of their generosity, the Frewen brothers suffered from ill feeling on the part of their neighbors. "I begin to believe that being a gentleman is much against one here," he said, "as in the colonies generally." Frewen's assessment of their character is summed up in an exasperated outburst to Clara: "[T]hese western men, at least some of them, are the most impracticable, aggressively independent people possible, and I often long to thrash one or two but for the want of dignity in such a proceeding."[2]

Nor was the complaint of the "native" westerner solely against the "visitors" who came for a casual hunt in the West; there were also barbs directed at the Britishers and other foreign gentlemen who came to manage the new investments in the United States. In the first year of the Frewens' operations on the Powder River, their style of operation had already offended at least one editor in Cheyenne. "The 'B. S.,' which upon translation means British Subject who is located on Powder River, it is said, points with his dexter finger and claims, presumably by right of conquest (?) all the country from the old post of McKinney to the Big Horn Mountains, thence north and west to Crazy Woman's fork and has hoisted the 'Union Jack' over his tent. However, . . . my Briton is being elbowed, and will be crowded. . . ." Frank M. Canton, the stock detective in the Powder River basin, was puzzled by the animosity shown: "I can't understand why Frewen is so unpopular," he said. "He seems to want to do all he can for the interest of the country."[3]

Six years later, the Cheyenne *Leader* carried the story of another who wanted to "settle" in the Powder River Basin, only to be warned off by an "intensely English" cowboy, although he was at the time thirty-five miles from the ranch headquarters where the "Frewen Castle" stood. Later in the same year, John D. Sargent complained that he had been ordered off "his" quarter section in Sweetwater County, Wyoming, by the Wyoming Cattle Ranch Company, a Scottish enterprise, on the claim of "prior right." This possessiveness about range rights was hardly a "foreign" attitude, however; in Miles City, Montana, the Montana stockmen resolved not to work the J. H. Conrad cattle, because Conrad had encroached on the range of the Niobrara Cattle Company.[4]

In Texas the British consul, Walter Tschudi Lyall, complained about anti-British prejudice, which he attributed in part to the Irish American element, many of whom held official positions in the United States. Yet such comments have to be considered in the light of Lyall's motivation to steer new investment and settlement to Manitoba and other British possessions, rather than to the United States; the crown's representatives were not above making gross overstatements to further this objective, as when Victor Drummond, a British diplomat in Washington, wrote home regarding Texas, "the country is unfitted for English settlers of the better class."[5]

It is difficult to separate truth from trumpery. One young gentleman who suffered from a consistently bad press was Archibald John Marjoribanks, son of Baron Tweedmouth and comanager of the Rocking Chair Ranche in the Texas Panhandle. The Rocking Chair had its share of troubles, but the evidence does not suggest that Archie was at the bottom of them; certainly, one must suspect that Drew, the other comanager, may have been acting not altogether in the interests of his employers, having first sold the herd to them and then stolen part of it back. There were fires that were apparently arsonous, and assertions that during these incidents Archie was too frightened to come outside the safety of ranch headquarters. A reading of Archie's letters impresses one not so much with his arrogance—although there is a high tone in places ("See that the fruit is *good* and not wormy")—as with the fact that the suppliers *were* often palming off shoddy or spoiled merchandise on the ranch and Archie was rejecting it.

In the case of the Rocking Chair, a good bit of the settlers' ill will stemmed from an idea that apparently originated with Drew, not Archibald John. The settlers were not permitted to participate in roundups with the ranch crews, and they had to mount their own roundup (the so-called Blackball wagon). One account says that Drew would also intentionally disrupt the settlers' branding if he didn't feel well. This again points the finger at Drew, who was drawing the larger salary in compensation for his supposed ranching experience, while Archie, who seems to have been more devoted to keeping the books.

If we restrict ourselves to Archie's account, a much more sensible picture emerges. He was the one who clearly saw and reported to his brother that the time of the settler had come, and he was in fact expecting that the cattle herds would have to be liquidated and the land sold; indeed, he looked forward to the rise in land values as the golden goose for the ranch, and for this reason he wanted the farm crops to be good. It is true that he found it "trying, delicate and difficult" to get along with some of the settlers, but we must remember that he assumed they were stealing cattle from the ranch; it now seems that his comanager was the likely thief.[6]

It is not at all clear what Archibald John's problem was, if indeed he had one. On the one hand, we are told he could not look one squarely in the eye and that the cowboys enjoyed shooting about his head and feet and sending him on snipe hunts; we are also told that they taunted him for riding into town wearing a "scissor-tailed" coat, and that they called his English horses "pecker-necks" (a word that in any case would not have seemed vulgar to the British ear). We are even told that "no other" British outfit was so snobbish, and that the "Rockers" gave all British outfits a bad name. The cowboys' nickname for him ("Marshie" or "Old Marshie"), a mere shortening of the correct pronunciation of the family name ("Marchbanks") may carry no connotation at all or even an element of fondness. But the chief complaint seems to be that although Archie ate with the cowboys and was always polite, he did not discuss his personal life with them. Of course, at home he had been in the company of political leaders and such famous painters as Landseer, Millais, Wolff, and Gourdlay Steele (the last painted the family's prizewinning Angus and Highland cattle). It was not an environment that would have been familiar to the Texas cowhands, even if he had chosen to speak of it. John Clay, ever critical of the "younger sons" on the western plains, said that Archie was "troublesome" and that his job was a sinecure to keep him out of the way; but his criticism of Archie is not consistent with the grumblings of others, for he says that Archie liked to play cards and drink at the thirteen saloons in Mobeetie, a trait that could not have injured his reputation with the hands.[7]

It was also said that Archie tried some strange innovations that didn't work, as when he bought ten deer and foxhounds to hunt "loafer" wolves; however, the Spur also paid a man two hundred dollars to hunt wolves with hounds and felt that their money was well spent, not because many wolves were killed but because their depredations were considerably reduced during this period.[8]

Clay certainly knew the Marjoribanks family well enough to meet
with them a day or two a week on the hunting field back home,
and he should have had a good perspective for assessing Archie's
shortcomings, but his recollection of some of the facts is clearly not
accurate. According to Clay, after recounting that Archie married
"a beautiful Southern girl" (the daughter of Judge James Trimble
Brown of Nashville, Tennessee), "the pace had been too fast for
him, and he did not live long after leaving the ranch." These comments, written in 1916 or 1917, consigned Archie to a premature
grave, for he was very much alive when Clay's book was published
in 1924, having served as extra aide-de-camp to the earl of Aberdeen, when that worthy was governor-general of Canada (Archie
died in 1925).

The indignation of the gentlemen can also be forgiven in the
cases where the wealth of the big outfits was regarded as fair game
by their neighbors and suppliers. Col. B. H. "Barbecue" Campbell,
general manager of the XIT, once personally checked shipments
coming into the ranch and found that the freighters were selling off
ranch supplies. The Spur tried to reduce the stealing of wood by
extending wood-cutting privileges to neighbors. Indeed, this outfit
seemed to have such difficulties with nearly all of their neighbors,
except for a nearby colony of Quakers, who were scrupulous in their
respect of the big ranch's assets and performed many specialized
duties for them, such as quality blacksmith work and the introduction of fruit trees.[9]

The "presence" that came with position could sometimes be useful in dealing with the shadier elements. Thus, when Captain William French (son of Baron de Freyne), manager of the WS Ranch
on the San Francisco River in New Mexico, noticed that fifteen or
twenty of the calves on the range bearing the brand of the notorious
Clanton brothers had been "adopted" by WS cows, he had his men
"vent" (or cancel) the Clanton brands and rebrand them with the
WS. The Clanton brothers saw the results of this work and came
over to confront French, who proceeded calmly to account for the
number he had altered in this fashion, and expressed the opinion
that there would be others requiring the same treatment in the future. The Clantons were apparently so astonished at this speech
that they rode away without further action, and were not seen again
on the WS range. Moreton Frewen threatened to do the same thing
with cattle that were disappearing under the so-called "maverick"
brands, but it is not known whether he carried out that threat.[10]

The question of whether to engage in local politics was one that often vexed the foreign companies. Frewen worked hard to see Johnson County organized with people friendly to his interests. "I can only secure the right returns by being myself on the spot," he said. The outcome satisfied him. The Matador avoided local politics until after the last county on its range was organized in 1892; two years later, tax increases forced the company to take an active role to contain this cost. The Texas management of the XIT secured the election of Walter de S. Maud, the son of a substantial shareholder of the company, as county commissioner and at one time was pay-ing a Texas judge forty dollars per month to look after ranch inter-ests in the court. Of course, there were times when the big compa-nies accomplished what they sought. The Spur successfully made the interesting argument that fences should not be assessed, since their enhancement of the value of cattle and land was already re-flected in those other values. Thus, it would seem that a cow inside a fence was more valuable than one outside it.[11]

Some of the local governmental jurisdictions saw the big cattle companies as a source of funds that they tried to tap in rather inge-nious ways. The Prairie manager in Denver was upset when Beaver County, Colorado, which lay outside the Prairie range, devised the argument that the Prairie should pay taxes in the county because the county had to expend money to prosecute thieves who stole Prairie cattle. "[I]t seems to me that taxes should not be regarded as a sort of gratuitous donation for services rendered," he fumed. Nevertheless, the Prairie did on occasion dispatch its own men to apprehend cattle thieves, saying, "we must have those men what-ever it costs," so perhaps the county could be forgiven for assuming that the big company was a part of its law enforcement system and might therefore share its cost.[12]

While there was a common bond among the British companies and usually easy communication between them, the XIT did not cooperate with the other big outfits in some important areas. Thus B. H. ("Barbecue") Campbell, the manager, refused to have the company join the cattleman's association, and even refused to let Prairie hands come on the XIT range to look for Prairie cattle. Nor were E. S. R. Boughton's countrymen exempt from the occasional sharp letter, as when he wrote to John H. Douglas-Willan to demand that the fences of the Douglas-Willan Company be removed from Ione Company land.[13]

Relations with the railroad were often difficult for the British.

Though no one would say that the big carrier was more domineering than the Wyoming Stock Growers Association, it was such a huge economic factor that its rules were routinely observed by nearly everyone, even when grossly unfair. Indulging his talent for sarcasm, Boughton wrote to Union Pacific headquarters in Omaha to try to get the right to pay for freight by company check, saying, "I do not mind paying demurrage if I keep a car load of material waiting more than 24 hours as I accidentally did the other day & it pleases me & gives my men healthful exercise when ironwork in kegs & boxes arrive looking as if they had passed through the severest kind of railroad accident, but if the Co. would take my cheques in payment for the charges on the same, as I have said, it would facilitate my business."[14]

Early in 1887, Boughton wrote to the Union Pacific to request that the station agent at Hutton be replaced, following a fistfight between the agent and Whitaker, an Ione employee, and the ensuing threat of the agent, a Mr. March, to shoot Whitaker. "Now this state of thing renders business difficult," said Boughton, "although personally I doubt the accuracy of Mr. Marsh's aim, yet this . . . is liable to lead to trouble."[15]

The sophisticated irony and sarcasm the aristocrats often employed in their writing was sometimes a cause of irritation. Although it may have sounded condescending to American ears, the British used it indiscriminately with their friends and peers back home. Indeed, they often enjoyed a good barb, even directed at themselves: Winston Churchill is reported to have "chortled" when Lord Charles Beresford called him a "Lilliput Napoleon" during a Hyde Park rally.[16]

Of course, there were examples of good relations with the local community. John Douglas-Willan was popular in the Laramie area, and Claud Anson, son of the earl of Lichfield, apparently got on well with the folks in Texas, and his wife commented that the guard and brakeman called him Claud as a sign of popularity. (While there was a bit of shooting and threatening to shoot going on in the range country, Lady Anson was not concerned for her own safety, for "they never mix women up in these affairs out there, and [are] always civil to the wives of their enemies. . . .")

Up in the Powder River country, the Frewens also apparently got on well with their hands, at least when the industry was not in a wage-cutting posture, and in the spring of 1885, Moreton told Clara that there was not a good cowhand in the country who didn't want to work for Fred Hesse. Similarly, Lyulph Ogilvy was reportedly extremely popular with the cowhands, and his "splendid" horsemanship gained him a great deal of respect.[17]

On occasion the criticism of the foreigners went too far. A certain "Lord Thursby" (who was clearly not a lord although he may have been a baronet or the son of one) was singled out for keeping half a dozen young men at the state university, paying their expenses from his own pocket. He was also said to have given a thousand dollars to a local athletic club. But one recognizes in such behavior the marks of a gentleman, responding to the call to public service, and to an unbiased eye the criticism seems more peevish than substantive.[18]

Sometimes the gentleman *was* hard to love, however. When Galiot François Edmond, baron de Mandat-Grancey, came through Dakota Territory in 1883 and saw what the marquis de Mores was doing there, he thought the Americans should "throw down flowers" on the path before him; but unfortunately for de Mores, that sort of sentiment was all too rare for him (he was more likely to be defending himself in court). De Mandat-Grancey's lack of perception is understandable; the baron, who owned the Fleur de Lys Ranch in Dakota and Nebraska, had his own image problems with the Dakota cowboys. A drunken cowboy once charged into a livery stable, saying, "They tell me there's a cursed French baron here and I want to see a cursed French baron," whereupon the square-built Mandat-Grancey seized the poor cowhand by the gunbelt and threw him into an empty stall.[19]

The marquis de Mores never was able to overcome his problems with the local populace. Perhaps his army background made him too rigid, for he did not mix well with the more informal cowboys, in contrast with Theodore Roosevelt, who was very popular with them. When de Mores fenced his property, settlers squatting on the land were displaced, and they, together with some hunters who resented the obstruction presented by the fences, launched a campaign to drive the marquis from the Badlands despite the nobleman's expressed desire to be friends with "everyone." They had not reckoned with the Frenchman's ability to defend himself, however, and in short order he demonstrated that he was no mean shot. There was an exchange of gunfire, and afterward a man had to be buried. De Mores was tried for the crime and acquitted, but his tenure in the Badlands was thereafter troubled by rumblings of resentment, and doubtless it had a great deal to do with the decision to close down his operations in the West.[20]

The opinion of Theodore Roosevelt, who was ranching on the range just to the north, is of value in assessing the relations of the marquis with the Americans. In 1885 the two ranchers came into collision when the Frenchman sent his men, with fifteen hundred head of cattle, into some bottomland Roosevelt regarded as his own (of course, neither was entitled to exclusive use, but to credit this technicality ignores the customs and usages of the time). Both men acted through their employees: Roosevelt ordered the de Mores cattle off his range, and de Mores offered to rent the range for the large sum of fifteen hundred dollars for three weeks, which Roosevelt refused. When it looked as though real trouble would erupt, the marquis backed down, although he continued to fume and finally wrote Roosevelt to enquire whether he was an enemy. Roosevelt replied in the negative but was not overly conciliatory; the crisis passed, although Roosevelt was concerned for a time that the marquis might press to settle the conflict by duel.

But while there were evident conflicts between the two men, there is a more positive postscript. Some years later, after the marquis had met a violent death in the North African desert, Roosevelt described him in generous terms: "The credit belongs to the man who personally descends into the arena, who struggles valiantly, who makes mistakes, who tries and tries again, but who struggles with all his might in doing what he is doing, who knows great enthusiasms, great devotions, so fully that his place will never be at the side of those cool and timid souls who are ignorant of defeats, but of victory as well." It was a noble tribute, capturing in a few words what some of these gentlemen were trying to accomplish in the short time they were among us.[21]

Also in Texas was a most unfortunate investor in the American West. Heneage Finch, another of Frewen's friends, was the seventh earl of Aylesford, and his American experiences were the sad exile he bore after the events of 1876 had destroyed his life in England. In the fall of that year, Lord Aylesford, then twenty-seven, who had already a name for handling horses well and had also earned the nickname Sporting Joe, had departed with the Prince of Wales on an official tour of India, authorized by Victoria. After much negotiation, the Queen had finally approved the list of companions, who, besides Sporting Joe, included the duke of Sutherland, Lord Charles Beresford, and Lord Carrington; in the case of the latter two, Victoria's consent was on the condition they would agree to behave themselves.[22]

As it developed, high jinks in India were not the most serious risk entailed by the journey. Lady Aylesford, who had urged her husband to accept the prince's invitation, now moved her household to Packington Hall, one of the earl's estates in Coventry, where she would be closer to her lover, George Charles Spencer-Churchill, marquess of Blandford and eldest son and heir of the duke of Marlborough. Blandford, who was himself married to Bertha, daughter of the duke of Abercorn, visited the lady with some frequency, taking few precautions to avoid detection. But outside notice proved not to be the chief danger, for soon Lady Edith herself sent a hysterical letter to Sporting Joe, who was then hunting in India, telling him she was on the point of eloping with Blandford. Joe at once set off on the back of an elephant to make his way to England.[23]

Aristocratic society now swung into action to avert the unthinkable, for while affairs of this nature were widely condoned, public scandal and divorce were not. An old hand in such matters, Lord Hartington, was dispatched with Lord Hardwicke to settle the business quietly, and in due course Lady Edith and Blandford called off their elopement. But Joe's divorce action could not be stopped.

At this point Lord Randolph Spencer-Churchill, the hot-headed second son of the duke of Marlborough, who was later to be Frewen's brother-in-law, entered the fray and personally confronted the Princess of Wales with some letters the prince had unwisely written to Lady Edith; he threatened to publish them if the Prince did not force Aylesford to withdraw the divorce petition. As one might expect, the prince reacted to this blackmail in a rage and sent Lord Charles Beresford to challenge Randolph to a duel.

In due course there were apologies, and after a period of princely ostracism for Lord Randolph and Jennie, all was mostly forgiven on that side. Lady Edith went into exile, where she bore the son she had not given Sporting Joe; for a surname he was given the first half of his father's family name and thus became Bertrand Spencer. (Blandford never married Lady Edith, although his wife divorced him in 1883, leaving him free to do so.)[24]

Aylesford did withdraw his divorce action, but he deserted his homeland to take up ranching in Texas, where he seems to have been obsessed with the need to build a fortune for the benefit of his two daughters (the earldom's property was entailed in the male line, and in default of male heirs would descend to Joe's brother, not to Joe's female children). A final sad indignity arose when the earl found another he really wanted to marry and again asked for a divorce; the Queen's Proctor (an official in the High Court of Justice) stopped the case because the earl's life was not "blameless."[25]

Aylesford set himself up near Big Springs, Texas, in the fall of 1883, where he built a "plain" house (the tables were covered in oilcloth, and the windows had neither curtains nor blinds). Nevertheless, the house was plastered and wallpapered in chocolate and gilt, which must surely have distinguished it from those of the neighbors, and the earl maintained there a valuable collection of guns and hunting paraphernalia. One supply that was undeniably generous was liquor: When Aylesford died there was reportedly a pile of empties as big as a haystack in the house, three-fourths of them whiskey bottles.[26]

Aylesford was joined on the ranch by brothers Clement and Daniel, although the former soon returned home; the latter stayed on, earning the nickname "the Kid" from the cowboys (it was he who visited Frewen's Powder River Ranch for a hunt). The brothers reportedly did not come alone to Texas but brought with them five servants, thirteen dogs, and twenty or thirty horses, if we can believe newspaper reports of the time.[27]

Sadly, Aylesford had only three years in which to try to accomplish his purposes, for early in 1885 he died of cirrhosis of the liver and dropsy—byproducts of that pile of empty bottles. Although he was then only thirty-six, the news reports of his death stated he looked fifty.

What sort of man was Heneage Finch? His reputation in England was not high. His brother-in-law thought him unsavory, and the queen herself had said he was a fool. On the credit side of the ledger, Finch was robust, possessed great physical strength and endurance, and was said to have a handsome face. He was also a great favorite with the cowboys, and one writer said, "They will spill their blood in his behalf as readily as he opens his bottle for them, and many a gun has been pulled by an indignant cow-puncher at a fancied reflection on his Lordship's character and manners." The visitor to the ranch might awake in the morning to find bottles "thick as fleas," cowboys two deep on the floor, and Sporting Joe in the corner with a bottle in each hand. He entertained the hands with stories of Europe and India, and eagerly joined with them in wild and reckless sports; as a mark of their favor, the hands called him Judge and declared him a "boss" fellow.[28]

Lord Airlie's son Lyulph remained in Colorado after the ranching operation was closed down and in 1902 married Edith Gertrude Boothroyd, the daughter of a "humble ranchman," to the dismay of his family and with a reportedly disastrous effect on his allowances. He later served for a time as a sixty-dollar-a-month night watchman for the Union Pacific and then lived on the "Three Waters" ranch near Loveland, Colorado. He was also a special writer for the *Denver Post*.

Having the son of an earl nearby naturally piqued the interest of the Denver press, and there were colorful stories about Lyulph; we have no way of judging their veracity. In one story, which may well have been totally fanciful, Ogilvy is supposed to have taken a rooster to his room at the Brown Palace Hotel one night. The clerk responded to complaints from other guests and accused Ogilvy of harboring a pet in his room. "This is not a pet," said he, brandishing a pistol, "this is an alarm clock. The last time I was here, you let me miss a train, and this time I've brought something I can rely on to call me at 6 o'clock."[29]

If there were criticisms of the foreigners on the American side, the feeling was sometimes reciprocal. Some Britishers, such as Frewen and Lord Airlie, fell in love with the Americans and their scene, but Plunkett never gained great fondness for the Americans in the West. Even at the Cheyenne Club, he said of his fellow members from the local community, "They don't like us naturally & on the whole I don't like them. They are to a certain amount clannish & feel our intrusion. The exact feeling they would express thus— 'You have a social position. We have hardly any. You compare us with your "society!" We don't compare favorably perhaps. But we are members of a greater nation than yours & just as good as you, tho you don't know it!'" While the comment is typical of Plunkett and reflects his acerbic style, it does reveal an essential point of friction between the two groups. The fiercely independent American, acutely conscious of the wealth and growth of his native country, resented the old society and what he saw as its pretensions. Nevertheless, much of that society was unabashedly imitated, as the success of the Cheyenne Club clearly showed. There was love and hate in varying proportions that made for a lively exchange.[30]

# Hard Times

## A Fatal Winter and a Private War

———◆———

arly in 1887 a rancher near Sundance, Wyoming, was seeking
signs of life on his range in the Powder River country when
he chanced on a six-month-old calf marooned in the deep snow with
a single tree as his sole living companion. The starving youngster
had stripped the bark from the tree as far up as it could reach, for it
could not escape the snow bank that formed its prison. The rancher
rescued the survivor, luckier even than some of the cowhands, since
there were human victims as well as cattle in that awful winter.[1]

The range-cattle industry as it was practiced on the northern
plains first fell victim to overcrowding and later destroyed itself in
the foolish adventure known as the Johnson County War. Linking
these two causes is the winter of 1886–87, which serves as a convenient watershed. That the winter was a bad one was undeniable,
and it may have been worse than those in the memory of the men
on the plains, but it was not the only reason for the demise of the
big outfits on the free-grass range.

By the summer of 1885, there were distinct signs that all was not
well on the plains, although they did not often find their way into
the public press. Certainly, Frewen saw it all coming, for his initial
1883 purchase of the Rawhide range was intended to protect the
Powder River range from overcrowding, and with the same idea in
mind, he also tried to move herds north to Canada. Plunkett remarked that the bad times had depressed the spirits of the ever-

optimistic Moreton Frewen, and he was casting about for ways to cut costs on his own operations. That they were not alone in these efforts was brought home to Plunkett in a most direct way on a journey to a neighboring ranch, where he arrived at noontime. To his great surprise he was not offered a meal. "Col. Pratt not home, of course," he noted in his diary; obviously the breach of range etiquette was due to the bad times. "I only hope the open house system is going to be done away with," Plunkett wrote. "But it won't do to be the victims of both systems."[2]

Thus, overcrowding had already begun to bite the operations of the big cattle companies, even before the celebrated winter of 1886–87 took its toll. At the Wyoming Stock Growers Association meeting in October 1885, the cattlemen sat in session for six hours and set up a group to establish a fair but reduced scale of wages for cowhands, and to abolish free board at ranches.[3]

A wage reduction of five to ten dollars was made (although it was not uniformly observed); in a somewhat timid response, some of the hands formed what the Cheyenne papers called a sort of "labor league." Others with less faith in the democratic process talked openly of shooting the proponents of the cutback, notably Horace Plunkett, who was then managing the Powder River Cattle Company that Frewen had started. In these straitened circumstances, the extra hands were laid off *between* the two roundups (as well as in the fall); the hapless cowboys were also charged for winter meals, eliminating even the small abatement of the harshness of range life represented by the "grub line."

Even when the cutbacks brought friction with the hands, the basic hospitality of the range did not entirely fail. Plunkett, under fire (figuratively, if not literally) for his efforts to reduce wages, was riding across country with a cowboy and a miner when darkness overtook them; putting aside Plunkett's unpopular economic argument, the other two men insisted on a fair division of blankets, since he had only one and they were more providently supplied.

By the following spring the dissension caused by these cost-cutting measures was showing up in press reports. A letter in the *Big Horn Sentinel* from a cowboy complained that he couldn't work for five months for thirty dollars a month and then pay thirty dollars a month for board the rest of the year. Roundup No. 23 was subjected to a strike for forty dollars per month, a demand that was met by all except Judge Carey's CY outfit; the *Rawlins Journal* reported that as a result, CY cows with "maverick" calves were "thick as the flowers."[4]

A confrontation with the cowhands was clearly on the way, and while the cattlemen wanted to cut wages, there had already been a strike for *higher* wages in the spring of 1884 in the Powder River country, and apparently some of the outfits there acceded to the demands, according to John Clay. He was with the Seventy-One Quarter Circle outfit at the fall roundup when the men demanded that they be paid through to the end of the year rather than be laid off after the roundup, as was the general custom. Clay resisted the demands and bluffed the men. Although there were only five men to handle six hundred beef animals and some old cows, they were successful in holding the herd through the night, and when the hay crew arrived with ten additional men, the crisis was over. Three of the strikers returned to work, but one of the foremen quit out of feelings of solidarity with the other men.[5]

When overcrowding on the ranges in the United States became evident to everyone (ranchers such as Plunkett saw this problem as early as 1884), some herds were moved to Canada before that country began imposing duty on such movements. Frewen's Powder River Company made one drive of seven thousand head in 1886.

Meanwhile, Plunkett's Frontier Company was beset by more trouble than it could overcome. By the end of the year 1885, it was apparent that a new fattening operation the Frontier Company had established at Herman, Nebraska (north of Omaha), was a failure, causing Plunkett to comment morosely that many of his speculations were failing. He mused that he had expected to be a rich man; now he was not only at a financial low ebb but was beginning to be concerned about the security of his backers. Early the next year Lord Dunsany gave him three hundred pounds to help him through the crisis. In the spring, Plunkett attended the roundup at Paint Rock Creek, on the west side of the Bighorn Mountains, and there the hands were far from cordial; "They have been talking of shooting me all winter as I have been made the scapegoat of the attempt to reduce wages," he said. Another weakness was Plunkett's difficulty in selecting and keeping good foremen; once his foreman was arrested for horse stealing at the crucial roundup time. He finally decided that the best way to cut further losses was to liquidate, but while this was going on, a disastrous prairie fire hit the range, followed by the winter of 1886–87. The remnant of the once-extensive herds was sold in 1888 for fifteen thousand dollars.[6]

Another source of trouble for the cattlemen stemmed from an action of President Grover Cleveland, shortly after he began his first term of office. In the summer of 1885 the president gave cattle ranchers only forty days to remove their herds from the Cheyenne and Arapaho Indian reservations in Indian Territory. These leases covered about 3 million acres; when they were cancelled at the urging of the Indians, apparently about three hundred thousand head of cattle were thrown on other ranges. Another 6 million acres in the Cherokee Strip were also under lease, and the removal order was eventually extended to this area as well. Thus, many new southern herds were suddenly introduced into the already crowded northern ranges.[7]

Cattle prices were low in 1885, and even lower the following year. Many cattlemen tried to hold for winter feeding as many animals as they could, even though forage was poor (in some places, such as eastern Montana, there had been a plague of grasshoppers). The rains came later than normal in the fall of 1886, and there were range fires in a number of places. Wolves and coyotes were reported to be especially plentiful.

Thus, the ranges were heavily overstocked in 1886, and even the *Northwestern Live Stock Journal* (at other times a wildly optimistic industry organ) was admitting the problem. In the fall of that year, John Clay was riding the range in Wyoming and he described conditions there: "Cattle were thin and green grass was an unknown quantity except in some bog hole, or where a stream had overflowed in early spring." Over on the Belle Fourche, a normally heavily grassed country, the same conditions were observed. By August, it was apparent that losses would be high even if the winter was mild. Even the normally optimistic Moreton Frewen was distressed by the condition of the range. "[T]he business has quite broken down on these ranges," he said. "There can never be any recovery." Prophetically, he said in September, "I dread the coming winter; if it is a severe one half the cattle in Wyoming will die for sure."[8]

In the fall, for the first time in their memories, the Montana cattlemen saw the white Arctic owl in the Judith Basin; the Indians gathered their blankets tightly around themselves when they saw the strange northern birds. The winter came early and it was not mild. In November the cattlemen in the Powder River Basin pooled manpower to form a line from the head of the Powder River to the Montana line. Feed was scarce along the river, and it was necessary to keep the hungry animals from drifting down to the river bottom. This system was still working the following January. By January hungry cattle were roaming the streets of Cheyenne itself, and by March the police had given up trying to keep them out.[9]

With the coming of the wind and cold, the *Northwestern Live Stock Journal* returned to its optimistic stance, admitting that Montana had experienced "a more severe winter than average" (not a word about Wyoming), but then discounting the reports by saying that word from Montana was "simply marvelous in the way of exaggeration." The *Journal* put forth its own estimate of losses in the Dillon area, which it gauged at only six or seven percent. Strangely, word of the disaster was slow in crossing the ocean, for in far-off London, the Swan company annual meeting in March was told by the chairman that "this winter has so far been a favorable one," and the assemblage applauded; Mr. Swan himself then seconded the remark with the observation that the winter was "very fair." As late as the end of April the *Journal* was running articles limiting the losses to "scrawny" or "ill-favored" animals, and explaining away reports of greater loss as the products of envy by those outside the livestock business.

Granville Stuart, in his book, *Pioneering in Montana*, told a different story; he said that in the great January storm of 1887, which lasted for two weeks (the thermometer reached −47°), fat young steers froze to death, and his seasoned range herd took a 50 percent loss). Cowboys were marooned on the range, often without supplies. The *Big Horn Sentinel* finally lost patience with all the editorial optimism and growled that "occasionally" there could be a "few" truthful remarks; and the editor in Albright, Montana, complained that the foremen of the big companies only stirred from the fire to go to town or to tell the editors "all is well," while cattle died by the thousands.[10]

As late as February, John Hunton, a Wyoming rancher who was then in Cheyenne, admitted that the ranchers were still talking about 5 and 6 percent losses, although they knew better, but he also thought that losses north of the Platte (the worst area in Wyoming) would only be fifteen percent or so. He had fed over three hundred tons of hay to his eighteen-hundred-head herd and hoped he could get by with a two-hundred-head loss. By April more somber news had caused him to place the northern losses at 30 to 50 percent; his own herd continued to suffer, and to die, so that by the end of May he had lost more than three hundred and considered himself lucky the good spring weather had saved one hundred fifty or two hundred more from the same fate.[11]

At long last it was over. An editor in Miles City, Montana, greeted the long awaited warm chinook wind with the sad comment, "At the risk of a great setback, we cannot refrain from a third and last call. Springtime has surely come, gentle Annie."

For all the optimism that had poured from the *Journal*'s offices in Cheyenne during the winter, the losses *were* greater than usual, and not just in Montana. An estimated three hundred persons died, but the toll among the unprotected livestock was collossal. Some outfits did not even bother to gather the remnants. For one herd of 5,500 three-year-olds, about 100 head were found, and Conrad Kohrs recovered 300 head from a herd of 35,000. The painter Charles M. Russell spent most of the winter on Jesse Phelps's O.H. Ranch in the Judith Basin of Montana, and when a Helena business-man wrote for word of the 5,000-head herd he owned jointly with Phelps, Russell prepared a poignant watercolor called *Waiting for a Chinook*, showing a single steer surrounded by five wolves; he wrote the words "the last of 5,000" as the only message in response.[12]

Some herds were lucky and had drifted over onto the less-crowded Indian reservation west of the Missouri, where there was more grass, but for the most part it was a disaster, all the way from southern Colorado to the Canadian line, from the hundreth merid-ian almost to the Pacific slope. When Horace Plunkett joined the roundup on the Powder River in the summer of 1887, he found only two wagons working the North Fork of the Powder River, where there had been ten a year earlier. He was "floored" by the news of the calamity, and estimated that 75 percent of the female stock and 10 percent of the steers had perished. He thought the Powder River Company herds, with a book count of 33,000, would only prove to have 12,000 head left; the calf crop was only 1,200. The Johnson County tax assessment for 1887 was prepared on the basis of an assumed 25 percent loss by the ranchers, but Plunkett fought for the more realistic 50 percent suffered by his own EK operations and those of the Powder River Cattle Company. The Swan may have suffered lower-than-normal losses; one estimate placed their losses at 25 to 50 percent west of the Black Hills of Wyoming and not over 5 percent east of that range.[13]

In Alberta conditions were better because there were far fewer cattle, and they came through the winter in excellent condition, even though the flat range on Mosquito Creek offered less shelter than Wyoming's Powder River ranges.[14]

The Swan and Sturgis outfits both went down, and Kohrs, Gran-ville Stuart, and other big outfits were badly hurt. Most of the east-ern men and the British simply went away, as Clay put it in his memoir. The ensuing summer was a dry one, causing some of the survivors to ship to a market fed by continuing liquidation sales, where prices were disastrously low. Clay sent to market a herd bought for twenty-seven dollars a head in 1885; even though the losses from the winter had been less than for other ranches (only 25 to 30 percent), the total price realized was considerably below their cost in 1885.[15]

No one can be sure who first told the anguished cattlemen huddled about the winter fire while their herds froze on the plains, "Don't worry, the books won't freeze," or words to that effect, but figuring out how bad the winter had been was hampered by the accounting system of the big outfits, the so-called "book count." Transactions among the big outfits were often conducted not by actual tally, but by book count, and the system worked reasonably well so long as the herds were roaming the range under normal conditions and reproducing in normal numbers. When a disaster struck, the book count meant next to nothing, since the losses were obviously greater than the assumed "standard" loss, but no one could be sure precisely how much was attributable to the weather and how much to a faulty book count.

If the winter of 1886–87 was the main cause of the hard times on the northern plains, there were equally severe causes in the Texas Panhandle. One writer saw the beginning of the end in the prairie fires of 1883–84, which were fought for six days and nights by the big outfits. When the fires died down, the ranges were ruined and fences had to be cut to let the cattle drift in search of food. There was no spring beef that season, and the following winter was also unusually severe; some cattle drifted as much as 450 miles, and thousands perished, so that the ranchers had to sell off the breeding stock to pay expenses and dividends to shareholders.[16]

In the midst of the winter of 1886–87, a long letter signed by a number of Wyoming cattlemen was published in the *Boston Journal*. It was mainly an effort to defuse the arguments made in an earlier story in the *Boston Daily Advertiser* that the cattle business in Wyoming was ruined, but in countering those arguments, the cattlemen made a special effort to denigrate the role of English capital. Criticisms of the industry were put down as the opinion of Englishmen in "their" club in Laramie City, wherever that might have been. It was noted that of the 450 members of the Wyoming Stock Growers Association, only 14 were directly or indirectly involved with foreign capital, and that those enterprises were "by no means" as successful as American ranches, since they were conducted by young aristocrats from abroad "unaccustomed" to economy or work, so that the enterprise took on the nature of a "grand picnic."

While some of these generalities could scarcely be proven, there was much in the letter that was patently false. The letter claimed that most losses "in the past two or three years" were Texas cattle, and although that was probably true, it begged the question about what was at that very moment happening on the western ranges, where many seasoned range cattle were dying. The cattlemen also tried to explain away the exodus to Montana and Canada as no more than a search for paradise in the next country, but the creatures that perished in that terrible winter yearned not so much for paradise as for mere survival.

Finally, the letter stated that the Wyoming ranges were as well grassed and as capable of supporting cattle as they had been five years earlier, which was emphatically not true. Perhaps no more than 1 percent of the cattle raisers were insolvent or "anything near it," in December of 1886, as the cattlemen claimed, but that was because no banker had the information to judge the real financial condition, since the only data then available were in the unfreezable tally books.[17]

Frewen's Powder River Cattle Company had been set on the road toward liquidation early in 1887, not because of the winter but as a condition of the continued management of the property by Horace Plunkett, so when the results of the winter of 1886–87 were announced for that company, they proved anticlimactic. The same was true of Richard Frewen's Dakota Company, which closed out in 1886.[18]

Further south, the Ione Company was also in trouble. By late 1886, Boughton was writing to Horace Plunkett to describe a "bona fide crisis" involving overdrafts and overdue notes at the bank; he predicted darkly that the company would soon go under. However, disaster did not descend so quickly, and a year later Boughton was still writing to a shareholder about hopes for "next spring," saying, "Any alteration in business takes place with far greater rapidity in America than in England." That assessment may have been accurate, but the operation ultimately did fail.[19]

Others were leaving, too, and a number of companies closed their western offices. In September 1886, Moreton Frewen was at the Cheyenne Club and remarked how deserted the city was. "No one in Cheyenne has got a bob left," he said. "I never saw such a depressed place." A few days later, he found similar conditions in Miles City, Montana. Still, he saw the possibility to make money for "two or three years" in Alberta, but as to the Montana and Wyoming ranges, he said, "it is all over here." Unfortunately, the reins were not in his hands any longer, and the old Powder River Company would not have even two or three years in Alberta.[20]

The Wyoming Stock Growers Association noted the reduced income from the sale of mavericks and acknowledged the straitened circumstances by asking the territorial veterinarian to take a salary cut and reducing the chief of detective's and the secretary's salaries. They also proposed to abandon operations in Dakota unless the members there paid for them. The fall of 1887 was farewell time for a number of the "imported Dudes," as Plunkett called them. Alston of the Peters and Alston spread lacked even enough money to return to Britain and was depressed and talked of suicide; Ralph Stuart Wortley left the same outfit and went to New York, where he later headed a brokerage firm; Jim Winn shut down the Big Horn Cattle Company and went to Cheyenne to find another job.[21]

Plunkett made ready to leave Cheyenne for what he thought would be the last time (he actually did return the following year), and the Cheyenne Club gave him a farewell dinner with thirty members present; there were many speeches, which pleased the withdrawn Plunkett, and in his diary he made one of his rare gracious comments about the people there: "They have had my good will & all the help I could give them. That's true." Plunkett in turn gave a dinner for a number of the British investors, including Boughton, Peters, Pryce, Quin, Alston, and Wortley, but his motive was mostly to provide some money for Mrs. Peters, who was reduced to running a boardinghouse in Cheyenne to support her family. The exodus was also hurting the Cheyenne Club and, in the fall of 1888, the board asked the city and county to reduce the tax assessment; two years later they would levy members to pay the club's debts.[22]

In the aftermath of the terrible winter, and in an action that heaped insult on the injuries of the crippled industry, President Cleveland authorized a cavalry troop at Cheyenne to aid the enforcement of antifencing laws, and soon he abandoned his policy of appointing local governors for the territories by naming Col. Thomas Moonlight governor of Wyoming. Governor Baxter had been removed the previous December because of his own enclosures of the public domain; the man who replaced him was apparently guilty of nothing more serious than the hanging of two Indian chiefs.

Moonlight was now a Democrat (as was the president), although he had once been a Republican, and if he felt a certain ambivalence in political affiliation, there was no doubt about the way he felt about cattlemen. In office he devoted himself to a crusade against the cattle industry, once writing, "There is a future for this territory, as soon as men begin to satisfy themselves that Cattle! Cattle!! Cattle!!! are not the only things." While these comments were at least partly inspired by politics, they serve as a symbol of the change that had overtaken an industry that had once been all-powerful in the territory. The reasons for the fall from power stem from more than a bad winter: There were simply too many other interests to be served, even though these regions would never yield to intensive farming in the midwestern style. Never again would the cattle industry be able single-handedly to direct the operation of government.[23]

But the venture that represented the symbolic end of the cattle king era on the plains was the Johnson County invasion of 1892. This sad incident, devised and promoted by the large operators in the cattle business, was carried out after the foreign investors had for the most part withdrawn from the scene. In consequence there is none of the harsh invective directed against the foreigner in accounts of the raid.

After the events of 1886–87 forced a new look at the realities on the range, the cattlemen had agonized over the changing situation. Settlers were coming in some numbers now. By 1886 there were only three employees left in the surveyor general's office in Cheyenne, as compared with thirty-six to thirty-eight just four years earlier; the work of surveying the public domain was essentially finished, and when the 1890 census came to be published, those charged with the analysis of the results could no longer find a frontier line. It is in northern Wyoming that the symbol of that disappearing frontier was perhaps last seen, for it was to those ranges that the cattlemen drove Oregon cattle east to pasture, and others drove Texas cattle north for the same purpose. It was in this region where the great cattle trails debouched, and when permanent settlers appeared at last on these virgin prairies, the great free-range era was over.[24]

If the range was now crowded with settlers and other cattlemen, it also attracted those poaching off the bounty represented by the ranging beef animals. At first it was the Indian, who saw the beef as a somewhat less fleet version of the mighty herds of buffalo that once provided sustenance for himself and his family. In 1877 the Lawrence County, Dakota, commissioners tried to halt Indian raids on livestock by offering a $250 bounty for Indians, "dead or alive." Nor were the Indian agents particularly sympathetic with stockmen; the Pine Ridge agent had the reservation brand placed on all strays found on that agency's land. Along the Canadian border, U. S. ranchers had to cope with roving bands of Canadian Indians, who apparently found it easier to "hunt" beef in the United States than under the watchful eyes of the Mounties. But reservation life soon sapped the Indians' ability and inclination to launch forays into the cattle region.[25]

There was also the white "rustler," who existed in numbers we cannot know and who stole uncounted head of animals. For when a cow hid herself in some remote gully while the roundup "circle" made its way across the range, she was as surely beyond the grasp of the cattleman who owned her as if she had been eaten by a wolf (as some were), killed in a winter storm (as many were), or taken captive to pass under the running iron and change her apparent ownership (as many others were). To sort out all the causes of loss is impossible. But when the fall shipments were short of the expectations not only of the boards of directors in England and Scotland but also of the experienced foremen and cowhands on the range, there was gloomy talk about the need for action.

Moreton Frewen had advocated a law making it illegal to possess a short branding iron (because it could be concealed in the saddle) and on at least one occasion threatened to have his hands rebrand with the 76 all animals found with "rustler" brands. The maverick law itself was blamed for the loss of animals, as the roundups produced few mavericks and the big ranchers assumed the missing calves were out there somewhere in the hills being held for the running iron. Sometimes the losses were especially large and detectable, as when a herd of fifteen hundred from Kansas passed through the country, and ninety head were waylaid and held in the hills until the main herd had passed; their brands were then burned out before they were sold in South Dakota. These men were caught, but how many others were not? And even when the guilty were brought to justice, conviction was not assured; a Buffalo, Wyoming, judge openly admitted that three rustlers were clearly guilty, "but the jury turned them loose."[26]

Finally the big cattlemen resolved to act. In the fall of 1891, John Clay was in Wyoming, and while there he took a long walk with Major Frank Wolcott, the man who had hosted young Owen Wister on his ranch five years earlier. Major Wolcott, whom most hated, many feared, and only a few loved, had served in the Civil War and afterward came to Wyoming Territory, where he was U. S. marshal—a "fire eater, honest, clean, a rapid Republican with a complete absence of tact," in Clay's description. Clay later admitted that Wolcott had told him of a planned "lynching bee" but claimed he strongly advised against it; whereupon, he said, "the matter left my mind."[27]

In any case, Clay returned to points east and the winter dragged on; when the subsequent invasion had passed into history, Clay reminded the world that he had been in Europe at the time, "innocent as a newborn babe" and "unconscious of any cattle war." In the early spring of 1892, the Wyoming Stock Growers Association presumably went about its business as usual, although we lack proof of that fact, for the voluminous files of correspondence, minutes, and other papers are remarkably sparse for that year, and an observer with no other knowledge beyond what the records reveal might well conclude that these garrulous men of meetings and writings had suddenly fallen silent.

At the end of March agents were sent to Texas to recruit men willing to take orders and to kill, if need be—and to keep their mouths shut. A number of such men, and some who fell short of the standard in varying degrees, were at length engaged. Then supplies were laid in, a railway train was hired—these men operated with a certain style—and the expedition headed north.

This was not the first or only occasion on which the cattlemen had taken up the job of enforcing the law. The stock detectives had been doing so for years, but they at least were covered with some color of authority, although their orders came from Tom Sturgis in Cheyenne and not from some elected county or state official. Then, of course, there was the unfortunate story of the supposed rustlers Cattle Kate and Jim Averell, who were hanged at a spot now covered by the waters of the Fontenelle Reservoir. And there were other such incidents. But the force sent to Johnson County did not bother with any pretense at being a legal posse or deputation of the constituted law-enforcement authority of the State of Wyoming; it was the creature of those who bankrolled it, and it would be their last hurrah in such a role.

The story of the raid has often been recounted, although there
is still controversy over some of the details. It was on the KC ranch,
one of Frewen's old line camps (and named for one of his brands),
that suspected rustler Nate Champion died. While assessing his in-
creasingly grim situation—which culminated in the firing of the
cabin where he lay—Champion penned a diary that, if not epic, at
least in a few words may redeem his memory; he was, after all, once
a respected employee of Horace Plunkett on the EK outfit, and perhaps there was even someone who mourned him in Texas (his
brand, the open A, N, open A, supposedly honored the memory of
a woman called Anna). It is pointless to expend much effort trying
to decide whether Champion's end was justified by his deeds, whatever they may have been. But the aftermath of his death was a
surprise to the invaders, for it suddenly dawned on them that they
had totally misjudged the temper of the people they had come
among.

While many of the townsfolk in Buffalo and the small ranchers
and farmers undoubtedly had no sympathy for thieves, there was a
totally different and very hostile reaction when they were faced
with an invasion by an extralegal army of gunmen: Popular revul-
sion was widespread. Soon the invaders, who had gathered at the
nearby TA ranch, found *themselves* surrounded and besieged; indeed, had the siege continued longer, there would have been a
much larger number of long guns bombarding the beleaguered cattlemen behind their log barricades. Thus the invasion failed mostly
because it alienated the decent element of the countryside; it was
largely for this reason that Fred Hesse found it prudent—even essential—to absent himself and his family from the state for a time,
while his house was vandalized by persons whose identity was never
the subject of any serious investigation.

The army arrived in time to save the lives of the cattlemen and
their hired guns and to conduct them away in safety. There then
followed the slow process of gaining the release of the cattlemen,
now prisoners; this was carried out in the courts in the southern
part of the state, where they had been removed for their own safety.
Meanwhile, on the northern ranges, cattle bearing the brands of
those invaders simply melted away in some cases, seemingly beyond
the concern of their former owners as well as those empowered to
enforce the law. If there was any question about the existence of
anarchy before the invasion, there could be none afterward. Judge
Carey warned a friend that he should avoid travel to his ranch in

Fremont County and commented that the "reign of terror" in Johnson County was so severe that, according to two returning cattlemen, "they would feel safer among Apache Indians on the war
path."[28]

The invasion did not quite mark the end of violence and vigilantism on the range. One further incident perhaps has the distinction
of representing that final watershed. In 1909 another dispute arose
in northern Wyoming, not this time with the rustlers but with the
sheepmen. It was then still the passionately held opinion of many
cattlemen that sheep ruined the range for cattle grazing, and they
would kill the woollies when they could. It was the practice in the
Bighorn country (as in many places elsewhere) to erect an imaginary
barrier beyond which sheep were not permitted on the range. This
so-called "deadline" was the Rubicon across which a band of sheep
and their four herders passed in the spring of 1909, on Spring Creek,
a tributary of the Nowood River. On a moonlit night, the two owners of the band were ambushed and shot, one of them with his
hands in the air, the killer remarking laconically, "It's a Hell of a
time of night to come out with your hands up." The body of the
other man was incinerated in the fire of their wagon; the only ten-
derness shown that night was by a puppy who lay pitifully on his
master's lifeless form, and by the gunman who spared the dog while
slaughtering the sheep.

Four men in a nearby cabin, awakened by the rapid gunfire, went
outside in their nightclothes to watch the flames and listen to the
fireworks, which continued for nearly two hours; then they returned
to bed, not to venture near the scene of the crime until after day-
break. At the trial no one asked the four why they had not investigated further that night: There was no need to ask.

After the bloody work was over, the seven men whose deed it was
sent the two surviving sheepherders away with the admonition to
keep quiet; as hired hands they were not required to pay for their
masters' trespass on the cattle range. The herders untied their own
horses from the sagebrush nearby and rode back to their homes a
short distance away, arriving by one o'clock in the morning. But this
was hardly an event that could be kept quiet, and soon even the
participants ignored their own injunction. One of them actually returned the following day to view the bodies, after the sheriff had
arrived to begin his investigation; nor was he shy about his part in
the attack, confiding the awful truth to at least one cowhand and

very probably another. It was as though they had no fear of punishment.

But this was not 1892. The trial of these killers was attended by the National Guard to give security to the proceedings. One man who was to be called as a witness had committed suicide, but with the grant of immunity to two of the participants, four others quickly pleaded guilty and the fifth was convicted at trial; in a final anachronism, the defense tried unsuccessfully to introduce evidence of the deadline rule, perhaps in explanation if not mitigation. One of the prisoners later walked away from a prison work gang, never to be seen (officially) again. But the reign of violence and vigilantism was over; henceforth, killing was punished by law, and it was no longer a more serious crime to steal a cow than to kill a man.[29]

The ranches that survived the 1886–87 winter were few, including the Matador, the Prairie, and the JA ranch, plus Western Ranches in Wyoming. The story of the last of these was told by John Clay himself. In the fall of 1883, Clay had proposed to his Scottish masters that the properties of the Dickey brothers (Wyoming ranchers) be added to Western Ranches, Limited, either on the basis of book count with guaranteed brand or on the basis of an actual count. To his dismay the Scots refused to accept the deal. However, the Dickeys needed three hundred thousand dollars, and on the basis of Clay's recommendation, this amount was advanced on a loan by Thomas Nelson, against the security of the Dickey herds. In the year that followed, the Dickey brothers moved to Chicago, where their expenses increased, and only with difficulty could they produce the hundred thousand dollars due at the end of 1884. The next two winters were hard, and Clay estimated that losses ran 50 percent or 60 percent.

Then came the winter of 1886–87, leaving the Dickeys badly strapped. Their notes at the First National Bank of Chicago could not be met, and that institution took a loss of around 50 percent in its indebtedness; however, the Scots took possession of the herds and ran them with their own VVV outfit for one dollar per head per year. In addition to the Dickey herds, the Scots received fifteen thousand dollars in cash and some Hereford bulls that had not been included in the mortgage, in all about thirty-five hundred head of cattle. Even though he had this security, Nelson was furious with the result, and Clay settled down to recoup the losses.

Expenses were light in the following years, and by the summer of 1891 there were ten thousand four- and five-year-old steers fat and ready to ship, which brought $55 a head. After expenses $110,000 could be paid to Nelson, and in 1892 a further $60,000 was paid; thus, in 1894, Nelson's executors took delivery of a fine herd. It was quite a success story. Indeed, the record of Western Ranches in the 1890s was unmatched among the big companies; dividends of 14 to 20 percent were paid in the period 1889–95. Eventually, the shareholders got back more than double their initial investment while enjoying a 9 percent dividend for thirty-one years.[30]

It is interesting that Clay blames the Dickeys for their profligacy, but it was the wealthy banker with the resources to wait for the turn of the market who clearly held the long odds to win such a contest. Although the bankers were skittish about agricultural loans after the winter of 1886–87, Clay and the well-heeled companies he represented were able to lay their hands on some fresh locally borrowed money (the investors back home had ceased sending new money across), and from 1888 on they made good purchases from the floundering operators on the range. Profits "multiplied rapidly."[31]

The Matador was also an unusual story of perseverance in the face of adversity, for it continued to grow and add to its acreage over the years, peaking at over eight hundred thousand. Although it lost money in 1931 and there were a number of years when no dividend was paid, the big ranch continued to make at least some money, and eventually paid its stockholders well (dividends were 15 to 20 percent in the years 1942 and 1950). Ironically, it was not difficulties of the business but the impact of the tax laws that eventually dictated the transfer of ownership back to the United States. The company was finally acquired by an American investors' group in 1951, paying the old shareholders nearly $19 million and yielding them a handsome profit. Although the ranch still had over forty-six thousand head of cattle, the real estate was a far larger asset; the land purchases by the Scots eventually overcame all the other vicissitudes the old company had encountered.

Another survivor of the winter of 1886–87 was a man who had not previously loomed large in the industry. Born in Roubaix, France, in 1858, Pierre Wibaux was from a family of commercial distinction that had been operating cotton and woolen mills since 1810. After a trip to England, where he met some English gentlemen whose sons were in the American cattle business, he came to the United States in 1882, at the age of twenty-four. A chance meeting with the marquis de Mores in Chicago brought him to the high plains just west of de Mores's ranch in 1883. There he selected a range in the Beaver Valley of eastern Montana Territory, and started a cattle ranch, at first in partnership with another Frenchman, but later on his own. The partnership's first herd was said to be ten thousand head, although another source contends the herd was not larger than eight hundred until after 1886.[32]

Wibaux devoted his resources first to the expansion of the herd under the W-bar brand, so that during the first winter in Montana, his new English bride had to make do in a log cabin with a sod roof. But Wibaux was lucky. While the winter of 1886–87 was laying waste the Montana cattle ranges, Wibaux was in France, where he had gone to raise more funds for expansion. When he returned in the spring with five hundred thousand dollars, he saw at once that there were bargains to be had on the range. Many large outfits were closing out and would sell their remnant—by definition the hardiest of their former herds—for very low prices. And the range was no longer overstocked. All through 1887, Wibaux bought up the decimated herds, at prices averaging twenty dollars per head; that fall, he sold enough beef at forty to forty-five dollars over cost to pay for his entire remaining herd. One such deal involved the remnant of the Powder River Company herd; Fred Hesse explained to Horace Plunkett that although the contract demanded more than would be allowed to any other purchaser, "Mr. Wibaux was the only man I suppose in America who could or would have bought as large a herd of she stock as ours." In this deal, Wibaux got 7,419 head of cattle and 100 horses for just over $139,000, or less than $19 per head. Wibaux commented that he had 16,000 head which had cost him nothing, and that he had made quite a fortune.[33]

From this beginning Wibaux became one of the biggest stockmen in Montana. In 1890 he replaced his log cabin with a handsome house some eighty feet long, which presented a nice contrast with the sod or log structures on the range; its white-painted exterior earned it the nickname White House. Water was pumped into the house by a windmill, and its appointments were elaborate, with papered walls and a billiard room and wine cellar. By this time Wibaux was running sixty-five thousand head of cattle, and the little town of Mingusville, which had been named for his former partner, was renamed Wibaux in his honor; a county was also named for him in 1914.[34]

Among the other survivors were some of the hardy old animals themselves. Although the Powder River Company had been set on the road to liquidation in 1885, there were still enough cattle left to make a major sale in 1889, and two years later they were still show-ing up "very well." Over near Belle Fourche, in Dakota, when the VVV herds of Western Ranches were wound up, there was a mam-moth longhorn steer who had lived his long life on the free range. His head, sporting perfect horns that measure more than seven feet between their points, still graces a wall in the house of James T. Craig's grandson, and he is a fitting reminder of those larger-than-life years.[35]

The grim story of the 1886–87 winter and its aftermath mark the demise of the range-cattle industry, but the evaluation of Moreton Frewen's downfall is more complicated. One reason for that down-fall was Frewen's vast ambition: He initiated an incredible number and diversity of projects during the short time he was ranching in Wyoming. The ranch itself, the refrigeration facility at Sherman, the plan to export live cattle, the expansion on the Canadian range, and the projects for cattle fattening and real-estate development at Superior each could have been full-time undertakings for someone permanently residing in the United States or in Canada, but More-ton at times pursued all of them while continually crossing and re-crossing the ocean in the days before jet airplanes. So it is easy to understand that the gentlemen in London and Dundee should look askance at the proliferation of plans for the use of their money, even though the ideas were for the most part sensible.

Moreover, the proper strategy for the investment of money was something they often disagreed about. Moreton's view was always long term: He was continually telling Clara that next year, or two years hence, they would be rich, and he was willing—even eager—to forgo his current salary with the prospect in view of enhancing the future value of his own shares (and, incidentally, those of the other common shareholders as well). But the other shareholders, and in particular the Scottish preferred shareholders, wanted an as-sured dividend *now.* These attitudes were at bottom irreconcilable.

For his part Moreton contributed handsomely to the venture, both in money and work. He took 20 percent of the common shares and agreed not to sell them for a time, became the American man-ager at no salary, and at length gave up that job while paying the replacement from his own pocket. It is not difficult to understand that in the circumstances he felt he was being wronged when the board turned against him and criticized his judgment, finally cutting him off altogether from the operations. And when the wisdom of the Canadian move he had advocated was underwritten by the dead bodies on the plains, it was a bitter thing for him to see his own rightful place of authority occupied by Horace Plunkett, who took the job on condition that he have the right to liquidate the old Powder River Company—thereby making certain it would finally fail.

# The Legacy of the Free Range
## What the British Left Behind

---

**I**n the fall of 1882, the Union Pacific Railroad asked Moreton if he would agree to their naming a station in his honor. He told Clara of the request, saying, "Perhaps in our children's time it may be a western metropolis!" Unfortunately, no such naming ever occurred, so that the place where the town of Frewen might have been is as empty of that connection as are the vast ranges to the north. Indeed, there are few reminders of any kind to evoke memory of the English cattlemen. Although hundreds of thousands of cattle roamed the ranges of northern Wyoming in the eighties, if one consults the records in the county seat at Buffalo, Wyoming, there are few entries relating to the great companies that owned these herds. The Matador did not even register to do business in Texas until 1887; the Powder River Cattle Company, Limited, never bothered to qualify with Wyoming Territory to do business there (an unrelated corporation with the similar name of Powder River Live Stock Company was registered in Wyoming); and the Rocking Chair Ranche never registered its brand in Texas. Thus, there is little "paper trail" behind these giant outfits. As for Frewen himself, the big house he built on the Powder River has long since been pulled down, and only the modest one he used as a stopping place in Cheyenne still testifies tangibly to his presence in Wyoming.[1]

Before considering the legacy of the free-range system, it is necessary to say a word about one myth that has arisen. It has frequently

185

been said that the frontier profoundly influenced the development of American society, and doubtless this was so. But when the open-range cattle industry is discussed, writers often use the word *freedom* to describe the working environment of the cattlemen. But how felicitous is that description? When we refer to the "free" range, we are speaking in economic terms, for what made the industry workable during the brief period when it reigned supreme on the plains was the discipline and control exercised by the men who sat in its councils of power. Therefore, while Walter Farwell (of the family involved in the XIT) described the range experience as "free and unregenerate," a less apt illustration of freedom could scarcely be found. The XIT itself held absolute sway over parts of ten counties in Texas, and its western boundary fence ran nearly two hundred miles with scarcely a jog to offend the eye. This empire—for so it was—was the fief of a board of directors, and they ruled as surely within their boundaries (and sometimes beyond) as did many sheriffs of the day.[2]

Thus, it was not freedom that the foreign gentlemen brought to the western plains of America. Rather, the brief era was a time when men confronted the savage country and tried to wrest financial rewards from it. The work was carried out according to their rules, with little thought of compromise or adaptation, consequently the touches of the culture they introduced to the plains were sometimes a source of amusement and even derision for some of their employees and others who observed them. But it was precisely because they refused to compromise their native culture that anachronistic trappings appeared—such as a House of Lords pub in Iowa or a polo field on the Powder River range.

Some of the criticism directed against the foreign gentleman was doubtless deserved, and there were widely publicized examples of profligacy and arrogance on their part. But there were also stories so overblown as to be ridiculous, as the storytellers succumbed to the temptation to spin a colorful tale. Likewise, their management style was sometimes flawed, but no more so than that of others; much of the difficulty was caused by the awful obstacles of distance and time that interfered with efficient communication. Moreover, the technology and science of animal husbandry they introduced had a lasting effect on the development of the West. And their personal failings were at least matched man for man by those of their American colleagues, who were also trying to survive in a harsh and unpredictable business environment.

Some of their business ventures failed because of market thinness and premature timing rather than a flawed concept, but there were other forces against them, too. Thus, the failure of the de Mores packing plant did involve competition from the "beef trust," which both he and Frewen regarded as a key factor in the demise of their slaughtering operations on the high plains. The management of the Matador also blamed the beef ring for reduced cattle prices; although Murdo Mackenzie was reluctant to say so publicly ("we have a great many cattle to sell"), nevertheless he believed the policies of the packers were controlled by only two or three men. Nor were the foreign aristocrats alone in this belief; certainly some leading newspaper editors thought the beef monopoly and the railroads were restraining competition unfairly. (Indeed, the Federal Trade Commission later concluded that much of the impetus for antitrust legislation in the United States stemmed from the discontent of cattlemen with their access to markets.)[3]

Moreover, de Mores—a Frenchman who had the audacity to fence his own land—was targeted by some whose reputation and background could stand rather less scrutiny than his. Although he was acquitted in court for killing a man while defending himself, he was obliged to stand trial again and again, as though it was unconscionable that a French nobleman should be able to prevail in an American legal proceeding.[4]

Unfortunately, the troubles the marquis encountered after leaving the United States, including the killing of a Jewish army captain in a duel, so colored American editorial opinion that it is hard to find a fair assessment of his earlier activities here. His countryman, Maurice Barrès, commented on the marquis' death, saying he had been "a practical 'Americanist,' and the last reader of novels of chivalry." Perhaps Barrès was saying he was an Americanized gentleman.[5]

Much has been made of the contrast between the English and Scottish business methods in those years, and the Scots made more money from their investments. It is easy to have perfect perception in hindsight, of course, but in fairness it is clear that the Scots were in a different business than the English. From the beginning the Scots were in the real-estate business, and they were constantly at pains to guarantee their land tenure. This was a capital-intensive strategy, but the resulting land position made it possible for the Scots to make a lot of money by selling it off when the big Scottish companies were liquidated; some of them paid their shareholders off handsomely.

The English, on the other hand, had slightly different objectives.

It was exciting to contemplate building a sizable business on the public domain—where feed could be had for the taking—and controlling it only by the presence of one's own cowboys and those of other like-minded gentlemen. The scale they had in mind and the style they insisted on was grand enough to attract the attention of men who had been schooled for the leadership of great enterprises. The game was risky, for, as they freely admitted, their claim to the land was of trifling account, but they relied on discipline and the authority inspired by their own presence to make up for these legal deficiencies. While it is easy to lose sight of the promise of that early idea, we must remember that the returns could be very high—30 to 50 or even 80 percent per annum—far more than the Scots could hope to realize by investing in the grazing land itself.

For a time it worked; but that time was all too brief. When they realized that failure was upon them, the English met that crisis, too, differently than did the Scottish merchants. The Scots reacted to the difficulties of the late eighties by cutting costs, adjusting to the new environment, and largely turning their cattle companies into land companies. The English pondered the changed environment and found that it no longer interested them; to them the game was up. In the end they fell back on their training as leaders of men, both in the military and in parliamentary politics. They cut their losses and withdrew.

Thus, the Rocking Chair Ranche liquidated its land rather than "hunker down" and wait for a better day, while the Matador continued to duck and weave and adapt to each new adversity that appeared. The drawback of this strategy was that it committed the shareholders to the awkward American situation for a number of years, sometimes with no dividends at all, while those who had funded the Rocking Chair were long since engaged in other pursuits. It is not easy to say which was the better choice, and perhaps there is no useful answer to such a question, for these "other pursuits" included more than making money.

If the gentlemen cut their losses and went home, unlike their Scottish rivals, what did they leave behind? A first answer lies in the cattle themselves, for there was scarcely a blooded herd that did not owe its pedigree to the Scottish and English stockmen, who bred them with care and introduced them to the West either through their own operations or directly from Great Britain.

A second answer is supplied by John Clay, although he did not intend it as a compliment to the British investors. At the Wyoming

Stock Growers Association meeting in April 1922, Clay reminisced about the events of 1886–87, comparing those bad times to the more recent economic troubles of 1919 and 1920:

> Of course, some of you remember '86 and '87. You know how we were all broke at that time, but we were broke in a different way than we were in 1919 and '20, because all of the cattle in the West, in Wyoming, were financed by eastern men, in England, in Boston and New York, and all over the country where they have money, and when we had that terrific disaster the people who were working here in a small way and the banks that were scarcely hurt at all, *because the men who lost the money were foreigners to them* [emphasis added], and the consequence was we passed over that crisis easily because we were still alive, and what is far more than that, a great number of our people had courage and better still, they had lots of virgin range.[6]

John Clay's comment suggests the importance of the financial contribution made by the British companies to the growth of the American West. The fact that a major disaster of this kind could be survived with relative ease by the sparsely populated region is testimony to a hidden legacy of the foreign investors. W. Turrentine Jackson counted thirty-three companies organized in the period 1880–88 and estimated that the equity capital paid in, together with the borrowings of these companies, poured something like $45 million into the American cattle industry. Much of this investment went into the lightly populated West, which had only just emerged from being little more than a well-traveled highway connecting the population centers on the East and West Coasts. Although we have no detailed analysis of the impact of the foreign money, it must have been disproportionately large, perhaps accounting for as much as 15 percent of the agricultural wealth of the region. Most of it was never repaid, but remained to enrich the American economy. It was indeed a rich legacy.[7]

Granville Stuart was finished in the cattle business when the winter of 1886–87 was over, but his retrospective on the era is interesting precisely because he had no reason to burnish the memory of the big foreign investors who had vanished from the scene. Stuart remembered these scions of wealthy families as men who loved the business and were anxious to learn. He vehemently disputed allegations of extravagance, contending that their usual fare on the range was the cowboy's diet of "beans, bacon, coffee, syrup, bread and beef." And he recalled the fact that millions of dollars in capital had come from those big outfits and vanished into the maw of the western economy. Without those millions, the pace of development of the West must surely have been slower.[8]

Finally, indictments such as those of John Clay must be weighed against the background of bitterness and prejudice that typifies many such critics; the foreign gentlemen were marching to a different drummer, and "different" too often becomes "wrong" in the mind of an unsympathetic observer. The local press was eager for sensational stories, and even a man as unassuming as Lyulph Ogilvy was moved to anger at the bias that was evident in stories about him; when a flamboyant soul like Frewen appeared, there was no limit to the "color" in the news accounts.

When an account in the press or elsewhere was wrong, it generally went unchallenged because a gentlemen does not descend to the level of a muckraking journalist. Thus the story of the Rocking Chair Ranche must depend on the testimony of John Clay, who held only 26 shares, not Lord Tweedmouth, who held 552.

The number of head of breeding stock they brought and the amount of money they spent in the West may at least be expressed on a numerical scale, but what of the more intangible contribution the British gentlemen made? Evidence of their influence abounds, if only in vulgar imitation and in the almost hysterical interest displayed by the Americans in royal weddings, engagements, and other social goings-on. But beneath all of these surface trappings, there was the ethos of the gentleman's approach to life, which had been subtly imparted in his numberless encounters on the plains. After they had gone, of course, few remained who could read Greek and converse comfortably in Latin; but other cultivated virtues took hold in the land and may be due in part to their presence there: the love of nature and the admiration for order, symmetry, balance, and restraint. In the otherwise unrestrained West, these civilized ideas made a spectacular contrast, and much of the criticism the gentlemen endured stemmed from the uncompromising character of that contrast. In short, they had a sense of style; and when they left there were still some who upheld the lofty principles they had so briefly espoused here.

British investors and cattlemen came to work and play in a new land, and to do so in a manner consistent with their training and ideals. The work they did was typically well planned, and they made use of the best available technology. That they did not succeed is largely due to the ephemeral nature of the range-cattle industry itself; it cannot be taken as a comment on the effectiveness of gentlemen as leaders in the economic arena (as they had long been in their country's military and political spheres). They gave of their fortunes and sometimes their lives, and some were scarred by the experience. But in so doing they enriched that part of the United States that grew up in the West, and when that region burst on the twentieth century, it did so with a richness, both financial and cultural, that would not otherwise have been possible.

Moreton Frewen was very much a part of this great adventure, contributing much from his boundless store of energy and enthusiasm. He was fascinated by the American scene and worked hard to understand Americans; he knew every president of the United States from Grant to Wilson, and while his political and economic ideas did not always persuade, they always had an audience. On the financial side Frewen exhausted his fortune in the American West, yet he could see the promise of his investments with a vision that was always long term. Nor did the later disasters kill the spirit that animated him, and even the "war to the knife" that once raged between him and Horace Plunkett finally cooled. Although their first chance meeting after they had both returned to England produced only "utter silence," older ties ultimately prevailed, and there was once again correspondence between them—although not about cattle but about British politics and the question of Ireland.

It was flood tide for the empire, but the strange anomaly of an island race governing half the world grew out of that collection of contradictions and contrasts that made up the British system. While the British fought many military skirmishes during the Victorian era, there was never a thought that those encounters were decisive in the exercise of power. Their empire was never a surly rabble presided over by uncounted legions, for these men ruled by presence rather than firepower. When at length the British left their colonies, much remained; and even though the statues of Victoria may have been pulled down, the new rulers and their descendants would still address the United Nations (and each other) in the tongue the British gave them, while their systems of law and government still bore traces of the original British pattern.

Even at the height of Empire, however, the world leadership of the mother country was beginning to give way to that of the new society across the Atlantic, a society in the midst of change and

turmoil. A searing national conflict had divided the nation only two
decades before Frewen and his colleagues came West, and that
war's end also dashed the South's dreams of national independence.
While the outcome of the Civil War was still in doubt, British sym-
pathies were often with the South, perhaps because, despite the
British abhorrence of slavery, the two societies shared some of the
same ideals. After the war, many of the leaders of the defeated Con-
federacy moved out on the raw plains to rebuild, and there they
met these other gentlemen of an older stripe; the heroic composite
that was "the Virginian" was Owen Wister's way of describing those
men and that encounter. They had much in common, indeed, for
men who had relied on breeding rather than guns to save their lives
in India and Africa were not so different from Wister's natural aristocrat, a man who could face down a gambler's insult with the now-
famous remark, "When you call me that, smile," rather than simply
shooting him.

Out on the range, the far-flung cattle operation was almost a domestic microcosm of the British Empire itself and some of the same
principles were employed to govern it, for scattered bands of intensely English cowboys could scarcely even count the masses of
cattle, let alone control them. Rather, the right to rule the range was
underwritten by a compact of like-minded men, and their presence
and agreement were enough to guarantee that it would function.
But it deserves to be remembered that the reason they were able to
agree on such a compact stemmed from their common attachment
to the principles of gentlemanly conduct.

These were the principles that Wister held up for admiration in
his book, and we can never know in what proportion he derived
them from the two sets of gentlemen. Of course it would be wrong
to make too much of the analogies between them, but it would also
be a mistake to neglect their true relationship. The ground of that
relation is a concept of nobility and honor; and these values have
lived on in our society, although they are no longer expressed in
terms of duty to sovereign and country, nor even in the simpler
formulations Wister chose for his Virginian. And while perhaps we
would not choose to trace the modern concept of a Peace Corps
back to Kipling's "white man's burden," the two ideas share a certain kinship. It is precisely in such kinships that one sees the deepest
legacy of all.

# Those Who Stayed Home

---◆---

While a number of aristocrats worked in the cattle industry in the United States in this period, an even larger number were connected with the range-cattle industry only as investors, rarely or never setting foot on the properties themselves. They are not the chief focus of our story, but they did have a profound impact on some of the companies and thus deserve comment.

It would be tiresome to list even a representative number of these more or less passive investors, but here we try to show some of the striking similarities among them (other than their titles) and to indicate some of the relationships. As one might expect, a sort of "culture" grew up around individual companies or groups of companies. A number of the shareholders were related, not only in the small companies (such as the Ione, in which E. S. R. Boughton and his brother-in-law, Sir Offley Wakeman, were both shareholders), but also in the larger public companies. Investments often showed up in groups of relatives, as the idea was passed around the family, although the Oxley Ranche was an extreme example of this tendency—all of the directors there were family members.

Dunraven took his brother-in-law into the Estes Park venture, and in the Powder River Company the duke of Manchester and his nephew were both shareholders. A number of directors and shareholders of that company were also clustered around the Beckett name. Ranching attracted the Anson family and their in-laws, the Beresfords; both were represented on the plains, although in only a few of the public companies. The Rocking Chair Ranche included not only Lord Tweedmouth and his sons, but also the earls of Ilchester and Aberdeen, who were family members and in-laws. In other companies, geography mattered more than anything else, and this was particularly true of those companies promoted in and around Dundee.

We shall first consider a fairly long list of men who were directors or shareholders in the Powder River Company. The chairman of that company was William Drogo Montagu, seventh duke of Manchester. The duke had been educated at Sandhurst and advanced to the rank of major in the army; he was also aide-de-camp to the governor of the Cape in 1843–44, and lord of the bedchamber to the Prince Consort. After marrying the daughter of Count von Alten of Hanover, he received the order of Iron Cross of Prussia.

Another member of the Powder River Company board was Manchester's nephew, Frederick Augustus Ker Bennet, second son of the earl of Tankerville. Bennet's brother-in-law, John William Ramsay, thirteenth earl of Dalhousie, was also an investor in the American cattle-ranch industry. Born in 1847, he was married to Lady Ida Louisa Bennet, daughter of the sixth earl of Tankerville.[1]

One of those who wanted to be a more passive investor than the trials of the Powder River Company would permit was the fourth earl of Rosslyn, Francis Robert St. Clair-Erskine, born in 1833; he was educated at Eton and Oxford before his military service, where he rose to the rank of brigadier general.

Then there was the Beckett group. A member of the Powder River Company board was Lord Henry Ralph Gilbert Nevill, born in 1854, son of the marquess of Abergavenny. Lord Henry was educated at Eton, and his second wife was the daughter of William Beckett (brother of Baron Grimthorpe), also a large shareholder of the Powder River Company; she was said to be the most celebrated hostess in London in an era when such a distinction was very lofty indeed. Her brother was Ernest William Beckett, another Etonian and later the second baron Grimthorpe, whom Lady Aberdeen called the most prominent member of the Parliamentary bar; he was a friend of Lord Randolph Churchill (and ultimately one of his executors) and was also on the Powder River Company board. Still another was Sir Frederick George Milner. A baronet born in 1849, educated at Eton and Christ Church, Oxford, and a member of Parliament in 1883–85, Milner was married to another daughter of William Beckett.[2]

Edward Plunkett, sixteenth baron Dunsany, born in 1808, was a representative peer from Ireland (only those Irish peers specially elected could sit in the House of Lords), and was married to Anne Constance Dutton, daughter of Baron Sherborne. A shareholder of the Powder River Company, he labored fruitlessly to make peace between Moreton Frewen and his son Horace Plunkett.

A number of Powder River Company shareholders were relatives or friends of the Frewens, and one such was Hugh Lowther, son of the earl of Lonsdale. When Moreton Frewen went to the United States, his good friend Hugh bankrolled him, in part by buying his horses (which were subsequently sold at a loss) and apparently also in part by direct loan. In any case, when the Frewen partnership was turned over to the new Powder River Company, Lowther consented to take shares in lieu of repayment of the debt from Moreton. Lowther's brother-in-law, Lord Douglas William Cope Gordon, third son of the tenth marquess of Huntly, was a director and shareholder of the Swan Company, until he resigned because of the pressure of parliamentary duties. Born in 1851, Gordon served in Parliament in the years 1876–85.[3]

Another friend of Moreton Frewen was Rowland Winn, first baron St. Oswald of Nostell Priory, who was born in 1820, educated at Eton and Cambridge, and sat as member of Parliament for North Lincolnshire from 1868 until he was ennobled in 1885.

Alfred Urban Sartoris, father of Lionel of the Douglas-Willan, Sartoris Company, was also a Powder River Company shareholder. He was born in 1826, and was married to the daughter of Viscount Barrington (she was also the aunt of Lady Clarendon). His brother had married Adelaide Kemble, an opera singer (and sister of the famous actress, Fanny Kemble), and their son married the daughter of President Ulysses S. Grant in an 1874 White House ceremony.

The Clarendon connection gave the Sartoris family in-laws a tie to the Oxley Ranche group. Edward Bootle-Wilbraham, first earl of Lathom, was married to Lady Alice Villiers, daughter of the earl of Clarendon. Born in 1837, Lathom was the son of Richard Bootle-Wilbraham, a member of Parliament; he was educated at Eton and Oxford and succeeded to his grandfather's title of Baron Skelmersdale in 1853. He was appointed lord in waiting to the queen in 1866 and created earl of Lathom in 1880. In 1874 he was named captain of Yeomen of the Guard and became lord chamberlain of her majesty's household in 1885. Lathom and Alexander Staveley Hill were the moving forces in the Oxley Ranch, and all of the board seats were held by them and their in-laws; Hill also served on the Spur board.

Edward Montagu Stuart Granville Montagu-Stuart-Wortley-Mackenzie, first earl of Wharncliffe, sat on the Powder River Company board and was chairman of the company after Manchester stepped down from that post. Born in 1827 and educated at Eton, he was created Viscount Carlton and earl of Wharncliffe in 1876. His wife was daughter of the earl of Harewood.

Still another Powder River Company shareholder was Thomas Francis Anson (Viscount Anson), eldest son and heir to the second earl of Lichfield. Born in 1856, Viscount Anson was educated at Harrow and Trinity College, Cambridge. He married Lady Mildred Coke, daughter of the earl of Leicester. Lady Anson's sister was married to Henry Strutt, second baron Belper, who was also on the Powder River board. He was born in 1840, educated at Trinity College, Cambridge, and sat in Parliament (1868–74 and again in 1880) until he succeeded to the peerage. Viscount Anson's younger brother, Claud, was in ranching in Texas. Born in 1864 and educated at Harrow, he married Lady Clodagh de la Poer Beresford, daughter of the marquess of Waterford and niece of Lord Delaval James de la Poer Beresford, who ranched in Mexico.

Sir John Leslie was another Powder River Company shareholder; his sister, Christina, was the marchioness of Waterford and aunt of Lord Delaval James de la Poer Beresford. (Another of the Waterford family, and a brother of Lord Delaval Beresford, was Lord William Leslie de la Poer Beresford, Frewen's friend, who had a thoroughbred horse venture with Pierre Lorillard.) Sir John Leslie, a baronet, was born in 1822 and educated at Harrow and Oxford; he was married to Lady Constance Wilhelmina Frances, sister of the earl of Portarlington, and his son John Leslie married Leonie Jerome, the sister of Clara Frewen and Lady Randolph Churchill.

William J. Mackenzie, an important preferred stock shareholder of the Powder River Company and a member of its board, became involved in the Prairie Company (chaired by the earl of Airlie), buying 200 of the 12,500 outstanding shares in that company. He was also the man behind the organization of Britain's largest mortgage investor in the United States, the Alliance Trust.[4]

David Graham Drummond Ogilvy, earl of Airlie, was descended from an ancient Scottish family that had sided with the Stuarts at the time when that unhappy family was in Catholic exile (while the sturdy Protestant Hanoverians reigned in London), and this fealty earned the Ogilvies the attainder of their titles by George I and George II. David, the ninth earl, was born in 1826, just a few weeks before George IV signed the law reversing the attainder of the house of Airlie.

Earlier in their history, their participation in other political struggles had resulted in the burning of Airlie Castle. According to family legend, the drummer boy charged with the responsibility of sounding the alarm was of the Cameron clan, and the Ogilvies suspected his failure of duty was deliberate; they therefore left him to perish in the burning castle, where he beat the drum to protest his innocence until overcome by the flames. Thereafter, so the legend goes, the Airlie drummer was always heard before the death of a member of the family. In fact, the daughter of the duke of Buccleuch, Lady Margaret Cameron, said she heard the drummer at Achnacarry Castle on the night in 1881 when the earl of Airlie died in far-off Denver.

Although this is the stuff of which drama is made, the Ogilvy family prided itself on the principles by which it lived and prospered, and sometimes suffered. Opposition to the English was carried to the point at which it was the ninth earl who first broke tradition by attending an English school and, more important, was also the first to marry outside Scotland. But he did not marry a shabby bride: She was the second daughter of Lord Stanley of Alderley, and it was said of the Stanleys (whose lineage could be traced all the way back to William the Conqueror) that they did not marry, they created alliances.

Lord Airlie was chairman of the Prairie Company and later set up his son Lyulph in ranching in Weld County, Colorado; his daughter, Lady Maude Josephy Ogilvy (who had accompanied him on trips to the West), was married to Theodore Whyte, the man who leased Estes Park from the earl of Dunraven to raise cattle in that beautiful setting. Lord Airlie was also chairman of the Dundee Mortgage Company and held three hundred shares in it; merchants and manufacturers were the other major shareholders. The Airlie estates were extensive, and much attention was devoted to their improvement; the earl was particularly interested in his herd of blooded Aberdeen Angus cattle on the Cortachy Castle estate.[5]

The man who headed the XIT ranch in Texas was William Montagu Hay, tenth marquess of Tweeddale, born in 1826 and educated at Haileybury. He was deputy commissioner of Simla and was a member of Parliament for the Taunton and Haddington district. His sister, Lady Elizabeth Hay, was the duchess of Wellington and had been Queen Victoria's mistress of the robes.

Then there was the Marjoribanks group. Dudley Coutts Marjoribanks, first baron Tweedmouth, was born in 1820 and educated at Harrow and Oxford. He was a barrister of the Middle Temple and sat as a member of Parliament from Berwick, where he owned a large estate. He was a shareholder in Meux and Company's brewery, and for a time director of the East India Company. He was created a baronet in 1866 and Baron Tweedmouth of Edington, County Berwick, in 1881. His wife, Isabella, was daughter of Sir James Weir Hogg, a baronet, who was chairman of the East India Company, a member of the India Council, and a member of the Parliament for Beverley and Honiton (his son, Isabella's brother, was created Baron Magheramorne).

Two of Tweedmouth's children also married well: Edward married Lady Fanny Octavia Louisa Spencer-Churchill, daughter of the duke of Marlborough, and Ishbel Maria married the earl of Aberdeen, as we have already noted. Daughter Mary Georgiana married Sir Mathhew White Ridley, a baronet, who sat as member of Parliament for Northumberland and Newcastle-upon-Tyne, and was also undersecretary of state for the Home Department and financial secretary to the Treasury. Sir Dudley's son Edward Marjoribanks, who received the Rocking Chair Ranche reports from his brother Archibald John, was educated at Harrow and Christ Church, Oxford, and was a member of the Inner Temple bar. He served in Parliament from 1880 until he succeeded to his father's title in 1894. A third son, Coutts, was briefly engaged in ranching in Dakota and then managed Lord Aberdeen's farms in British Columbia. As with so many of these men, the descriptions we have are far from complete; we only know that Coutts had huge feet.

Tweedmouth's son-in-law, John Campbell Gordon, seventh earl of Aberdeen, was born in 1847, the second son of the fifth earl. Educated at St. Andrew's and at Oxford, he succeeded to the title in 1870, when his brother George was swept overboard from the ship on which he was serving as mate under the alias George H. Osborne, a name he had used for the past four years in travels around the United States and at sea. Because of these peculiar circumstances, it was more than two years before John could establish to the satisfaction of the authorities that he was entitled to inherit the titles and the estate. Gladstone appointed him lord lieutenant of Ireland in 1881, and he served in that post until 1885. When the Liberals returned to power, Aberdeen hoped he would be returned to Ireland, but instead he was appointed governor general of Canada (1893), where he served until 1898. In 1905 he again served as lord lieutenant of Ireland, and in 1916 was created marquess of Aberdeen and Temair.

Aberdeen was a shareholder in both the Rocking Chair Ranche and the XIT. In 1887, the Aberdeens visited the Rocking Chair Ranche, a journey requiring Lady Aberdeen to spend the night on the floor of a wagon, and the last three days in a buckboard (although they stopped for the night at ranches along the way). The Coldstream Ranch in British Columbia was the first to establish orchards in the Okanagan Valley; from this beginning it was a profitable operation under Lord Woolavington, who bought it from Aberdeen.[6]

A nephew of Tweedmouth was also a Rocking Chair Ranche shareholder. He was Henry Edward Fox-Strangways, fifth earl of Ilchester, born in 1847 and educated at Eton and Oxford. He was married to Lady Mary Eleanor Anne Dawson, daughter of the earl of Dartrey.

Another gentleman of the Marjoribanks set was Lord George Granville Campbell, a younger son of the eighth duke of Argyll, who was important in the syndication business in Scotland; it was he who organized the syndicate that brought out the Cattle Ranche and Land Company, Ltd. Born in 1850, Lord George was the younger brother of the marquess of Lorne, who was for a time Governor General of Canada; another brother, Lord Archibald Campbell, was a partner in Coutts and Company.[7]

# Notes

---

**INTRODUCTION**

1. Owen Wister diary, July 21, 1885. University of Wyoming, Laramie.
2. *Denver Times*, April 11, 1896.

**CHAPTER 1**
Before the Herds Came

1. Kenneth L. Holmes, ed., *Covered Wagon Women: Diaries & Letters From the Western Trails, 1840–1890* (Glendale, Calif., 1983), 100.
2. Moreton Frewen to Clara Frewen, June 19, 21, 1884, Frewen papers, American Heritage Center, University of Wyoming, Laramie.
3. The silk hat had already appeared to displace the beaver hat, but demand for beaver furs remained strong for a time. Robert A. Murray, *Fort Laramie: "Visions of a Grand Old Post"* (Fort Collins, Colo., 1974), 12.
4. There are several stories of "spent" oxen turned loose on the range in the fall and found to be alive and fat in the spring. A Colonel Jack Henderson reported this phenomenon in Colorado in the spring of 1859 ("The Range Cattle Industry," University of Wyoming, Laramie microfilm). Granville Stuart reported that Captain Richard Grant and his sons were trading for spent stock as early as 1850. A similar story is told regarding Saskatchewan in the winter of 1873–74. (Granville Stuart, *Pioneering in Montana: The Making of a State, 1864–1887* [Lincoln, Nebr., 1977], 97, and *New York Times*, March 29, 1885).
5. T. R. Fehrenbach, *Comanches: The Destruction of a People* (New York, 1983), 541–42; Brian C. Pohanka, ed., *Nelson A. Miles: A Documentary Biography of His Military Career 1861–1903* (Glendale, Calif., 1985), 79;

and J'Nell L. Pate, "Ranald S. Mackenzie," in Paul Andrew Hutton, ed., *Soldiers West: Biographies from the Military Frontier* (Lincoln, Nebr., 1987), 177–92.

6. Jack D. Forbes, ed., *The Indian in America's Past* (Englewood Cliffs, N.J., 1964), 59–60.

7. House of Representatives, 49th Congress, 1st sess., *Ownership of Real Estate in the Territories* (July 31, 1886), 2.

8. William Curry Holden, *The Espuela Land and Cattle Company: A Study of a Foreign-Owned Ranch in Texas* (Austin, Tex., 1970), 80.

9. Bob Lee and Dick Williams, *Last Grass Frontier: The South Dakota Stock Growers Heritage* (Sturgis, S. Dak., 1964), 222–23, and *Sartoris, Douglas-Willan vs. U. S.*, 3 Riner 288–309 (1889) and *Canfield et. al., vs. U. S.*, 66 Federal 101 (1895). Bartlett Richards, a cattleman and banker, was the brother of future Wyoming Governor De Forest Richards. L. Milton Woods, *Sometimes the Books Froze: Wyoming's Economy and its Banks* (Boulder, Colo., 1985), 36.

10. Stibbard Gibson & Co. to Messrs. Fraser Stadart & Ballingall, February 16, 1883. Swan file, Western Range Cattle Industry Study, Colorado Historical Society, Denver; hereafter WRCIS.

CHAPTER 2
A New Class in a New Land

1. Frewen diary, June 1, 1883 (American Heritage Center, University of Wyoming, Laramie).

2. Daniel J. Boorstin, *The Americans: The Colonial Experience* (New York, 1958), 105.

3. Anita Leslie, *Clare Sheridan* (New York, 1977), 11.

4. Victoria succeeded William IV, the last of the Hanoverians, whose line ended with "an imbecile, a profligate and a buffoon," to quote Sir Sidney Lee. William fathered ten children, all of whom would have outranked Victoria in the succession had they been legitimate; in society they were collectively referred to as *les bâtards*.

5. In 1609, under Henry VII, the peers numbered only 44, a third of the total three hundred years earlier. By 1900, there were 522 peers, with dukes, marquesses, and viscounts accounting for fewer than 30 each, in the company of over 120 earls and 320 barons. John Cannon, *Aristocratic Century: The Peerage of Eighteenth-Century England* (Cambridge, 1984), 13, and John V. Beckett, *The Aristocracy in England, 1660–1914* (Oxford, 1986), 471.

6. One of Lord Pembroke's natural sons (by Catherine Elizabeth Hunter) attended Eton under the amusing name Augustus Retnuh Reebkomp,

the last two names being anagrams for Hunter and Pembroke. John Chandos, *Boys Together: English Public Schools, 1800–1864* (Oxford, 1985), 23, 34, and Cannon, *The Peerage of Eighteenth-Century England*, 40, 41.

7. Cannon, *The Peerage of Eighteenth-Century England*, 34, 35, and Chandos, *Boys Together*, 32.

8. Chandos, *Boys Together*, 177, 221, 222.

9. Ibid., 74–75.

10. Cannon, *The Peerage of Eighteenth-Century England*, 47, 48.

11. Cannon, ibid., 38; Chandos, *Boys Together*, 74, 218; Plunkett diaries, May 22, 1887; and Philip Mason, *The English Gentleman: The Rise and Fall of an Ideal* (New York, 1982), 163.

12. Owen Wister diaries, July 10, 1885 (American Heritage Center, University of Wyoming, Laramie).

13. The fifth duke of Norfolk, to name only one example of lunacy among dukes, was "an incurable maniac" who lived his later life confined in Italy; on the other hand, there have been so many examples of brilliant politicians, speakers, and writers among the dukes of Bedford as to cause one commentator to say that there are no "ordinary" Russells. Brian Masters, *The Dukes* (London, 1975), 18, 46.

14. Walter Edwards Houghton, *The Victorian Frame of Mind, 1830–70* (London, 1957), 283.

15. Byron Farwell, *Queen Victoria's Little Wars* (New York, 1972), 364–71.

16. Ibid., 32; and idem, *Eminent Victorian Soldiers* (New York, 1985), 93.

17. Moreton Frewen to Clara Frewen, October 13, 1880, Frewen papers, American Heritage Center, University of Wyoming, and Howard B. Lott, ed., "Diary of Major Wise: An Englishman Recites Details of Hunting Trip in Powder River Country in 1880," *Annals of Wyoming*, 12:2 (April, 1940), 85–118.

18. Anita Leslie, *The Marlborough House Set* (New York, 1973), 81.

19. Clodagh Anson, *Book: Discreet Memoirs* (London, 1931), 181.

20. David E. Shi, *The Simple Life* (New York, 1985), 164, 178, 192.

21. Plunkett diaries, May 31, 1887.

22. Lillie Langtry, *The Days I Knew* (New York, 1925), 38.

23. John V. Beckett, *The Aristocracy in England, 1660–1914* (Oxford, 1986), 350, 358.

24. Moreton Frewen to Clara Frewen, September 21, 1880. Frewen papers.

25. Ron Tyler, "Alfred Jacob Miller and Sir William Drummond Stewart," in idem, ed., *Alfred Jacob Miller: Artist on the Oregon Trail* (Fort Worth, Texas, 1982), 20, 21n, 36; John C. Ewers, *Artists of the Old West* (New

York, 1973), 98 ff., and Robert Combs Warner, *The Fort Laramie of Alfred Jacob Miller* (Laramie, 1979), 157 ff.

26. John I. Merritt, *Baronets and Buffalo: The British Sportsman in the American West, 1833-1881* (Missoula, Mont., 1985), 9.

27. Frances Fuller Victor, *The River of the West: The Adventures of Joe Meek* (Missoula, Mont., 1983), 234.

28. On one occasion, Gore and Bridger were discussing the Battle of Waterloo, and Bridger remarked that the British had fought better on that occasion than they had against the Americans at New Orleans. When Gore suggested that the later engagement was of lesser importance, Bridger disagreed, saying, "You can bet your pile on it!," Merritt, *Baronets and Bufffalo*, 92 ff, Milo Milton Quaife, ed., *Kit Carson's Autobiography* (Lincoln, Nebraska, 1935), 52–53; and Mari Sandoz, *The Beaver Men* (New York, 1964), 306.

29. After the French surrender, French guerrillas in the countryside were still harassing the German troops. Sheridan advised Bismarck to adopt the tactics he had used in the Shenandoah during the Civil War. Although Dr. Moritz Busch termed Sheridan's advice "somewhat heartless," Bismarck promptly issued orders to adopt it. Paul Andrew Hutton, *Phil Sheridan and His Army* (Lincoln, Nebr., 1985), 202, 204.

30. Gordon Hendricks, *Albert Bierstadt: Painter of the American West* (New York, 1974), 206 ff.

31. Marshall Sprague, *Gallery of Dudes* (Lincoln, Nebr., 1966), 97 ff.

32. Frewen to Clara, October 8, 1883.

33. Moreton Frewen to Clara Frewen, October 8, 1883, American Heritage Center, University of Wyoming, hereinafter cited as "Frewen."

34. Lord Fairfax was sixth baron Fairfax of Cameron. Rowland Berthoff, *An Unsettled People: Social Order and Disorder in American History* (New York, 1971), 83; and David Duncan Wallace, *South Carolina: A Short History* (Columbia, S. C., 1966), 196.

35. Michael Kamman, *Colonial New York* (New York, 1975), 281.

36. Near Roundup, Montana, was Rawdon George Grey Clifton, Baron Grey de Ruthyn, grandson of the marquess of Hastings (the baron had the right to bear the great gold spur at the coronation ceremony).

37. Wallop's enjoyment of the American West was cut short in 1925, when his brother unexpectedly died and the earldom descended on Oliver. He returned to England to estates that were even larger than his ranch, a reported 30,000 acres that earned him an annuity of $15,000. His son remained to carry on the ranching business, and his grandson, Malcolm Wallop, was sent to Washington to represent Wyoming in the United States Senate. *Washington Post*, December 28, 1917; C. Watt Brandon, "Wyoming Rancher Will Sit in Britain's House of Lords,"

*Wyoming Stockman Farmer*, January, 1932; and Jean Mead, *Wyoming in Profile* (Boulder, Colo., 1982), 113–14.

38. Lillie was extremely circumspect in her recollections of the men in her life. She recalled that the Prince was so intimidating that "he would have been a brave man who . . . attempted a familiarity with him." Perhaps so, but then, the Prince was more attracted to women. Lillie Langtry, *The Days I Knew* (New York, 1925), 71.

CHAPTER 3

The Serious Business of Ranching

1. Horace C. Plunkett diaries, September 3, 1883, University of Wyoming, hereinafter cited as "Plunkett diaries."

2. Scully bought some wet prairie land in Logan County, Illinois. Although the purchase price from the government would have been $1.25 per acre, he bought warrants for less than $.90 per acre, so that 8,520 acres cost him less than $8,000. Eventually, the specter of so large an operation in the hands of a foreigner drew considerable adverse comment, and it was largely because of him that the states in which he operated passed alien land legislation; Scully himself finally took American citizenship in 1900, apparently to protect the value of his estate for his heirs. The story of Scully's investments is told in detail in Homer E. Socolofsky, *Landlord William Scully* (Lawrence, Kans., 1979).

3. Plunkett diaries, May 17, 1881.

4. W. Turrentine Jackson, *The Enterprising Scott: Investor in the American West After 1873* (Edinburgh, 1968), 74–75.

5. Goodnight's name is associated with the Goodnight Trail from Fort Belknap, Texas to Fort Sumner, New Mexico, and with the Goodnight and Loving Trail from Fort Sumner to Cheyenne. J. Evetts Haley, *Charles Goodnight: Cowman & Plainsman* (Norman, Oklahoma, 1936), 198; and Anita Leslie, *Mr. Frewen of England* (London, 1966), 36.

Adair's estate in Ireland included 27,000 acres of grazing land. He came to the United States in 1866, and three years later married Cornelia Wadsworth, daughter of a Union general. He ran a brokerage firm in New York and then moved to Denver in 1875, after enjoying a buffalo hunt in Kansas in 1874. Adair was briefly a director of the Texas Land and Mortgage Company (he resigned in 1885). He and his wife were said to know everyone of note on two continents, and in any case, they were well-enough connected in London society to host the Prince of Wales. Dale calls Adair a British general, but apparently he had no military rank at all; Mrs. Adair was amused that he was successively "promoted" by Americans as he traveled, eventually becoming "Colonel" Adair. Edward Everett Dale, *Cow Country* (Norman, Okla., 1945), 102, Cornelia Adair, *My Diary: August 30th to November 5th, 1874* (Austin, Tex., 1965), 105, and Haley, *Charles Goodnight: Cowman and Plainsman* (Norman, Okla., 1949), 279–80.

6. It is said the name derives from the experiences of Francisco Vasquez Coronado's men, who crossed the plain in 1541 and set stakes along the trail, so they would not lose their way on the return journey. George A. Wallis, *Cattle Kings of the Staked Plains* (Denver, 1957), 7. David Dary says the name derived from the need to tie horses to stakes, since there were no trees. David Dary, *Entrepreneurs of the Old West* (New York, 1986), 273. Other students of Spanish argue that the name is a contraction of *llano destacado*, to denote an elevated area.

7. Donald R. Ornduff, *The First 49 Personalities in the Honor Gallery of the AHA's Hereford Heritage* (Kansas City, Mo., 1981), 56.

8. Jot Gunter, who worked with a firm of land locators out of Sherman, Texas, was surveying the canyon. Goodnight, who did not have enough money from Adair to buy the entire canyon, was able to get Gunter to agree to let him select 12,000 acres at 75 cents per acre. Goodnight then proceeded to make the selection, in a pattern he described as the "Old Crazy Quilt," covering all the water, "every place a man was liable to come." He also got the right to select another 12,000 acres the following year. Eventually, Adair authorized Goodnight to buy more land, and Goodnight bought "anywhere and everywhere," paying 20, 25, 30 and 35 cents; in one purchase in Tule country, he got 170,000 acres for 20 cents per acre.

When the first five-year partnership expired in 1882, it was possible to repay all of Adair's advances with interest at 10 percent, and show a clear profit of $512,000—a remarkable return. The partnership was extended for a further five years, with Adair again providing the financing to be repaid with interest at 8 percent and Goodnight now to receive $7,500 per year to manage the ranch. While this agreement was still running, Adair made his third trip to the ranch; he died in St. Louis on the way home, on May 14, 1885. Adair's interest in the ranch passed to his wife Cornelia, who divided the properties with Goodnight and continued to operate her share for a number of years thereafter. (She now made her home in England, where she was referred to as an "American hostess.") Anita Leslie, *The Marlborough House Set* (New York, 1973), 180.

9. Moreton Frewen, *Melton Mowbray & Other Memories* (London, 1924), 137–38.

10. Allen Andrews, *The Splendid Pauper* (London, 1968), 17, 27.

11. Frewen to Clara, October 29, 1881.

12. Lorah B. Chaffin, *Sons of the West* (Caldwell, Idaho, 1941), 177.

13. Dictated by Howard Michael, *Annals of Wyoming* 5:2 (October 1927), 46; and Plunkett diaries, October 2, 1884.

14. *Cheyenne Daily Sun*, May 1, 1879.

15. Frewen to Leonard Jerome, February 5, 1881; and Frewen to Clara, July 25 and October 15, 1880; and February 15, 1881.

16. Lowther's story is an interesting one. Born in 1857 and educated at Eton, he married the daughter of the marquess of Huntly. As a younger son, he thought it unlikely he would succeed to his father's title and, needing a source of ready cash, he sold outright his chance at the reversion of the Lonsdale estates; the price was reportedly £40,000, or nearly $200,000. When his brother, who was then earl, learned of the sale, he made the Lonsdale trustees buy back the reversion from the purchaser; as a consequence, when the earl unexpectedly died, so that Hugh did succeed to the title as the fifth earl, he did not receive the estates, since they now belonged to the trustees. (He did, however, receive a generous annual allowance.)

    Lowther did not lead a dull life. He reached the rank of major in the army and, on a trip to the Arctic, confirmed the presence of gold in the Klondike; he was an ardent sportsman, and crowds turned out to watch him ride to the royal enclosure at Ascot. He maintained splendid country establishments, and the sheep on his own land provided the wool for his clothes in Lonsdale tweed—the lighter gray for family members and the darker for the household.

17. Frewen to Clara, August 3, 1880.

18. Frewen to Clara, April 2, 1881.

19. Geoffrey C. Ward, *Before the Trumpet: Young Franklin Roosevelt, 1882–1905* (New York, 1985), 132. Stafford, then thirty, was still unmarried, and someone asked if the occasion stirred similar thoughts for him. He graciously complimented the ceremony ("pretty") but begged off on the marriage business, saying that his brother was already married and had heirs, which presumably was the only imperative then that could have urged him to the altar. Later, Stafford married another of Frewen's friends, the daughter of Lord Rosslyn.

20. When he died, Pierre Lorillard left his New Jersey stud farm to his mistress of long standing, a Miss Lilly A. Barnes. There was a persistent story that Lorillard had arranged for a mock wedding between Lilly and another woman dressed as a man, so that Lilly could be presented in society as a married woman. Woods, *Moreton Frewen's Western Adventures* (Boulder, Colo., 1986), 56.

21. *Cheyenne Daily Sun*, June 16, 1881.

22. A man using these loops was called a "dally welter," or one who wrapped the rope around the horn in the Oregon style rather than tying it fast, Texas style; the words are the cowboy's corruption of the Spanish *de la vuelta* (literally "of the turn"). Edward Charles Abbott and Helena Huntington Smith, *We Pointed Them North: Recollections of a Cowpuncher* (Norman Okla., 1982), 38n, 44. See also *Cheyenne Daily Sun*, June 3, 1879.

23. Walter Prescott Webb, *The Great Plains* (New York, 1931), 210.

24. It is interesting that if one turned the running W over, the mark was very like the rolling M used by the Wyoming Stock Growers Association for branding all mavericks.

25. There are two versions in the Antiquarian Press edition of the Clay book, xiv and 116, giving Luke Murrin's saloon and the Cheyenne Club as sources; the former version was apparently furnished by Ichabod S. Bartlett in an 1885 newspaper story. *Cheyenne Daily Sun*, February 14, 1885. Also, fourth annual report of the Hansford Land and Cattle Company, Ltd., for the year ended November 30, 1886. WRCIS.

26. Francis E. Warren to George H. Hull, Jr., December 18, 1885, American Heritage Center, University of Wyoming.

27. Harmon Ross Mothershead, *The Swan Land and Cattle Company, Ltd.* (Norman, Okla., 1971), 77–78.

28. The Spur used a 5 percent loss deduction, while the Powder River Company used 4 percent. Holden, *op cit.*, 57.

29. Plunkett diaries, June 22, 23, 1886.

30. Ibid., August 6, 1888.

31. Ibid., June 10, 12, 1883.

32. Ibid., May 20, 1887.

33. Frewen to Clara, October 11, 1886.

34. Frewen to Clara, May 13, 1880.

35. Abbott and Smith, *We Pointed Them North*, 57.

36. Ibid., 67; and Geoffrey Millais to Mrs. John Edward Millais, June 21, 1885, American Heritage Center, University of Wyoming, Laramie.

37. Edgar Beecher Bronson, *Reminiscences of a Ranchman* (New York, 1908), 52 ff.

38. A. S. ("Bud") Gillespie, "Reminiscences of a Swan Company Cowboy," *Annals of Wyoming*, 36:2 (October 1964), 199.

39. Abbott and Smith, *We Pointed Them North*, 129; and William Curry Holden, *The Espuela Land & Cattle Company: A Study of a Foreign-Owned Ranch in Texas* (Austin, Tex., 1970), 123.

40. Holden, *Espuela*, 161.

CHAPTER 4

Launching an Enterprise

1. Trevor West, *Horace Plunkett: Co-operation and Politics, an Irish Biography* (Washington, D.C., 1986), 24.

2. On a trip to Sherman to try to sell Frewen's cold-storage facility for used lumber, Plunkett saw the stone monument the Union Pacific had erected to the memory of Oakes Ames. He mused, "Funny the two monuments on the Rocky Mtns at Sherman, one on the south side of the track to Oakes Ames of Credit Mobilier fame & the other side the monument of Frewen's folly & the British investors' gullibility." Plunkett diaries, November 6, 1887.

3. The picturesque name Crazy Woman Creek is the subject of several stories: in one, a whiskey trader was killed by Indians in the presence of his young wife, who thereupon went mad; in another, a squaw survivor of an attack on an Indian camp thereafter lived alone on the creek. A third story is of a white woman, sole survivor of an Indian attack; she was said to have disappeared in the night following her discovery by white men. Mae Urbanek, *Wyoming Place Names* (Boulder, Colo., 1967), 50; and *Cheyenne Daily Sun*, February 20, 1881. Plunkett's choice is told in Margaret Digby, *Horace Plunkett, an Anglo-Irishman* (Oxford, 1949), 15, 21. Also Lawrence Milton Woods, *Moreton Frewen's Western Adventures* (Boulder, Colo., 1986), 189, Digby and R. A. Anderson, *With Horace Plunkett in Ireland* (London, 1935), 1, 2.

4. The company found a contractor to do the drilling for thirty-five dollars per linear foot. Plunkett diaries, November 17, 1882, May 9, 1883, and July 8, 15, and October 13, 1884.

5. Ibid., May 8, 15, 1884 and Ione Land and Cattle Co. Letterpress Book, 1884–1888, January 1, 7, 1887, University of Wyoming, Laramie, hereinafter cited as Ione Letterpress.

6. Plunkett periodically visited doctors with his physical complaints, with little satisfaction; on one occasion, he took an extremely sore throat to the doctor at Fort Fetterman, whose hospital was full of "broken & bullet pierced cowboys." The doctor looked at Plunkett's throat and pronounced it "a Hell of an old throat" but said that he would "scatter it," whatever that meant. Plunkett remarked, "He was the roughest looking practitioner I ever saw." Plunkett diaries, June 16, 23, 1884.

7. Dunraven was educated in Rome (and briefly in Paris) before going to Oxford; on his second visit to the United States in 1871, he met General Sheridan in Chicago, where they may have spent some time comparing notes on the Franco-Prussian War (Dunraven had covered the short conflict as a reporter for the *London Daily Telegraph* and Sheridan had visited the German command). Marshall Sprague, *A Gallery of Dudes* (Lincoln, Nebr., 1966), 150–52.

8. The valley was named for its first settler, a Kentuckian argonaut named Joel Estes, who had squatted on the land, built a couple of houses, and brought in a herd of cattle. Estes later became unhappy with the venture, as the snow was too heavy to permit winter forage without the need to feed hay, and the altitude did not agree with him. The Estes family lived there for only six years; he reportedly sold out his "claim" for a yoke of oxen. Ibid., 153; Edwin J. Foscue and Louis O. Quam, *Estes Park* (Dallas, 1949), 42; and Milton Estes, *The Memoirs of Estes Park* (Fort Collins, 1939), 13.

9. The secluded valley is drained by the Big Thompson River, which debouches down a canyon that was then impassable, and when Dunraven made the trip the only access was through an obscure trail guarded by Mountain Man Jim Nugent, who was supposed to be an English desperado. The Estes Ranch had by then been taken over by Griff Evans, a Welshman, who had about a thousand head of cattle grazing there.

10. Whyte, then twenty-six, had met Dunraven at the Corkscrew Club; he was the son of an Irish hussar and had trapped for the Hudson's Bay Company. Although Dunraven could not file on the land directly, it was easy to find ranch hands or other willing souls who would make the necessary filings, and by May 1874, four thousand acres had been filed on, with a thousand more in the next two months. It is said that most of the required buildings on the filings were merely four logs laid in a square, and there are allegations that the filings effectively controlled ten or fifteen thousand acres, but the land actually owned by Dunraven's company was considerably less.

All of this filing activity attracted attention, and soon a man named Thorn called the attention of the *Denver Tribune* to it; a scorching article resulted. At this point, Dunraven decided to abandon the homestead filings and purchase some of the land outright; he paid $1.25 per acre (although it is said that middleman costs raised the price to $5.00 per acre).

11. Dunraven seemed to think the range conditions were attractive and said the snow did not lie on the ground so as to cover the forage—the opposite of the experience of Estes a decade earlier. Nevertheless, the cattle venture under the Dunraven company was not a success—whether from poor grazing conditions or the lack of land (both reasons have been given)—and the earl then turned to development, constructing some facilities in the park, including the Estes Park Hotel (built in 1878 and known locally as the English hotel), on a site selected for it by Albert Bierstadt. (The artist had come to the park with Dunraven in 1876 and was commissioned to paint "Long's Peak," for which he was paid fifteen thousand dollars. The Bierstadt painting now hangs in the Western History Room of the Denver Public Library.)

June E. Carothers, *Estes Park, Past and Present* (Denver, 1951), 37, 41; Enos A. Mills, *The Rocky Mountain National Park* (New York, 1926), 1, 66; and Curt W. Buchholtz, *Rocky Mountain National Park: A History* (Boulder, Colo., 1983), 48, 69.

12. Later the earl returned to the United States in two attempts to win the America's Cup (in 1893 and 1895). Success also eluded that venture.

Dunraven still owned the Estes Park land, and by 1907, he had been joined in that investment by Arthur Hugh Smith-Barry, Baron Barrymore, whose first wife was Dunraven's sister (Lord Barrymore's second wife was the sister of John George Adair, the man who had introduced Moreton Frewen to ranching). In 1907, Dunraven and Lord Barrymore sold the Estes Park land to B. D. Sanborn and Freeman Oscar Stanley, of Stanley Steamer fame. Of course, the beautiful park was not destined to be a cattle ranch or even a mammoth development project. On January 26, 1915, President Woodrow Wilson signed the legislation creating Rocky Mountain National Park, containing 358.5 square miles; with enlargements in 1926 and 1930 the park now covers 405 square miles. W. Turrentine Jackson, *The Enterprising Scott: Investor in the American West After 1873* (Edingurgh, 1968), 102, Woods, *Moreton Frewen's Western Adventures*, 90, H. A. Doubleday and Lord Howard de Walden, eds., *The Complete Peerage*, (London, 1940), vol. 13, 16; and Carothers, *Estes Park, Past and Present*, 75. Whyte did stay on in the West, to become a Colorado cattle rancher whose hands learned to like him after they became used to his habit of using gates as hurdles to jump his horse. In 1896, Whyte left Colorado for England, where he later died. Damson Scrapbook, 43:539, Colorado Historical Society, Earl of Dunraven, *Past Times and Pastimes* (London, 1922), 151; Carothers, *Estes Park, Past and Present*, 42.

13. Edward used the "97" brand, which could be applied with the "76" branding irons, for an interesting labor-saving device.

Moreton was remarkably casual about Clara's flirtations with other men, although he did warn her about Lorillard's reputation for womanizing, saying, "It would not do for you in my absence to be about with him." Nonetheless, he was not above asking her to try to extract a better business deal from Pierre: "Work on PL if you can to sell me Taylor's calves." Frewen to Clara, September 6, 1882, and May 6, 1884. In London, Clara was besieged by Milam Obrenovich, exiled king of Serbia, who sent her daily floral offerings until she stopped him for appearance's sake; yet, when Moreton came to town, he went shooting with Milam! Woods, *Moreton Frewen's Western Adventures*, 92.

14. Woods, *Moreton Frewen's Western Adventures*, 56–58.

15. Consuelo was not especially inhibited, and on one occasion she removed her corset while riding in a carriage to a court ball. Another story is told of her return from Ireland, when a man teased her by

suggesting that she could give him the benefit of the wisdom of the Blarney Stone by giving him a kiss. Lady Mandeville thereupon informed the startled gentleman that she had sat upon the stone! Ralph G. Martin, *Jennie* (New York, 1972), vol. 2, 219.

16. The family name is confused in the records, since by royal license they were authorized to resume the Beckett name in lieu of Denison, and both names were used, with no apparent pattern.

17. Plunkett diaries, February 4, 1886.

18. Frewen to Clara, October 8, 1882, and Moreton Frewen to Messrs. Vivian, Gray & Co., June 25, 1882. Frewen papers.

19. In his prospectus for the company, Moreton claimed 10,000 head, but 3,247 of this count was really "97" brand stock, the separate property of Edward Frewen, who paid one-third of the expenses as well, and this herd was purchased directly from him by the Powder River Company. Tally book for Powder River Cattle Company, Ltd., in the possession of Fred E. Hesse, Buffalo, Wyoming, and Frewen to Clara, September 5, 1880. Moreton claimed he and Dick took $125,000 out of the partnership and still had a remaining value of $192,000, all from an investment of $114,000. There is no way to verify this, but Moreton's accounting was never particularly accurate. Woods, *Moreton Frewen's Western Adventures*, 70–71; and Frewen to Clara, September 18, 1882.

20. The checkerboard sections owned by the government were to be taken up by filings under the Desert Land Act, permitting a fence to be built around the whole property without leaving company land. The irrigated lands had been purchased for $5.00 per acre, and the pasture lands for $.50 per acre. The first payment of $.25 per acre had been made on the desert land filings, but soon the government returned the filings for more "proof." Ione Letterpress, October 27, 1884, and December 13, 1885.

21. John H. Douglas-Willan was born in Dublin in 1852 and came West in 1875, first to Colorado and then to Wyoming in 1877, at a time when, as he said, the Indians were still stealing cattle and horses and killing "a few men." In 1883 he and the Sartoris brothers formed the Douglas-Willan, Sartoris Company, which owned a 1,330-acre ranch and was capitalized at $543,000. In 1889 the partners branched out into mining and bought the Keystone mine and other mining properties on Douglas Creek, but the entire operation failed three years later. John J. Clay, Jr., *My Life on the Range* (Chicago, 1924), 151–52; Woods, *Moreton Frewen's Western Adventures*, 64–65, and interview with John H. Douglas-Willan, microfilm, Bancroft collection, University of Wyoming.

22. Marvin B. Rhodes, "Livestock in the Big Horn Basin," microfilm, University of Wyoming and Woods, *Moreton Frewen's Western Adventures*, 81; and Frewen to Clara, October 9, 24, 1880; July 16, 1883.

23. Geoffrey Millais to Mrs. John Millais, August 23, 1884, American Heritage Center, University of Wyoming, Laramie.

24. Frewen to Clara, August 4, 1883.

25. Frewen diary, October 23, November 26, December 10, 1884.

26. Ibid., January 7, 1884.

27. Frewen to Clara, March 7, 1881.

28. Frewen to Clara, October 20, 1882.

29. De Mores was heir to the Duc de Vallombrosa, and his mother was the daughter of the Duc des Cars, a French general who had been involved in the conquest of Algeria. De Mores was born in Paris in 1848 and spent two years at St. Cyr, the prestigious military school; he then attended Saumur, the cavalry school, in 1879. After all this fine military training, the marquis resigned his commission in the army because he could not stand the monotony of garrison life in peacetime. In Paris, de Mores met Medora von Hoffman, daughter of a New York banker, and they were married in Cannes in 1882; the couple made their way to New York, where the young marquis, who spoke polished English although with a French accent, joined von Hoffman's bank, learned about exchange, and made a study of the range-cattle business. His cousin, Count Fitz-James, had hunted in Dakota Territory, and it was his description of the area that gave the marquis the impetus he needed to launch his venture in the West.

30. The growth of Medora soon swamped Little Missouri, the existing town across the river, and by the middle of 1885, Medora had three hotels, a dozen stores, a church, a brickyard, and a teeming population. Although de Mores's house is called a château, it should not be confused in the reader's mind with the châteaus of France. The frame house had sixteen rooms downstairs and ten upstairs, but it was by no means opulent. The furniture was mostly American (often from Minneapolis), not French, and the china was Minton. There was a bathtub upstairs and a novel indoor "outhouse" in the bathroom. The marquise had her own bedroom, with connecting door to that of the marquis, which he shared with his "gentleman's gentleman," van Driesche.

31. The company, formed in 1883, had a capitalization of $200,000, and was 60 percent owned by de Mores; the balance of the stock was in the hands of Herman Haupt, Jr., and C. Edgar Haupt. Von Hoffman was treasurer of the company, and the ubiquitous van Driesche was vice president and cashier. The packing plant cost $250,000, and the massive foundations of some of the facilities can be seen at Medora today. The facilities were supposed to be the best technology available, and by the middle of June 1885, the plant was ready to receive cattle. It was expected that one hundred men would be continuously employed by the slaughterhouse, and in the winter more men would be

employed to fill the icehouses with ice cut from the Little Missouri River. In the winter of 1884, four thousand tons of ice were cut and stored in the icehouses, and the following year six thousand tons were stored.

To supply beef to the slaughterhouse, de Mores acquired rangeland, some in the name of the company, and some in his own name. There were 8,800 acres in Billings County and 12,000 acres in Burleigh County, most purchased from the Northern Pacific, although the marquis purchased scrip to buy some additional land.

32. De Mores's herd apparently was never larger than five thousand, since it was cheaper to buy beef than to raise it; soon, of course, there were no operations at all. The marquis left Medora in the fall of 1886, although he returned in 1887; his cattle losses in that terrible winter were fewer than for many, because his cattle were seasoned three- to five-year-olds. His last visit to Dakota was in 1889, and thereafter he devoted himself to causes in France. His courage at last brought his death in 1896 at the hands of the Tuaregs in North Africa. His widow remained in France, where his son inherited the dukedom he had not lived to receive. Arnold O. Golplen, *The Career of the Marquis de Mores in the Bad Lands of North Dakota* (Bismarck, N. Dak., 1979), 16–17; and Frewen to Clara, February 16, 18, 1885.

33. Frewen to Clara, September 3, 1884.

34. Ibid., May 16, August 1, 1884.

35. Ibid., Sept. 13, October 11, 16, 24, 1884.

36. Frewen to Clara, September 13; October 11, 13, 16, 24, 1882.

37. Woods, *Moreton Frewen's Western Adventures*, 95, 11.

38. Frewen to Clara, October 11, 1886.

39. Frewen to Clara, February 18, 1885, November 19, 1886.

40. Ibid., November 25, 1886.

41. Morton Frewen, *Melton Mowbray & Other Memories* (London, 1924), 234.

42. Lord Rosslyn to Frewen, August 15, 1885.

43. Woods, *Moreton Frewen's Western Adventures*, 130, 187–88.

44. Frewen, *Melton Mowbray*, 235.

45. Plunkett diaries, August 19, 1888.

CHAPTER 5
Kindred Spirits on the Range

1. Frewen to Clara, September 18, 1882.

2. *Live Stock Markets*, 44:7 (March 29, 1934).

3. John Clay, Jr., *John Clay, A Scottish Farmer* (Chicago, 1906), 32, 132–33, and *My Life on the Range* (Chicago, 1924), 226, 231.

4. Transcript of interview by John Cornelison of the Wyoming State Archives and Historical Department with Magnus Larson of Cheyenne, April 20, 1972, Wyoming State Archives and Historical Department, Cheyenne.

5. W. G. Kerr, *Scottish Capital on the American Credit Frontier* (Austin, Tex., 1976), 10; and John Clay to James A. Robertson, Esq., July 15, 1907, WRCIS.

6. Clay, *My Life*, 158; and Hansford Land and Cattle Company file, WRCIS. The company was liquidated in 1914.

7. Kerr, *Scottish Capital*, 24–25.

8. Clay, *My Life*, 131–32. Clay gives numbers slightly different than those presented by Richthofen. Walter Baron von Richthofen, *Cattle-Raising on the Plains of North America* (Norman, Okla., 1964), 54; and W. Turrentine Jackson, *The Enterprising Scot: Investor in the American West After 1873* (Edinburgh, 1968), 76, 90, 94.

9. Clay, *My Life*, 130; and Kerr, *Scottish Capital*, 19.

10. Mackenzie later left the Matador for eleven years to manage the Brazil Land, Cattle and Packing Company in São Paulo; its operations were on an even larger scale than the Matador, with three hundred thousand head of cattle on 10 million acres. Unfortunately, it collapsed after World War I, and Mackenzie returned to the Matador.

11. Clay, *My Life*, 130–39; and Jackson, *Enterprising Scot*, 125–26.

12. Clay, *My Life*, 20–24.

13. Ibid., 168–71.

14. Ibid., 158–66.

15. Ibid., 40–41, 85; and Bob Lee and Dick Williams, *Last Grass Frontier: The South Dakota Stock Growers Heritage* (Sturgis, S. Dak., 1964), 106, 255; and Kerr, *Scottish Capital*, 44.

16. Lee and Williams, *Last Grass*, 258; and Nellie Snyder Host, *Boss Cowman: The Recollections of Ed Lemmon, 1857–1946* (Lincoln, Nebr., 1969), 182–83.

17. Ibid., 49–50; and Donald R. Ordnuff, *The First 49 Personalities in the Honor Gallery of the AHA's Hereford Heritage* (Kansas City, Mo., 1981), 40.

18. Harmon Ross Mothershead, *The Swan Land and Cattle Company, Ltd.* (Norman, Okla., 1971), passim; and Swan file, WRCIS.

19. *New York Times*, May 18, 1887; and Jackson, *Enterprising Scot*, 88.

20. Swan file, WRCIS; and Mothershead, *The Swan Land and Cattle Company*, 80.

21. Clay, *My Life*, 209–229.
22. W. M. Pearce, *The Matador Land and Cattle Company* (Norman, Okla., 1964), 16.
23. Ibid., 23–24, 26.
24. Ibid., 28, 45.
25. Ibid., 84, 97, 49–50, 148–49.
26. Ibid., 34, 222, 225; and Kerr, *Scottish Capital*, 7; and Ordnuff, *First*, 49, 106.
27. Lewis Nordyke, *Cattle Empire: The Fabulous Story of the 3,000,000 Acre XIT* (New York, 1949), 62, and Rocking Chair Ranche file, WRCIS. John Clay, Jr., and his father each held £1,300 in shares, which explains Clay's knowledge of the inner workings of the ranch; they were the smallest shareholders. The Aberdeen story is in Archie Gordon, *A Wild Flight of Gordons* (London, 1985), passim.
28. John Campbell Hamilton Gordon and Ishbell Gordon, Lord and Lady Aberdeen, "*We Twa*": *Reminiscences of Lord and Lady Aberdeen* (London, 1926), vol. 1, 293.
29. Clay, *My Life*, 24. Clay refers to Drew as "Francis" in his book.
30. *New York Times*, October 14, 1887.
31. Some of the reports to the home office are on microfilm at the Panhandle Plains Museum, Canyon, Texas.
32. Estelle Tinker, *Archibald John Writes the Rocking Chair Ranche Letters* (Burnett, Tex., 1979), passim; "Nobility's Ranche: A History of the Rocking Chair Ranche," *Panhandle Plains Historical Review*, 15 (1942), 81–88; and liquidation notice, July 4, 1898, WRCIS.
33. Clodagh Anson, *Book, Discreet Memoirs* (London, 1931), 230.
34. Burke's *Peerage* sternly writes "unm." in its biography of Delaval, which may count for something against Flora's claims of marriage. Sir Bernard Burke and Ashworth P. Burke, *A Genealogical and Heraldic History of the Peerage and Baronetage* (London, 1930), 2423; also Anson, *Book*, 25, 230; *Washington Post*, January 1, 1907; Dawson Scrapbook, January 18, February 15, 1907; and Colin Richards, *Bowler Hats and Stetsons* (New York, 1966), 183 ff.
35. William Curry Holden, *The Espuela Land & Cattle Company: A Study of a Foreign-Owned Ranch in Texas* (Austin, Tex., 1970), 42–45, 52, 87; and Jackson, *Enterprising Scott*, 98.
36. Ibid., 143–45, 150, 152.
37. Ibid., 96, 99–100.
38. Ibid., 244.
39. The Capitol Reservation provision was approved by the voters in 1876, as a part of the new Texas constitution. Nordyke, *Cattle Empire*, 20, 22–24.

40. Ibid., 148, 187. Haley said flatly that the British owners had "almost nothing" to do with operations of the XIT. J. Evetts Haley, *The XIT Ranch of Texas and the Early Days of the Llano Estacado* (Norman, Okla., 1953), 73.

41. Cordia Sloan Duke and Joe B. Frantz, *6,000 Miles of Fence: Life on the XIT Ranch of Texas* (Austin, Tex., 1961), 109.

42. Lee and Williams, *Last Grass,* 162.

43. Nordyke, *Cattle Empire,* 190, 219, 251.

44. Duke and Frantz, *6,000 Miles of Fence,* 6, 7; and Nordyke, *Cattle Empire,* 246, 248.

45. *Washington Post,* January 13, 1918; and *Denver Post,* September 4, 1911; May 24, 1914.

46. Sand Creek Land and Cattle Company File, WRCIS.

CHAPTER 6

A Style of Business

1. John Roderick Craig, *Ranching with Lords and Commons: or Twenty Years on the Range* (Toronto, 1903), 14.

2. Plunkett diaries, June 6, September 1, 1881; July 22, 1885; and Frewen to Clara, August 15, 1880.

3. Bancroft collection, microfilm, University of Wyoming, Laramie.

4. John Clay, Jr., "The Cheyenne Club" *Breeders' Gazette,* December 21, 1916.

5. John Clay, Jr., *My Life on the Range* (Chicago, 1924), 272.

6. Ione Letterpress, November 9, 1884; May 7, 26, June 1, and September 16, 1886; and August 18, 1887.

7. Ione Letterpress, February 15, 1885.

8. Ibid., May 27, June 1, 1885.

9. Ibid., December 6, 1885.

10. Plunkett diaries, May 9, 30, June 3 and August 6, 1884.

11. Frewen to Clara, May 18, 1884.

12. Frewen to Clara, May 18, September 7, 1884, Lawrence Milton Woods, *Moreton Frewen's Western Adventures* (Boulder, Colo., 1986), 113–14; and Cheyenne Club minutes, July 7, 1881, American Heritage Center, University of Wyoming, Laramie.

13. Plunkett diaries, May 27, 1883; Geoffrey Millais to George Millais, July 31, 1886, American Heritage Center, University of Wyoming, Laramie; and Woods, *Moreton Frewen's Western Adventures,* 41.

14. Frewen to Clara, August 12, 1883.

15. William Curry Holden, *The Espuela Land & Cattle Company: A Study of a Foreign-Owned Ranch in Texas* (Austin, Tex., 1970), 53.

16. Frewen to Clara, October 7, 1882.

17. W. M. Pearce, *The Matador Land and Cattle Company* (Norman, Okla., 1964), 16, 41.

18. Ibid., 60.

19. Holden, *Espuela*, 196, 198; and Lewis Nordyke, *Cattle Empire: The Fabulous Story of the 3,000,000 Acre XIT* (New York, 1949), 175.

20. *Democratic Leader*, April 7, 1885.

21. Frewen to Clara, January 29, 1881.

22. Woods, *Moreton Frewen's Western Adventures*, 11.

23. A printed example of the blacklist was dated September 2, 1885. Wyoming Stock Growers Association files, American Heritage Center, University of Wyoming, Laramie. Also, Thomas Sturgis to Fred G. S. Hesse, April 23, 1884, Wyoming Stock Growers Association collection, Western Heritage Center, University of Wyoming and Woods, *Moreton Frewen's Western Adventures*, 14.

24. Nandi Moore, *Brands on the Boswell* (Glendo, Wyo., 1986), 29.

25. Canton gave 1854 as his birthdate in an interview with Ashley Bancroft in connection with the research on the Bancroft history of Wyoming. Interview (microfilm), September 16, 1885, Bancroft Collection, University of Wyoming, Laramie. His publisher gave the 1849 date in a 1930 letter, and when Canton died in 1927, the obituaries claimed he was seventy-six. Unsigned letter from Houghton Mifflin Company, October 9, 1930, American Heritage Center, University of Wyoming, Laramie.

    So much controversy surrounds Canton that it is difficult to sort the truth from the tall tales. Canton was supposed to have been one of the men Owen Wister used as a model for the Virginian in his eponymous novel. In any case, Canton was working for the Wyoming Stock Growers Association by 1877 or 1878, as field detective in Miles City, Montana, one of the extraterritorial posts maintained by the Wyoming association; in 1880 or 1881 he took the job of detective in Johnson County, Wyoming. The next year, he was elected sheriff of Johnson County and was reelected two years later, thereby joining in a single office the most important law-enforcement posts in the region.

26. Bob Lee and Dick Williams, *Last Grass Frontier: The South Dakota Stock Growers Heritage* (Sturgis, S. Dak., 1964), 197–98.

27. Mercer was born in Illinois in 1839, and had already lived a colorful life by the time he reached Wyoming. In Washington Territory, Governor William Pickering had appointed Mercer to stimulate immigration to Washington, and he headed east on a mission to hire twelve schoolteachers to come west; they all got married, according to Mercer. With this initial success behind him, Mercer hired a further three hundred

women the following year, and all of them also married, except one (who preferred to continue teaching).

From Washington territory, Mercer went to Oregon, where he engaged in shipping, but then started a newspaper at Albany, Oregon, called the *Oregon Granger*. Five years later, he went to Texas, where he started a number of papers; at one time, he was said to have owned all except one of the newspapers between Decatur, Texas, and the New Mexico line, including the *Texas Panhandle* at Mobeetie, the *Cross Timbers* at Bowie, and the *Wichita Herald* and the *Vernon Guard* at Vernon.

One story in the Cheyenne papers claimed that Mercer was the great-grandson of a man who owned one hundred acres in Manhattan that would soon be reclaimed at the end of a ninety-nine-year lease, but soon a newsworthy event arose nearer home. Mercer and Marney got into a dispute that erupted in a melee involving the entire Mercer family, the siblings armed only with rocks, and Mrs. Mercer wielding first a paperweight shaped like a bull, and later a majolica spittoon, which unfortunately was shattered by Marney's head. Asa S. Mercer interview with Ashley Bancroft, February 24, 1885. Bancroft Collection, American Heritage Center, University of Wyoming, Laramie.

28. The original printing of the *Banditti* is now rare, but there is no real evidence that its rarity stems from a "book burning" by cattlemen, as has sometimes been asserted.

29. *Morning Oregonian* (Portland), December 29, 1904.

30. Woods, *Moreton Frewen's Western Adventures*, 72–75.

31. Ibid., 69.

32. Ibid., 83–85; Frewen to Clara, September 17, 1883; and Plunkett diaries, September 12, 1883.

33. Nordyke, *Cattle Empire*, 160–61.

34. Harriet Ritvo, *The Animal Estate: The English and Other Creatures in the Victorian Age* (Cambridge, Mass., 1987), 45 ff.

35. Donald R. Ornduff, *The First 49 Personalities in the Honor Gallery of the AHA's Hereford Heritage* (Kansas City, Mo., 1981), 56, 58, 100; *Denver Post*, October 11, 1916; and *Rocky Mountain News*, October 1, 1879.

36. Ornduff, *First 49*, 41, 42 and Woods, *Moreton Frewen's Western Adventures*, 81.

37. Ibid., September 6, 1881.

38. Ibid., August 7, 1885; June 19, 1886.

39. Craig's story is told in John Roderick Craig, *Ranching with Lords and Commons* (Toronto, 1903); and it is also covered in Edward Brado, *Cattle Kingdom: Early Ranching in Alberta* (Vancouver, 1984), 81 ff.

**CHAPTER 7**
The Pearl of the Prairies

1. Agnes Wright Spring, *The Cheyenne Club: Mecca of the Aristocrats of the Old-Time Cattle Range* (Kansas City, Mo., 1961), 19; and Stelter, 439.

2. Edward Ring, "Denver Clubs of the Past," *The Colorado Magazine,* 19:4 (July 1942), 140. The club appears in the Denver city directories in 1885–86 and 1890–94.

3. Curtis Harnack, *Gentlemen on the Prairie* (Ames, Iowa, 1985), 7, 139–41; and Lawrence Milton Woods, *Moreton Frewen's Western Adventures,* (Boulder, Colo., 1986), 128.

4. Clay, *My Life,* 68.

5. *By-Laws, Articles of Incorporation and House Rules, with List of Officers and Members of the Cheyenne Club* (Cheyenne, 1888); John Rolf Burroughs, *Guardian of the Grasslands* (Cheyenne, 1971), 87–90; and Cheyenne Club Minutes, October 20, 1881.

6. Minutes of special board meeting of the Cheyenne Club, September 16, 1882, American Heritage Center, University of Wyoming, Laramie.

7. Thomas Mesker's painting, a copy of Paul Potter's "Two Bulls," has two holes in it. See also Spring, *The Cheyenne Club,* 6; and Cheyenne Club Minutes, September 15, 1895.

8. Ibid., 4.

9. Ibid., 4–6.

10. Ibid., 7.

11. Ibid., 10.

12. Plunkett diaries, June 26, July 1, 15, October 4, 1884; and Spring, *The Cheyenne Club,* 6.

13. *Cheyenne Daily Leader,* October 1, 1881.

14. *Cheyenne Daily Leader,* March 25, 1882; and *Cheyenne Daily Sun,* March 25, April 8, 1882.

15. *Cheyenne Daily Sun,* June 3, 9, 12, 1884; and December 30, 1885.

16. Plunkett diaries, September 26, 1883, October 14, 1884; and Gilbert Arthur Stelter, "The Urban Frontier: A Western Case Study, Cheyenne, Wyoming 1867–1887" (Ph.D. diss., University of Alberta, Edmonton, 1968), 444.

17. *Cheyenne Daily Sun,* June 16, 1881.

18. Spring, *The Cheyenne Club,* 20.

19. Woods, *Moreton Frewen's Western Adventures,* 11.

20. Ibid., 3, 10, 12, 15, 21, 25.

21. *Cheyenne Daily Sun,* December 8, 1882; April 19, 1884.

22. Ibid., December 9, 1882.
23. Spring, *The Cheyenne Club*, 27–29.

CHAPTER 8
Relations with the "Natives"

1. *Cheyenne Daily Sun*, August 14, 1881. Although Ogilvy's father was an earl, only the eldest son could enjoy the courtesy title "Lord Ogilvy."
2. Frewen to Clara, February 20, May 2, 1881.
3. Plunkett diaries, October 11, 1881; and Frank M. Canton to Thomas Sturgis, November 11, 1881, Wyoming Stock Growers Association Collection, American Heritage Center, University of Wyoming.
4. *Cheyenne Daily Leader*, September 4, 1879; *Democratic Leader*, March 3, 1885; and *New York Times*, August 18, 1885.
5. W. G. Kerr, *Scottish Capital on the American Credit Frontier* (Austin, Tex., 1976), 32.
6. Estelle Tinker, "Nobility's Ranche: A History of the Rocking Chair Ranche," *Panhandle Plains Historical Review*, 15 (1942), passim.
7. Lewis Nordyke, *Cattle Empire: The Fabulous Story of the 3,000,000 Acre XIT* (New York, 1949), 77.
8. William Curry Holden, *The Espuela Land & Cattle Company: A Study of a Foreign-Owned Ranch in Texas* (Austin, Tex., 1970), 180.
9. Estelle Tinker, *Archibald John Writes the Rocking Chair Ranche Letters* (Burnett, Tex., 1979), 3, 5, 6, 9, 49; John Clay, Jr., *My Life on the Range* (Chicago, 1924), 173; Holden, *Espuela*, 174–75; and Nordyke, *Cattle Empire*, 118.
10. William French, *Further Recollections of a Western Ranchman, New Mexico, 1883–1899: Being Volume II of Some Recollections of a Western Ranchman* (New York, 1965), 287–89; and Frewen Letterpress, August 9, 1883, American Heritage Center, University of Wyoming, Laramie.
11. Frewen to Clara, March 1, 1881; W. M. Pearce, *The Matador Land and Cattle Company* (Norman, Okla., 1964), 56, Holden, *Espuela*, 89; and Nordyke, *Cattle Empire*, 90, 148, 195.
12. Frank Law to Julius C. Gunter, December 10, 1895 and James C. Johnston to John Nelson, February 27, 1896. Prairie letterbook, WRCIS.
13. Nordyke, *Cattle Empire*, 105.
14. Ione Letterpress, November 9, December 6, 1884.
15. Ione Letterpress, March 8, 1887.
16. William Manchester, *The Last Lion: Winston Spencer Churchill* (New York, 1983), 454.
17. Ibid., 181, 186; Frewen to Clara, May 7, 1882; and *Denver Times*, September 30, 1907.

18. *Washington Post,* June 12, 1916.
19. Edmond, Baron de Mandat-Grancey, tr. William Conn, Intro. Howard R. Lamar, *Cow-Boys and Colonels: Narrative of a Journey Across the Prairie and Over the Black Hills of Dakota* (Lincoln, Nebr., 1984), Intro. (n.p.), 218; and WRCIS.
20. Herman Hagedorn, *Roosevelt in the Bad Lands* (New York, 1921), 62, 336–37.
21. Donald Dresden, *The Marquis de Mores: Emperor of the Bad Lands* (Norman, Okla., 1970), 114–16. See also Hagedorn, *Roosevelt in the Bad Lands,* 349.
22. Anita Leslie, *The Marlborough House Set* (New York, 1973), 57–58.
23. Ibid., 59–60.
24. Randolph S. Churchill, *Winston S. Churchill,* vol. 1: *Youth, 1874–1900* (Boston, 1966).
25. Ibid., 63; *Democratic Leader,* January 15, 1885; and Leslie, *Marlborough House,* 63.
26. Dawson Scrapbook, Colorado Historical Society, vol. 66.
27. Ibid.
28. Ibid., Leslie, *Marlborough House,* 64; and Aylesford file, American Heritage Center, University of Wyoming, Laramie.
29. Mabell Frances Ogilvy, Countess of Airlie, *Thatched with Gold* (London, 1962), 46; *Denver Post,* October 11, 1916; *Denver Times,* September 20, 1907; *Washington Post,* September 26, 1907; May 5, 1908; John Dugan, *Greeley and Weld County* (Norfolk, Va., 1986), 191; James H. Baker, ed., *History of Colorado* (Denver, Colo., 1927), vol. 4, 65–66; *Rocky Mountain News,* May 18, 1881; and *Denver Times,* April 11, 1896. See also Corinne Hunt, *The Brown Palace Story* (Denver, 1982), 45–46, where Hunt has Lyulph renouncing his title for a fair maiden. Alas, he had none to renounce.
30. Plunkett diaries, July 21, 1881.

### CHAPTER 9
### Hard Times

1. *Cheyenne Daily Sun,* February 4, 1887.
2. Plunkett diaries, June 19, September 8, 1885.
3. Plunkett diaries, October 26, 1885.
4. *Big Horn Sentinel,* March 27, 1886; and *Rawlins Journal,* June 8, 1885.
5. Lawrence Milton Woods, *Moreton Frewen's Western Adventures* (Boulder, Colo., 1986), 185–86, John Clay, Jr., *My Life on the Range* (Chicago, 1924), 123–28; and Plunkett diaries, December 19, 31, 1885; January 20, 1886.

6. Plunkett diaries, June 18, 1886.

7. *Democratic Leader,* July 26, 1885; and W. Turrentine Jackson, *The Enterprising Scott: Investor in the American West After 1873* (Edinburgh, 1968), 103.

8. Frewen to Clara, August 29, September 9, 1886.

9. *Democratic Leader,* January 8, March 3, 1887.

10. *Northwestern Live Stock Journal,* December 31, 1886; March 18, April 29, 1887; Granville Stuart, *Pioneering in Montana: The Making of a State, 1864–1887* (Lincoln, Nebr., 1977), 234–36; *Big Horn Sentinel,* January 8, 29, 1887; *New York Times,* February 17, 1887; and Swan file, WRCIS.

11. John Hunton to Mr. Tillotson, February 17, 1887; and Hunton to Col. W. G. Bullock, April 3, May 24, 1887, American Heritage Center, University of Wyoming, Larmie.

12. Bob Lee and Dick Williams, *Last Grass: The South Dakota Stock Growers Heritage* (Sturgis, S. Dak., 1964), 154; and Brian W. Dippie, ed., *"Paper Talk": Charlie Russell's American West* (New York, 1979), 22. The original of the letter is owned by the Montana Stock Growers Association in Helena; the painting based on it is in the Whitney Gallery of Western Art, Cody, Wyoming.

13. Plunkett diaries, June 2, July 2, 7, 1887; Woods, *Moreton Frewen's Western Adventures,* 187; and Alexander Bowie statement (taken in 1887), Swan file, WRCIS. Bowie said the Swan herds were divided equally east and west of the Black Hills.

14. Plunkett diaries, August 19, 20, 1887.

15. Clay, *My Life,* 176–80.

16. *New York Times,* March 6, 1887.

17. *Cheyenne Daily Sun,* December 31, 1886.

18. Lee, 107; and Plunkett diaries, February 15, March 1, 1887.

19. Ione Letterpress, November 13, 1886 and November 11, 1887.

20. Frewen to Clara, September 17, 1886.

21. Joseph M. Carey, "Early Days of the Cattle Business," April, 1915 (microfilm), University of Wyoming, Laramie; Fred G. S. Hesse to Frank A. Kemp, September 4, 1888, in possession of Fred E. Hesse, Buffalo, Wyoming; and Minutes of the Executive Committee, August 4, 1887, Wyoming Stock Growers Association collection, American Heritage Center, University of Wyoming, Laramie.

22. Plunkett diaries, October 20, 21, November 2, 6, 8, 10, 1887; and Cheyenne Club minutes, November 11, 1888, April 3, 1890, American Heritage Center, University of Wyoming, Laramie.

23. W. Turrentine Jackson, "The Administration of Thomas Moonlight," *Annals of Wyoming,* 18:2 (July 1946), 147; *Big Horn Sentinel,* May 28, 1887; and *Cheyenne Daily Sun,* December 9, 1886.

24. *Cheyenne Daily Sun*, January 16, 1886.

25. Lee, 62, 75; and Stuart, 148–49.

26. Fred G. S. Hesse to Horace Plunkett, July 10, 1889, in possession of Fred E. Hesse, Buffalo, Wyoming; and *Cheyenne Daily Leader*, December 21, 1883.

27. Clay, *My Life*, 142, 276.

28. Joseph M. Carey to Edward T. David, May 21, 1892, American Heritage Center, University of Wyoming, Laramie.

29. The transcript of *State of Wyoming* vs. *Herbert Brink* is in the William L. Simpson collection at the American Heritage Center, University of Wyoming, Laramie. The story of the raid is told in Jack Gage, *Ten Sleep and No Rest* (Casper, Wyo., 1958); Gage uses fictitious names for two of the participants and one of the witnesses, but the book is based on the actual transcript.

30. Clay, *My Life*, 91–97; W. G. Kerr, *Scottish Capital on the American Credit Frontier* (Austin, Tex., 1976), 25; and Jackson, *Enterprising Scot*, 128, 134.

31. Clay, *My Life*, 146.

32. Donald H. Walsh, *Pierre Wibaux: Cattle King* (Bismarck, N. Dak., 1953), 1–4; and Bertha M. Kuhn, "The W-Bar Ranch on the Missouri Slope," *Collections of the State Historical Society of North Dakota* (1933), vol. 5, 159–66.

33. Ibid., 9, 10; and Fred G. S. Hesse to Horace Plunkett, June 6, September 9, 1889, in possession of Fred E. Hesse, Buffalo, Wyoming.

34. Walsh, *Wibaux*, 5, 6.

35. Fred G. S. Hesse to Horace Plunkett, July 22, 1891, in possession of Fred E. Hesse, Buffalo, Wyoming.

CHAPTER 10
The Legacy of the Free Range

1. Frewen to Clara, September 1882.

2. Don D. Walker, *Clio's Cowboys* (Lincoln, Nebr., 1981), 85.

3. Jimmy M. Skaggs, *Prime Cut: Livestock Raising and Meatpacking in the United States, 1607–1983* (College Station, Tex., 1986), 89.

4. W. M. Pearce, *The Matador Land and Cattle Company* (Norman, Okla., 1964), 35–36, 100–101; and Lewis O. Saum, "The Marquis de Mores: Instrument of American Progress," *North Dakota History*, 36:2 (Spring 1969), 153–54.

5. Auguste-Maurice Barrès, *L'Oeuvre de Maurice Barrès* (Paris, 1966), vol. 5, 303.

6. Lawrence Milton Woods, *Sometimes the Books Froze: Wyoming's Economy and Its Banks* (Boulder, Colo., 1985), 102.

7. The 15 percent share is based on 1880 data for Montana, Wyoming, Colorado, New Mexico, and Texas, the states and territories where most foreign activity was concentrated. See Richard A. Esterlin, "State Income Estimates," in Simon Kuznets and Doroth Swaine Thomas, *Population Redistribution and Economic Growth: United States, 1870–1950,* Philadelphia, 1957), vol. 1, 929–30.

8. Granville Stuart, *Pioneering in Montana: The Making of a State, 1864–1887* (Lincoln, Nebr., 1977), 238–39.

**APPENDIX**
Those Who Stayed Home

1. Lawrence Milton Woods, *Moreton Frewen's Western Adventures* (Boulder, Colo., 1986), 150.

2. John Campbell Hamilton Gordon and Ishbell Gordon, Lord and Lady Aberdeen, *"We Twa": Reminiscences of Lord and Lady Aberdeen,* vol. 1 (London, 1926), 71.

3. Frewen to Clara, March 24, 1883; and Allen Andrews, *The Splendid Pauper* (London, 1968), 75–76.

4. W. Turrentine Jackson, *The Enterprising Scot: Investor in the American West After 1873* (Edinburgh, 1968), 26; and W. G. Kerr, *Scottish Capital on the American Credit Frontier* (Austin, Tex., 1976), 21, 182.

5. The attainders of the Airlie honors have created great confusion in identifying the earls by number. Burke's *Peerage* calls David Graham Drummond Ogilvy the ninth earl, while the *Scots Peerage* calls him the seventh and *The Complete Peerage* opts for seventh or fifth. Kerr, *Scottish Capital,* 171–72 and the Reverend William Wilson, *The House of Airlie* (London, 1924), 249, 253.

6. Archie Gordon, *A Wild Flight of Gordons* (London, 1985), *passim.*

7. Kerr, *Scottish Capital,* 20.

# Selected Bibliography

———◆———

ABBOTT, EDWARD CHARLES, and HELENA HUNTINGTON SMITH. *We Pointed Them North: Recollections of a Cowpuncher* (Norman, Okla., 1982).

ADAIR, CORNELIA. *My Diary: August 30th to November 5th, 1874* (Austin, Tex., 1965).

ALTER, J. CECIL. *Jim Bridger* (Norman, Okla., 1967).

ANDERSON, R. A. *With Horace Plunkett in Ireland* (London, 1935).

ANDREWS, ALLEN. *The Splendid Pauper* (London, 1968).

ANSON, CLODAGH. *Book: Discreet Memoirs* (London, 1931).

BAILLIE-GROHMAN, WILLIAM ADOLPH. *Camps in the Rockies* (New York, 1882).

———. *Fifteen Years' Sport and Life* (London, 1900).

BAKER, JAMES H. *History of Colorado*, 5 vols. (Denver, Colo., 1927).

BANCROFT, HUBERT HOWE. Bancroft Collection, University of Wyoming, Laramie. Microfilm.

———. *History of the North Mexican States and Texas* (San Francisco, 1889).

BARRÈS, AUGUSTE-MAURICE. *L'Oeuvre de Maurice Barrès* (Paris, 1966).

BECKETT, JOHN V. *The Aristocracy in England, 1660–1914* (Oxford, 1986).

BERTHOFF, ROWLAND. *An Unsettled People: Social Order and Disorder in American History* (New York, 1971).

BLAKE, ROBERT. *Disraeli* (New York, 1967).

BOORSTIN, DANIEL J. *The Americans: The Colonial Experience* (New York, 1958).

BRADO, EDWARD. *Cattle Kingdom: Early Ranching in Alberta* (Vancouver, 1984).

227

BRONSON, EDGAR BEECHER. *Reminiscences of a Ranchman* (New York, 1908).

BUCHHOLTZ, C. W. *Rocky Mountain National Park, A History* (Boulder, Colo., 1983).

BURROUGHS, JOHN ROLF. *Guardian of the Grasslands* (Cheyenne, 1971).

CANNON, JOHN. *Aristocratic Century: The Peerage of Eighteenth-Century England* (Cambridge, 1984).

CANTON, FRANK M. *Frontier Trails: The Autobiography of Frank M. Canton* (New York, 1930).

CAROTHERS, JUNE E. *Estes Park, Past and Present* (Denver, Colo., 1951).

CATTON, BRUCE. *The Coming Fury* (Garden City, N.Y., 1961).

CECIL, DAVID. *Melbourne* (New York, 1939).

CHANDOS, JOHN. *Boys Together: English Public Schools, 1800–1864* (Oxford, 1985).

CHAFFIN, LORAH B. *Sons of the West* (Caldwell, Idaho, 1941).

CHITTENDEN, HIRAM MARTIN. *The American Fur Trade of the Far West.* 2 vols. (New York, 1936).

CHURCHILL, RANDOLPH S. *Winston S. Churchill,* vol. I: *Youth, 1874–1900* (Boston, 1966).

CLAY, JOHN, Jr. *John Clay, A Scottish Farmer* (Chicago, 1906).

——. *My Life on the Range* (Chicago, 1924).

CRAIG, JOHN RODERICK. *Ranching with Lords and Commons* (Toronto, 1903).

DALE, EDWARD EVERETT. *Cow Country* (Norman, Okla., 1945).

DARY, DAVID. *Cowboy Culture: A Saga of Five Centuries* (New York, 1981).

——. *Entrepreneurs of the Old West* (New York, 1986).

DAVID, ROBERT B. *Malcolm Campbell, Sheriff* (Casper, Wyo., 1932).

DAVIES, GENERAL HENRY E. *Ten Days on the Plains* (Dallas, 1985).

DAVIS, ELMER. *History of the New York Times, 1851–1921* (New York, 1921).

DAWSON, THOMAS, Scrapbooks. Colorado Historical Society, Denver.

DIGBY, MARGARET. *Horace Plunkett, an Anglo-Irishman* (Oxford, 1949).

DIPPIE, BRIAN W., ed. *"Paper Talk": Charlie Russell's American West* (New York, 1979).

DONALDSON, Thomas. *The Public Domain: Its History with Statistics* (New York, 1970).

DRESDEN, DONALD. *Marquis de Mores: Emperor of the Bad Lands* (Norman, Okla., 1970).

DUGAN, JOHN. *Greeley and Weld County* (Norfolk, Va., 1986).

DUKE, CORDIA SLOAN, and JOE B. FRANTZ. *6000 Miles of Fence: Life on the XIT Ranch of Texas* (Austin, Tex., 1961).

ESTES, MILTON. *Memoirs of Estes Park* (Fort Collins, Colo., 1939).

EWERS, JOHN C. *Artists of the Old West* (New York, 1973).

FARWELL, BYRON. *Queen Victoria's Little Wars* (New York, 1972).

———. *Eminent Victorian Soldiers* (New York, 1985).

FORBES, JACK D., ed. *The Indian in America's Past* (Englewood Cliffs, N.J., 1964).

FOSCUE, EDWIN J., and LOUIS O. QUAM. *Estes Park* (Dallas, 1949).

FRASER, ANTONIA. *Cromwell: The Lord Protector* (New York, 1974).

FEHRENBACH, T. R. *Comanches: The Destruction of a People* (New York, 1983).

FRENCH, WILLIAM. *Further Recollections of a Western Ranchman, New Mexico, 1883-1899: Being Volume II of Some Recollections of a Western Ranchman* (New York, 1964).

FREWEN, MORETON. Frewen Diary. American Heritage Center, University of Wyoming, Laramie.

———. Frewen Letterpress. American Heritage Center, University of Wyoming, Laramie.

———. Frewen Letters. American Heritage Center, University of Wyoming, Laramie.

FREWEN, MORETON, *Melton Mowbray & Other Memories* (London, 1924).

FRINK, MAURICE. *Cow Country Cavalcade: Eighty Years of the Wyoming Stock Growers Association* (Denver, 1954).

GAGE, JACK R. *Ten Sleep and No Rest* (Casper, Wyo., 1958).

GATES, PAUL W. *The History of Public Land Law Development* (Washington, D.C., 1968).

GOFF, RICHARD, and ROBERT H. MCCAFFREE. *Century in the Saddle* (Denver, 1967).

GOLPLEN, ARNOLD O. *The Career of the Marquis de Mores in the Bad Lands of North Dakota* (Bismarck, N. Dak., 1979).

GORDON, ARCHIE. *A Wild Flight of Gordons* (London, 1985).

GORDON, JOHN CAMPBELL HAMILTON-, and ISHBELL GORDON, LORD and LADY ABERDEEN. *"We Twa": Reminiscences of Lord and Lady Aberdeen.* 2 vols. (London, 1926).

GOWANS, FRED R. *Rocky Mountain Rendezvous: A History of the Fur Trade Rendezvous 1825-1840* (Provo, Utah, 1976).

GREELEY, HORACE. *An Overland Journey From New York to San Francisco in the Summer of 1859* (New York, 1860).

HAGEDORN, HERMAN. *Roosevelt in the Bad Lands* (New York, 1921).

HAINLIN, LEWIS ALBERT. *Moreton Frewen: His Life*. Ph.d. dissertation, University of Missouri, Columbia, 1968.

HALEY, J. EVETTS. *Charles Goodnight: Cowman and Plainsman* (Norman, Okla., 1949).

———. *The XIT Ranch of Texas and the Early Days of the Llano Estacado* (Norman, Okla., 1953).

HARNACK, CURTIS. *Gentlemen on the Prairie* (Ames, Iowa, 1985).

HENDRICKS, GORDON. *Albert Bierstadt: Painter of the American West* (New York, 1974).

HIGGINSON, A. HENRY. *British and American Sporting Authors* (Berryville, Va., 1949).

HOLDEN, WILLIAM CURRY. *The Espuela Land & Cattle Company: A Study of a Foreign-Owned Ranch in Texas* (Austin, Tex., 1970).

HOLMES, KENNETH L. *Covered Wagon Women: Diaries & Letters From the Western Trails, 1840–1890* (Glendale, Calif., 1983).

HOST, NELLIE SNYDER. *Boss Cowman: The Recollections of Ed Lemmon, 1847–1946* (Lincoln, Nebr., 1969).

HOUGHTON, WALTER E. *The Victorian Frame of Mind, 1830–70* (London, 1957).

HUNT, CORINNE. *The Brown Palace Story* (Denver, 1982).

HUTTON, PAUL ANDREW. *Phil Sheridan and His Army* (Lincoln, Nebraska, 1985).

———, ed. *Soldiers West: Biographies from the Military Frontier* (Lincoln, Nebr., 1987).

IONE LAND and CATTLE COMPANY LETTERPRESS Book, 1884–1888. University OF WYOMING, LARAMIE. Microfilm.

JACKSON, W. TURRENTINE. *The Enterprising Scot: Investor in the American West After 1873* (Edinburgh, 1968).

KAMMAN, MICHAEL. *Colonial New York* (New York, 1975).

KERR, W. G. *Scottish Capital on the American Credit Frontier* (Austin, Tex., 1976).

KIM, SUNG BOK. *Landlord & Tenant in Colonial New York: Manorial Society, 1664–1775* (Chapel Hill, N.C., 1978).

KIPLING, RUDYARD. *The One-Volume Kipling* (New York, 1930).

LEE, BOB, and DICK WILLIAMS. *Last Grass Frontier: The South Dakota Stock Growers Heritage* (Sturgis, S. Dak., 1964).

LESLIE, ANITA. *Mr. Frewen of England* (London, 1966).

———. *The Marlborough House Set* (New York, 1973).

MANCHESTER, WILLIAM. *The Last Lion: Winston Spencer Churchill* (New York, 1983).

DE MANDAT-GRANCEY, EDMOND. *Narrative of a Journey Across the Prairie and Over the Black Hills of Dakota* (Lincoln, Nebr., 1984).

MARTIN, RALPH G. *Jennie.* 2 vols. (New York, 1972).

Mason, Philip. *The English Gentleman: The Rise and Fall of an Ideal* (New York, 1982).

MASTERS, BRIAN. *The Dukes: The Origins, Ennoblement and History of 26 Families* (London, 1975).

MEANY, EDMOND S. *History of the State of Washington* (New York, 1909).

MEAD, JEAN. *Wyoming in Profile* (Boulder, Colo., 1982).

MERRITT, JOHN I. *Baronets and Buffalo: The British Sportsman in the American West, 1833–1881* (Missoula, Mont., 1985).

MILLS, ENOS A. *The Rocky Mountain National Park* (New York, 1926).

MOORE, NANDI. *Brands on the Boswell* (Glendo, Wyo., 1986).

MOTHERSHEAD, HARMON ROSS. *The Swan Land and Cattle Company, Ltd.* (Norman, Okla., 1971).

MURRAY, ROBERT A. *Fort Laramie: "Visions of a Grand Old Post"* (Fort Collins, Colo., 1974).

NORDYKE, LEWIS. *Cattle Empire: The Fabulous Story of the 3,000,000 Acre XIT* (New York, 1949).

OGILVY, MABELL FRANCES, COUNTESS OF AIRLIE. *Thatched with Gold* (London, 1962).

ORNDUFF, DONALD R. *The First 49 Personalities in the Honor Gallery of the AHA's Hereford Heritage* (Kansas City, Mo., 1981).

OSGOOD, ERNEST STAPLES. *The Day of the Cattleman* (Chicago, 1929).

PEARCE, W. M. *The Matador Land and Cattle Company* (Norman, Okla., 1964).

PLUNKETT, HORACE C. Plunkett Diaries. University of Wyoming, Laramie. Microfilm.

POHANKA, BRIAN C., ed. *Nelson A. Miles: A Documentary Biography of His Military Career, 1861–1903* (Glendale, Calif., 1985).

QUAIFE, MILO MILTON, ed. *Kit Carson's Autobiography* (Lincoln, Nebr., 1935).

QUIN, WINDHAM THOMAS WYNDHAM-, LORD DUNRAVEN. *Past Times and Pastimes* (London, 1922).

RICHARDS, COLIN. *Bowler Hats and Stetsons* (New York, 1966).

VON RICHTHOFEN, WALTER. *Cattle-Raising on the Plains of North America* (Norman, Okla., 1964).

RITVO, HARRIET. *The Animal Estate: The English and Other Creatures in the Victorian Age.* (Cambridge, Mass., 1987).

SANDOZ, MARI. *The Beaver Men* (New York, 1964).

SHI, DAVID E. *The Simple Life* (New York, 1985).

SKAGGS, JIMMY M. *Prime Cut: Livestock Raising and Meatpacking in the United States, 1607–1983* (College Station, Tex., 1986).

SMITH, HENRY NASH. *Virgin Land: The American West as Symbol and Myth* (New York, 1950).

SOCOLOFSKY, HOMER E. *Landlord William Scully* (Lawrence, Kans., 1979).

SOMERSET, ANNE. *The Life and Times of William IV* (London, 1980).

SPRAGUE, MARSHALL. *Gallery of Dudes* (Lincoln, Nebr., 1966).

SPRING, AGNES WRIGHT. *The Cheyenne Club: Mecca of the Aristocrats of the Old-Time Cattle Range* (Kansas City, Mo., 1961).

STEWART, WILLIAM DRUMMOND. *Edward Warren* (Missoula, Mont., 1986).

STUART, GRANVILLE. *Pioneering in Montana: The Making of a State, 1864–1887* (Lincoln, Nebr., 1977).

SUNDER, JOHN E. *Joshua Pilcher, Fur Trader and Indian Agent* (Norman, Okla., 1968).

TINKER, ESTELLE. *Archibald John Writes the Rocking Chair Ranche Letters* (Burnett, Tex., 1979).

TYLER, RON, ed. *Alfred Jacob Miller: Artist on the Oregon Trail* (Fort Worth, Tex., 1982).

URBANEK, MAE. *Wyoming Place Names* (Boulder, Colo., 1967).

VICTOR, FRANCES FULLER. *The River of the West: The Adventures of Joe Meek* (Missoula, Mont., 1983).

DE VOTO, BERNARD. *Across the Wide Missouri* (Boston, 1947).

WALKER, DON D. *Clio's Cowboys* (Lincoln, Nebr., 1981).

WALLACE, DAVID DUNCAN. *South Carolina: A Short History* (Columbia, S.C., 1966).

WALSH, DONALD H. *Pierre Wibaux: Cattle King* (Bismarck, N. Dak., 1953).

WALLIS, GEORGE A. *Cattle Kings of the Staked Plains* (Denver, 1957).

WARNER, ROBERT COMBS. *The Fort Laramie of Alfred Jacob Miller* (Laramie, Wyo., 1979).

WEBB, WALTER PRESCOTT. *The Great Plains* (New York, 1931).

WEST, TREVOR. *Horace Plunkett: Cooperation and Politics* (Washington, D.C., 1986).

WESTERN RANGE CATTLE INDUSTRY STUDY. Colorado Historical Society, Denver. Files and Microfilm.

WILSON, WILLIAM. *House of Airlie* (London, 1924).

WISTER, OWEN. Wister Diaries, American Heritage Center, University of Wyoming, Laramie.

WOODS, LAWRENCE MILTON. "Evolution of Wyoming Territorial Legislation, 1869–1890," unpublished doctoral dissertation, New York University, 1975.

———. *Moreton Frewen's Western Adventures* (Boulder, Colo., 1986).

——. *Sometimes the Books Froze: Wyoming's Economy and Its Banks* (Boulder, Colo., 1985).

WYOMING STOCK GROWERS ASSOCIATION COLLECTION, American Heritage Center, University of Wyoming, Laramie.

YOST, NELLIE SNYDER. *Buffalo Bill: His Family, Friends, Fame, Failures and Fortunes* (Chicago, 1979).

# Index

---

235